Thomas Berry's War

C. W. Yocum

Thomas Berry's War

©2019 by George Yocum. All rights reserved.

No part of this book may be used or reproduced in any manner whatsoever without written permission except in the case of brief quotations embodied in critical articles and reviews or citations in academic works (including primary and secondary school reports).

Written by C. W. Yocum.

Designed through 31BY5,
distributed by Lulu.com, Morrisville, NC

Library of Congress Control Number: 2019906682

ISBN 978-0-359-68811-1

This book is dedicated to

who also suffered much.

Table of Contents

Acknowledgements	7
Preface: The Berry Family	9
Part 1: Advent of the Civil War	11
Part 2: Politics of the 1860s	17
Part 3: The First Letter	33
Part 4: The Chase After Bragg	53
Part 5: Battle of Stone's River	75
Part 6: Soldier on Parole	93
Part 7: Return to the Army of the Cumberland	117
Part 8: Battle of Chickamauga	141
Part 9: Chattanooga	157
Part 10: Knoxville	181
Part 11: Sherman's March on Georgia	209
Epilogue	231
Civil War Glossary Referenced to Thomas Berry Letters	238

Acknowledgements

Thomas Berry asked his wife to save his letters. She passed them to her daughter, Louella, who passed them to her son, Fredrick Yocum, who gave them to my father Carl Yocum.

My dad, mom, Myrtle Yocum, and sister, Joan Adamczak, transcribed Thomas' handwritten letters. My dad researched the letters and wrote the annotation in his retirement. As he neared completion he asked me to see if I could have his work professionally critiqued and then published.

Unfortunately, by the time I asked for and received several very thorough critiques, my dad was no longer able to work on the book.

Dad's mission was to preserve the letters in book form for his family. My mission is similar but in addition to preserving Thomas' letters I am preserving my father's writing. If he had implemented changes per the very thoughtful critiques the work would still be in his writing style. However, I did correct some grammar and misstated facts that were indicated.

I am very grateful for the generous writers who gave their time consuming best and thoughtful help even though much if it was not implemented. I accept responsibility for any errors and shortcomings. They are: Randolph Hennes, then Associate Director, College of Arts and Sciences, Honors Program, University of Washington; Robert Girardi, author of eight books on the Civil War; Birke Duncan, author; James F. O'Callaghan, author of *No Circuses* and other works; and Kent Morgan, author and lecturer on Civil War history. I am also especially grateful for the expertise of my very helpful designer, Chuck Veit of 31by5 and for Denise Merkling, who designed the dust jacket.

Finally, a gross summation of critiques is this: most of the annotation should have been either in footnotes or eliminated altogether. The story is about Thomas Berry and much of the annotation, which does provides a brief history of the Civil War, is a distraction from his letters. So, for those already familiar with Civil War history, or just not interested in it, read only the letters because they are the story.

Thanks also to the Library of Congress for each of the maps and pictures.

George Yocum

The Berry Family
Preface

Thomas Berry wrote an abundance of letters to his wife during his twenty-one month tour of duty with the Union army in the Civil War. He addressed those letters to Estelle Berry, Walnut Grove, Knox County, Illinois. Estelle did not receive all of the letters so addressed due to the hazards of mail delivery during that war. References to missing letters written by Thomas are found in his writings, letters which went astray through loss, interception or theft. Thomas wrote of his relatives, friends, and neighbors who were comrades in arms, describing camp life and battle experiences in detail; yet, his primary concern was for the welfare of the family he left behind. One hundred of those letters received by Estelle are presented in this book.

Thomas was born in 1837 at Rockingham, New Hampshire. His family moved to Victoria, Illinois, circa 1850. At that place on November 27, 1856, Thomas married Estelle, daughter of Isaac and Elizabeth Copley. Following their marriage, Thomas and Estelle moved to the farmland they acquired at Walnut Grove, Thomas' older brother George, also moved to Walnut Grove leaving their younger brother Charles with their widowed mother at Victoria.

Born to Thomas and Estelle were their daughter Louella on January 25, 1858, and a son, Sylvester, August 9, 1860. In that latter year the population of Walnut Grove had grown to 1120. Their farm at Walnut Grove produced grain, fruit, vegetables, livestock, and fowl, providing them food and income.

Isaac Copley married Elizabeth Rood in 1836 at Delaware County, New York. Five of their children were born to them in Delaware County including Estelle, born February 15, 1839. Following the deaths of two children in infancy, Isaac moved his family in the summer of 1844 to the State of Illinois, settling in an area 130 miles west of Chicago. To that new land Isaac also brought five of his brothers and one sister. Isaac was one of fifteen children.

The region grew with new settlers, forming towns and villages such as Walnut Grove, Knox County. Isaac, a pioneer of that county, resided with his family in his namesake town, Copley, Knox County, Illinois.

The years following Isaac's settlement in Illinois were prosperous and peaceful for the Copley and Berry families, but the developing social and political tumult between northern and southern states culminating in the Civil War put an end to serenity. The call for volunteers by the Federal army was heard at Knox County in the summer of 1862. Isaac Copley assumed recruitment duty in the towns and villages of that Illinois County. Among those he recruited were members of his own family, including his son-in-law Thomas Berry, Thomas' brother, George, and himself.

Thomas registered for duty August 9, 1862 at Altona, Knox County, Illinois. He left home in the evening of Monday August 25, "to fight for his country" as Estelle recorded in her diary, enlisting with his brother in Company G of the newly formed 89th Illinois Railroad infantry regiment at Altona. Company G arrived the following day at Camp Williams for basic training.

The 89th Illinois Railroad regiment was organized by the railroad companies of Illinois. Captain John Christopher, an infantry officer of the regular army was appointed as colonel, and Charles T. Hotchkiss as lieutenant colonel of the regiment. Officers of a company of volunteers were customarily selected by members of that company. In such manner Isaac Copley was made first lieutenant in Company G.

Thomas Berry began his letters to Estelle on his second day at Camp Williams. From then on he kept Estelle well informed of his camp life and of the location of his regiment. He was constantly concerned about the welfare of the family he left behind, and with his letters attempted to advise his wife on the operation of household and farm.

He struggled for writing paper and postage stamps. A scrap of brown bag paper and that portion of received letters not covered with writing were used to provide his link with home. Pen and ink were his favorite tools, but on many occasions he was forced to use lead pencil which considerably altered his handwriting. The use of ink produced a more structured and easily read script. In the use of pencil, which incidentally is better standing the test of time, Thomas paid little attention to penmanship.

Thomas apparently intended a chronicle of his military experiences since he admonished Estelle to "keep all my letters." That chronicle is the purpose of this book in which his letters are reproduced verbatim with original spelling left untouched. In addition to the letters, he carried a pocket diary into which, with few exceptions, he made daily entries. Names, places, and occurrences mentioned in letter appendages are based on recorded history. Appendages of a personal nature regarding people mentioned by Thomas are derived from historical documents or newspapers, or from manuscript handed down in the same manner as Thomas' letters, from Estelle to her great—grandson.

A brief sketch of historical events leading to the Civil War will bring us to the time Estelle receives her first letter from Thomas.

Part 1

Advent of the Civil War

The American Civil War was provoked in 1861 by action of eleven slave—holding southern states rebelling against the Constitution of the United States.

Four of the rebelling states, Georgia, North Carolina, South Carolina, and Virginia were charter members of the Constitution. South Carolina and Virginia had proposed the very foundation of that document which did not provide for withdrawal of any state from the Union for any reason. Yet, the attempt to secede from the Union was made, thereby challenging the validity of the Constitution. On that issue was the ostensible excuse for the Civil War.

The Southern states were aiming for expansion of slavery into new territories of the United States. Since they lost their bid in the political arena of 1860 for a pro—slavery president, the rebelling states immediately initiated political and military action in an attempt to be independent and free of Federal legislation.

Northern States entered the conflict initially to put down the rebellion and to recover Federal property confiscated by the Confederacy in its early attempt to prove state sovereignty.

Regardless of excellent southern oratory extolling state sovereignty and the right of states to secede from the Union as just cause for rebellion, the unmistakable, underlying cause of the American Civil War was the festering issue of slavery.

Contenders in that war were identified as the United States of America, and the Confederate States of America; otherwise identified as North vs. South, Federal vs. Confederate, Union vs. Secession, Yankee vs. Rebel, or Blue vs. Gray.

No such distinction can identify the many persuasions participating in the war's instigation or its execution. On both sides fought sympathizers of Union, secession, slavery, abolition, states' rights, Democrats, Republicans, northerners, southerners, and Colonists. (Colonists advocated the removal of freed black slaves to foreign soil where they would set up a nation of their own. Money was appropriated to pay slave owners for emancipation and for transport of those set free that chose emigration. President Lincoln was not opposed to colonization).

Loyalty to the federal government on the one side and loyalty to the Confederate cause of states' rights on the other, each took precedence over social and political ideologies which previously had fractured the nation in a multitude of unarmed camps. Emerging from those camps early in 1861 was a country armed and polarized, North and South.

At root of diverse social and political sympathies was the institution of slavery, an issue of contention in America for well over two centuries prior to the Civil War, and a legacy of Great Britain reluctantly accepted by the colonists.

Indentured servants were brought to the shores of American colonies in the year 1619, servants who had sold themselves to ship captains or to their agents for passage to America and whose bondages were sold upon arrival, to Colonial employers. That same year chattel slaves were sold in America. Unlike indentured servants in limited bondage who would fulfill their contract of service in the specified time and become free, chattel slaves and their progeny would live out their lives in servitude.

American colonists were themselves not totally free, subjected as they were to whims of the ruling monarch in England. Descendants and followers of the freedom seeking pioneers were powerless to attempt complete abolition of slavery while suppressed by England, and while yet living under an amorphous state of self-government approved only by the King's emissaries.

American colonists under the whip of British rule, flexed their muscles in 1765 with the first Colonial Congress. The result was a petition to the King of England with the 'DECLARATION of RIGHTS and GRIEVANCES' seeking redress of grievances suffered by the King's subjects in America, and seeking also treatment consistent with British citizens.

Disdain for that document by King George III and his ministers served to forge the colonies into a united cause of freedom from British rule. With that freedom in mind Americans no longer considered themselves Colonists of Britain and thus formed in 1774 the first of two Continental Congresses in which the 'DECLARATION of RIGHTS' was issued.

That action exploded with the shot 'heard round the world' at Lexington in Massachusetts where a nondescript American Army encountered a troop of British Regulars on April 19, 1775. The War of Independence had started and would not end until October 19, 1781. (The United States signed a peace treaty with Britain September 3, 1783.) The Second Continental Congress on July 4, 1776 issued the 'DECLARATION of INDEPENDENCE' in which was formed the United States of America, and in which was set forth the causes for declaring America free of British rule.

With slavery so imbedded in the colonies and advocated so passionately in southern states, one need not speculate too long regarding why the Continental Congress in phrasing that document did not cause slavery to be abolished from the land, or why such phrasing had been made but was lined out before being signed by all thirteen states. A united nation in pursuit of freedom from foreign rule was preeminent at the time.

'ARTICLES OF CONFEDERATION' approved by the Continental Congress in October 1777 and finally ratified by all thirteen states March 1781, stated rules under which the thirteen states would operate within the Union. Sovereignty remained for individual states to be exercised where not limited by the Articles.

One exercise not so limited was in choice of slavery. In other areas of state rule, individual state sovereignty proved to work in disfavor of the Union, particularly in recognition of the United States as a cohesive nation. In that regard, foreign governments in search of world trade looked with disdain upon the young nation.

The Second Continental Congress (in existence from 1775 to 1789) met regularly for "management of the general interests of the United States" and in special session to resolve problems of imminent concern. At one such meeting convened in Philadelphia on May 25, 1787 with George Washington presiding, and after weeks of debate, it became apparent to those assembled that the Articles of Confederation could not be effectively amended to provide efficient government. A resolution was adapted "That a National government ought to be established, consisting of a supreme Legislature, Executive, and Judiciary". The Continental Congress was compelled to give new form to the government of the United States.

Months of debate followed. The institutions of slavery and freedom met head-on. The former, with deep roots throughout history and continuing to enjoy support as a commodity of world trade, was permitted by much of the 'civilized' world, and would not die easily. The latter was an institution in which American citizens enjoyed a new found, unprecedented way of life. Many American citizens would persist in expanding that institution to embrace all residents of the United States and of its territories.

Resulting from that congressional meeting convened in 1787 was the document titled "Constitution of the United States". The Constitution was ratified on June 21, 1788 with the signing of the ninth state, New Hampshire.

Pressured by advocates of slave trade, the Constitution of the United States permitted 'importation' of slave labor 'as any of the states now existing shall think proper to admit'. Such importation would not be prohibited before the year 1808. (Beyond that year, it was presumed, reproduction of slaves within the United States would sufficiently meet the need of pro-slavers.) The Constitution further agreed, a person held to such labor escaping to a free state would summarily be returned to the party 'to whom such service or labor may be due'.

Though certainly not unanimous, the decision for such recognition of slavery was made again (as in 1776) to assure inclusion of all thirteen states in the Union; South Carolina and Georgia had threatened to withhold signature if slave trade became immediately prohibited. The Constitution of the United States finally embraced all thirteen of the original colony states with the signing by Rhode Island on May 29, 1790. The signing "required an unconditional adoption in toto, and forever" as phrased by George Mason, one of the framers of the document. Political balance at that time slightly favored the south.

From then on forces, both for and against slavery, would vie for dominance in American politics, and for sympathy and support of the United States citizens.

Colonies which became the original thirteen states by signature to the Constitution are as follows:

State	Colony Settled	Entered Union
Virginia	1607	(10) 06/25/1788
New York	1614	(11) 07/26/1788
Massachusetts	1620	(6) 02/06/1788
New Hampshire	1623	(9) 06/21/1788
Connecticut	1634	(5) 01/09/1788
Maryland	1634	(7) 04/28/1788
Rhode Island	1636	(13) 05/29/1790
Delaware	1638	(1) 12/07/1787
New Jersey	1664	(3) 12/18/1787
North Carolina	1660	(12) 11/21/1789
South Carolina	1670	(8) 05/23/1788
Pennsylvania	1682	(2) 12/12/1787
Georgia	1733	(4) 01/02/1788

Between the years 1619 and 1860 slavery had been absorbed into the lifestyle and economy of American communities. During that period slave population grew in excess of 3.5 million. Many statesmen, including signatories to the Declaration of Independence as well as to the Constitution, were slave owners. However, slavery became more and more unpopular in northern colonies where in 1774 Rhode Island abolished slavery from that colony, a bold commitment to freedom while yet under British rule. Such action was opposed in southern colonies where slavery was flourishing, spurred on by Eli Whitney's cotton gin and the use of steam for the sugar press. Both of those inventions permitted processing of greater quantities of cotton and sugar which in turn allowed greater production of those crops on larger plantations.

Large plantations depended heavily upon slave labor for producing, processing and exporting not only cotton and sugar, but other crops including tobacco. Those goods were shipped to the American north and to foreign markets where economy was geared to commerce and industry related to such products. Profiteers associated with those domestic and foreign markets would not be entirely sympathetic with the cause of abolition, nor would many influential politicians in either the northern or southern American states, since abolition would mean the end of cheap labor and the advent of stiff competition due to rise in cost of raw material produced in the south.

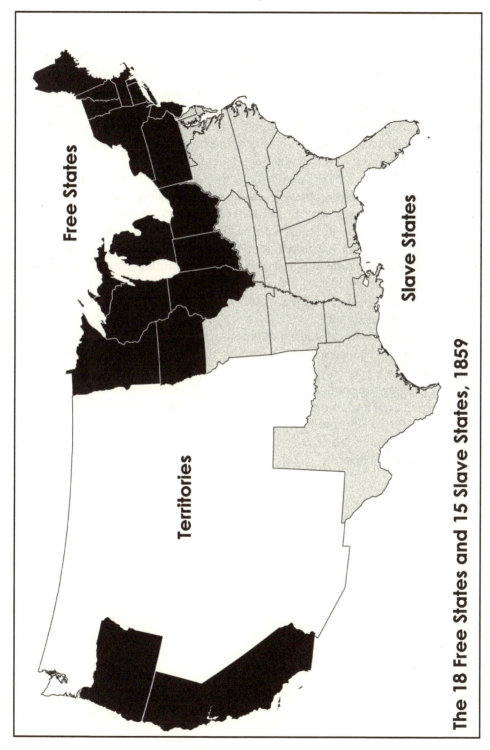

The 18 Free States and 15 Slave States, 1859

Northern colonies provided free-schools, encouraging scholastic development in literature, arts and sciences, a privilege generally denied Southerners (Boston established compulsory grammar school education as early as 1636). On that subject southern colonial Governor Berkeley of Virginia stated publicly, "I thank God there are no free-schools nor printing...for learning has brought disobedience, and heresy, and sects into the world, and printing has divulged them, and libels against the best government; God keep us from both". The philosophy of that 1671 statement prevailed for 90 years to the benefit of pro-slavery advocates, for within those words is found the seed of oligarchy, parent of slavery.

Between 1790 and 1860, twenty states were admitted to the Union. As each state was added the scales of political balance between slave and anti-slave would teeter until coming to rest with 18 free states and 15 slave states. In that same time frame laws of precarious durability were passed alternately permitting and limiting slavery within the states and territories. For several years various sentiments had been developing, not only about slavery pro and con, but Union pro and con, and colonization of the blacks, pro and con. Additionally, combinations of these sentiments were considered by many, and Democrats and Republicans were both factioned by various sympathies.

To pro-slavers it was not just a question of the continuation of slavery, it was a question of its expansion with or without protection under the Constitution. To the hard-line southern politician the aim was proliferation of slavery beyond arbitrary geographical boundaries within U.S. territories as imposed by congress. Political and social thinking of the southern populace was directed to that end, not too difficult in view of prevailing ignorance spawned through successful efforts of the southern oligarchy which controlled reading material and indeed even reading ability of southern citizens.

Part 2

Politics of the 1860s

The political scene taking shape for the presidential election of 1860 was not to the liking of southern pro-slave, anti-Union Democrats in power at that time. Slavery in the United States required hard-line politics for its growth and perpetuity, which meant controlling votes in the House and Senate, and a president sympathetic to that cause.

The Republican Convention convened May 16, 1860 at Chicago, nominating Abraham Lincoln for president on the third ballot. Following that nomination, South Carolina threatened to secede from the Union if Lincoln won election in November. The pro-southern cabinet of President Buchanan threatened treasonable acts if the Republicans were elected, and that shameless body in part did indeed commit such acts while still in office. The Secretary of War sent materials of war to forts within the borders of southern states and placed such forts where possible under command of U.S. officers of Southern birth. He also scattered the remaining small army to nonessential outposts in his efforts to undermine the next administration.

The Secretary of the Navy acted in like manner, dismantling many naval vessels and shipping the remaining fleet in all directions. That Secretary of the Navy was later indicted in a case of fraud concerning over eight hundred thousand dollars of Indian Trust Fund money. The Secretary of the Treasury made no secret of his sympathy and support for the southern cause, or for his desire to break the Union. The President of that administration, Buchanan, would do little to maintain the Union, a cardinal obligation to the people who put trust of their highest office in his hands.

President Buchanan, a southern Democrat, had won the 1856 election over the first Republican candidate John C. Fremont. During that campaign the state of South Carolina as on previous occasions threatened to secede if the anti—slavery candidate Fremont won election. Among further threats to the Union were the actions of Governor Wise of Virginia who asserted he would use the militia of his state and march upon Washington, seize archives of the Capitol, and thereby destroy the Federal Government if Fremont were elected. A majority of the electorate was strongly pro—Union and hoped for a conciliating means to resolve the slavery issue. More time was needed for that purpose than could be afforded by the upcoming election date. A united country was a bird in hand which would not be gambled by grasping at emancipation with the threat of disunity attached. The voters compromised at the polls and elected James Buchanan president, once again appeasing the South.

By 1860 Buchanan was anxious to rid himself of the office despoiled by Southern Democrats. Pro—slavery, anti—Union, Southern Democrats nominated John C. Breckinridge of Kentucky as their presidential candidate for the 1860 campaign. Breckinridge was the current vice—president under Buchanan.

Northern Democrats broke away from the staunch southern position and in

June, 1860 nominated Stephen Douglas of Illinois. For several years Douglas had been grooming himself for the presidency. He was popular in the north, and with that vote in hand he sought the southern vote when in 1854, as a senator from Illinois, Douglas attached a clause to his Kansas—Nebraska Bill which voided the Missouri Compromise Act, much to the liking of pro-slavers but a contemptible blow to the free states. The Missouri Compromise Act of 1820 had declared slavery illegal above the 36 degree, 30 minute parallel, with the State of Missouri the exception.

The Kansas and Nebraska Bill provided for the organization of those areas as territories of the United States with no restriction to slavery. Because of the balance of political power coupled with many of the Northern Congressmen's passion to remain at peace with the South, the bill was speedily passed. Its passing was much to the dismay of abolitionists throughout the states and territories.

A fourth candidate for the office of president was John Bell, a Tennessee slave holder, candidate of the newly established Constitutional Union party, made up in part of the old Whig and Know-Nothing parties. His supporters held no hope of his election but thought he would draw sufficient votes to prevent election of any of the four candidates. In that event the selection would be made by Congress for either Bell or Douglas to the exclusion of Lincoln. In that effort the pro-slavery parties outwitted themselves.

Diversity of sympathies in 1860 is demonstrated by the political platforms fielded in the presidential campaign that year:

Nominees: President	Vice President		
S. Douglas	H.V. Johnson	**Party, City/Date:** Democrat (free states), Baltimore, June 18	
		Platform: Right of people of territories to admit or exclude slavery. Accede to Supreme Count. Pro-Union.	
J. Bell	E. Everett	**Party, City/Date:** Constitutional Union	
		Platform: Uphold the laws and defend the Constitution. Maintain slavery. Pro-Union.	
A. Lincoln	H. Hamlin	**Party, City/Date:** Republican, Chicago, May 16	
		Platform: Free soil in territories. Non-interference with slavery in states where it presently exists. Pro-Union, pro-Constitution.	
J. Breckinridge	Gen. Lane	**Party, City/Date:** Democrat, (slave states)	
		Platform: Slavery or dis-Union. Slavery to be permitted in all territories.	

Note the absence of an abolition platform. Even though the abolition movement was growing, it was not a sufficiently popular issue on which to gamble political fortunes in 1860. Abolition had its champions in such people as Harriet Beecher Stowe with her book, Uncle Tom's Cabin. The abolitionist firebrand John Brown had brought attention to that movement through overt actions which saw his arrest by United States Marines, and his execution two months later in December 1859 by the State of Virginia, overstepping its bounds in a Federal case to its own ends. Many Northern states' citizens were advocates of abolition. Still, there was insufficient popularity in the movement to place the issue on the ballot.

Throughout the 1860 presidential campaign secessionist firebrands, north and south, resorted to insult, violence, and a continuing threat of disunion, intimidating pro-Union citizens in the north to vote once again for a pro-slavery candidate. At the same time the southern oligarchy was stirring up hatred for abolitionists in the minds of southern citizens, all for the apparent purpose of excusing acts of rebellion.

With the waning of political clout in support of slave trade and the unyielding pressure of abolitionists in the north, southern states reasoned political independence to be the answer to proliferation of slavery. In defense of the southern position, or rather in attempt to rationalize rebellion, one must look to slavery which had existed since biblical days, had found its way into the Colonies, and had become "the chief cornerstone in our new edifice" as Confederate Vice President A. H. Stephens referred to that institution.

The effect of abolition on the southern economy is better placed in perspective by review of population distribution in the eleven rebelling states according to the 1860 census. Total population of those eleven states was 9,103,014 of which 5,450,711 were white, 131,401 free colored, and 3,520,902 slaves. The removal of three and one half million slaves from southern labor would indeed have a devastating effect on domestic and foreign markets.

As the southern populace was being whipped into a frenzy against northern citizens, many northerners were being angered, not with their fellow citizens to the south as such, but with slavery, proponents of slavery, and the Democratic administration of the Federal Government. During Buchanan's administration the Supreme Court brought on further anger with the Dred Scott decision on March 6, 1857, nullifying existing laws against slavery. Dred Scott was a slave who had been taken by his owner to a free state where such ownership was illegal. On that technicality Mr. Scott petitioned the courts for freedom and lost. In the expanded decision regarding the Dred Scott case, the Supreme Court, loaded with southern sympathizers, declared as unconstitutional, previous laws passed by congress which limited slavery. That Supreme Court also declared the United States Congress could not pass laws prohibiting slavery in U.S. territories and such laws would be declared unconstitutional. Further, the same court ruled black men were to be denied citizenship.

Northern citizens were aware of the contempt displayed by President Buchanan's Cabinet for the Union, and the unprincipled leadership of the Democratic Administration which would allow such national unrest through sympathy for the southern cause.

Appeasement of the south by northern states was at an end.

Abraham Lincoln was elected President of the U.S. on November 6, 1860. His election set the wheels of secession in motion with vigor. Between that date and his inauguration on March 4, 1861, acts of southern rebellion included secession of the states of South Carolina, Georgia, Alabama, Florida, Louisiana, Mississippi, and Texas; the formation of the provisional "Confederate States of America"; seizure and confiscation of U.S. forts, arsenals, offices, and other U.S. property in Confederate territory; and the firing upon a vessel flying the U.S. flag. Between his election and his inauguration Lincoln was without official authority to interfere with the revolt against the Union.

With the Republican party soon to be in control of the Federal Government, lame duck administrators and Confederate states' officials wasted no time in their attempts to destroy the Republic.

In the early part of the year 1861, the Federal government appeared to be crumbling, however, when put to the test, the Constitution of the United States prevailed over the internal treachery and anarchy of a treason bent administration.

To Buchanan's credit, he did not do all that was demanded of him by the anti—Union people who helped put him in office; the oath of office bore too heavily and barely tipped the scales of duty on the side of the Union. Although the Federal Government was badly crippled, constitutional government was functional when President Buchanan left office.

Arkansas, North Carolina, Tennessee, and Virginia joined the Confederacy after Lincoln's inauguration. Kentucky and Missouri were termed borderline states, with sympathizers on both sides of the conflict. Those states did not attempt to secede from the Union; however, they were considered firmly in the Confederate camp. Both north and south struggled for borderline state support and many fierce battles were fought within their borders.

Following Lincoln's election on November 6, 1860 the secessionist movement was set in motion with these conspicuous events:

Dec. 20, 1860	South Carolina State Convention votes to secede (six more states secede before Lincoln's inauguration)
January 2, 1861	South Carolina confiscates Fort Johnson, federal property in Charleston)
January 3, 1861	Georgia state troops confiscate Fort Pulaski, federal property at Mobile
January 5, 1861	Alabama confiscates Fort Morgan and Fort Gaines, federal property at Mobile
January 6, 1861	Florida troops confiscate the federal arsenal at Apalachicola
January 7, 1861	Florida confiscates Fort Marion at St. Augustine
January 8, 1861	Federals at Fort Barrancas open fire at Pensacola
January 9, 1861	STAR OF WEST with U.S. flag fired upon at Charleston Harbor by South Carolina while attempting to refurbish Fort Sumpter
January 10, 1861	Louisiana state troops confiscate federal Forts Jackson and St. Phillip and the federal arsenal at Baton Rouge
January 11, 1861	Louisiana troops occupy U.S. Marine Hospital at New Orleans
January 12, 1861	Florida troops confiscate Forts Barrancas and McRee and naval yard at Pensacola
January 14, 1861	Louisiana confiscates Fort Pike, Federal property near New Orleans
January 20, 1861	Mississippi troops seize Fort Massachusetts on Ship Island in the Mississippi Gulf
January 24, 1861	Georgia seizes Federal arsenal at Augusta
January 26, 1861	Georgia confiscates Fort Jackson and Oglethorpe Barracks in Savannah
January 31, 1861	Louisiana takes over U.S. Branch Mint, Custom House and schooner *Washington* at New Orleans
February 1, 1861	Texas State Convention votes to secede
February 5, 1861	Confederacy initiated at Montgomery, Alabama
February 8, 1861	Confederate constitution is provisionally adapted
February 9, 1861	Jefferson Davis elected provisional president of Confederate States of America
February 12, 1861	Arkansas troops take U.S. munitions at Napoleon, Texas

February 19, 1861 Louisiana takes control of U.S. paymaster office at New Orleans

February 20, 1861 Jefferson Davis empowered to contract for war goods

March 4, 1861 Lincoln inaugurated. "...in your hands not mine..." is the issue of Civil War

Ordinances of secession from the Union were passed in various state conventions as follows:

State	Date
South Carolina	12/20/1860
Florida	1/7/1861
Mississippi	1/9/1861
Alabama	1/11/1861
Georgia	1/19/1861
Louisiana	1/26/1861
Texas	2/1/1861

The first six states listed above met in convention at Montgomery, Alabama, February 8, 1861 and inaugurated the Southern Confederacy. (This act is considered by some historians to proclaim the start of the Civil War). Texas delegates to that convention arrived too late to participate in the business of inauguration, regardless, the State of Texas was considered at that meeting to be a charter member of the newly inaugurated Confederacy. These seven states were called the cotton states.

States which later joined the Confederacy are listed here with dates of their respective ordinances of secession:

State	Date
Virginia	4/17/1861
Arkansas	5/6/1861
Tennessee	5/6/1861
North Carolina	5/20/1861

Slave states which did not secede but in part joined the Confederacy were Missouri and Kentucky. Slave states which did not join the Confederacy were Maryland and Delaware.

When Lincoln took office, there existed 34 States. Those states are listed below according to sympathy in regard to rebellion at that time, and in the order of their admission into the Union:

States loyal to the United States:

Delware*	12/7/1787	Pennsylvania	12/12/1787
New Jersey	12/18/1787	Connecticut	1/9/1788
Maryland*	4/28/1788	New Hampshire	6/21/1788
Massachusetts	2/6/1788	Rhode Island	5/29/1790
New York	7/26/1788	Ohio	3/1/1803
Vermont	3/4/1781	Illinois	12/3/1818
Indiana	12/11/1816	Michigan	1/26/1837
Maine	3/15/1820	Wisconsin	5/29/1848
Iowa	12/28/1846	Minnesota	5/11/1858
California	9/9/1850	Kansas	1/29/1861
Oregon	2/14/1859		

*slave state

Borderline slave states:

Kentucky	6/1/1792	Missouri	12/10/1817

Loyal to Confederacy (all slave states):

Georgia	1/2/1788	South Carolina	5/23/1788
Virginia	6/25/1788	North Carolina	11/21/1789
Tennessee	6/1/1796	Louisiana	4/30/1812
Mississippi	12/10/1817	Alabama	12/14/1819
Arkansas	6/15/1836	Florida	3/3/1845
Texas	12/29/1845		

There appears no rationale for deserting the Union in favor of the state. In his inaugural speech of March 4, 1861, Lincoln pledged protection of the southern way of life. No private or public land in the southern states was threatened, no chattel property in the south was endangered by the federal government, nor was the social structure of southern aristocracy. He left no doubt in anyone's mind regarding his intended role as president. Lincoln's primary objective and responsibility was to maintain the Union of the United States and defend its Constitution which, he said on that occasion, was his obligation to the nation through a "contract made in heaven".

There was however, one thorn in the side of southern politicians, and that was the loss of control of the federal administration. With the election of Lincoln, southern influence of the political arena came to an end. Expansion of slavery, prime concern of the Southern oligarchy, could no longer be secured through the office of the president against the will of the people, and although slavery as it existed under federal law would be defended under Lincoln's administration, it could not be secured against the electorate which had power to change law under the constitution administered by a responsive government. Therein lay a veiled threat to the southern way of life.

In the tormented mind of the southern politico, dissolution of the nation appeared the answer to proliferation of slavery. But that premise appears improbable since the states and territories not embracing slavery would remain in the domain of the Federal Government. A confederation of slave states demanding sovereignty resulted, its proponents either forgetting or totally disregarding the lesson learned by their forebears in the Continental Congress. Fealty of state, which should have been subordinate to fealty of nation, became an overwhelming devising element in the floodtide of brilliant but seditious oratory. Blinded by fire-brands, even the better educated lost sight of the glorious future which the United States Constitution promised.

Lincoln made no threats against established slavery in his inaugural address of March 4, 1861. We know he was passionately opposed to slavery from his earlier public statements, and as president he could exert extreme pressure to eliminate that institution; yet during the campaign and inaugural, on that subject he was passive. He was following the pattern of earlier patriots in the priority of constitutional government, a united government of, by, and for all its citizens, the collective minds of whom would ultimately determine the right course.

Rebuilding the administration for the Union left floundering by treason, commanding an army and navy seditiously impaired, and allaying fears of impending assault on the Capitol in Washington, D.C. by Confederates, were but a few of Lincoln's problems on his first inaugural, a day on which his life had been threatened. The cotton states sent letters to the new president notifying him of intent to secede and a notice of the election of Jefferson Davis to the presidency of the Confederate States, none of which Lincoln acknowledged as worthy of presidential reply.

Despite Jefferson Davis' inaugural address on February 18, 1861, in which he asserted "our true policy is peace", southern militia and fire-brands were extending their insidious anarchy outside the borders of the Confederacy to accomplish secessionist goals. United States military installations and Federal offices fell easy prey to the rebels as a result of the many seditious acts of the previous administration. Confiscation of federal property before and after Lincoln's inauguration was for the purpose of confirming the intent of the secessionists. No formal declaration of war had been made to that time by either North or South; however, the latter had been seizing federal property in Confederate states since January 2, 1861 with only passive resistance.

With so little to gain and the possibility of slavery being abolished by a showdown with the federal government, and with odds so patently in favor of victory for the North, what drove the South consisting of eleven agricultural states to provoke war with twenty—three States of the industrial north? It would appear the spirit of slavery foresaw its demise and was calling to task the growing spirit of freedom, to extract full price for its extinction through the evil of war; and the merciless, unyielding, oncoming wave of rebellion burst upon the walls of Fort Sumter on April 12, 1861.

Most northern citizens were not overly concerned about rebellious activities until the firing upon Ft. Sumter in Charleston Harbor. That overt action by a Confederate army under command of General Pierre Gustave Toutant de Beauregard in the secessionist state of South Carolina put an end to apathy of northerners. The fort was under rebel fire for two days beginning at 4:30 on the morning of April 12, 1861. Major Robert Anderson, the Federal commander of the fort, surrendered the fort after food and ammunition were exhausted. Miraculously no fatalities resulted on either side from the two-day bombardment, but a Union artillerist was killed by accidental explosion at the fort following the end of the battle.

Immediately after the surrender of Fort Sumter President Lincoln issued a proclamation calling for 75,000 men for muster into service and pay of the United States Army for the purpose of suppressing rebellion in the seven cotton states. That proclamation of April 15, 1861 was sent to the governors of non-seceding states with Oregon, California, and Kansas the exception due to distance. Enlistment of the 75,000 men was for a period of three months.

Kentucky governor Magoffin refused to honor Lincoln's call for troops on April 15, 1861, replying to the president that Kentucky would supply no men "for the wicked purpose of subduing her sister southern states." South Kentucky was predominantly pro-secession but the legislature and northern populace of that state were pro-Union. The governor, in an attempt to stymie the Federal government, qualified the State of Kentucky as neutral, with notification of that status sent to the Federal government and to the Confederacy. That indifferent stance could not remain long since supply and communication lines for both superpowers ran through the state. Kentucky's "sister southern states" disowned her for being an "insidious" neutral and for thereby showing "loyalty for Lincoln."

Military and political goals at the outset of hostilities in 1861 were defined and stated in simple terms by both sides. The South aimed to take and hold possession of Federal property within Confederate borders, establish state sovereignty, a secure nation of confederated states, and thereby continue the proliferation of slavery. The North set out to reclaim Federal property, put down rebellion, and preserve the Union. Limitations placed on those goals by both sides were short lived.

Determination of the Federal Government to maintain the integrity of the United States, and the commitment of northern citizens to that cause, came as a surprise to the Confederacy. In the early stages of state secession and prior to military action, Southern politicians predicted sudden collapse of the Union through apathy and an unwillingness of the Northern citizenry to take a stand against the South. Some of the seceding states were beguiled into the belief that secession was a bluff, designed to once again bring the United States electorate into compromise with the South and forbear proliferation of slavery within the Union. The South had gone to the well once too often.

The pillage of Federal property continued when, on May 6, 1861, after it became apparent the northern states would not tolerate such action, Jefferson Davis approved a DECLARATION OF WAR between the United States and the Confederate States of America. With that action the American Civil War was officially underway.

False pride in the superiority of southerners in combat and the stubborn arrogance of southern politicians stood in the way of reason when declaration of war against the United States was made by the Confederate President. That declaration altered considerably the military and political goals of both North and South.

Seizure of the United States capitol at Washington by the Confederacy would be an important political gain encouraging foreign intervention on the side of the South. A series of major military victories by the South was reasoned to accomplish the same result. The Confederacy therefore set about threatening the city of Washington.

Immediately, the Federal Government placed a hurried and temporarily effective defense around the Capitol. The first combat fatality suffered by the Union occurred with that maneuver on May 20, 1861 at Alexandria, Virginia, just across the Potomac River from the Capitol. That fatality resulted when a civilian shot a Union soldier who was in the act of removing a hoisted Confederate flag. Such was the hostile atmosphere within sight of Washington. Southern strategy called for the weakening of that defense by army movement around Washington to the northwest of that city and into border and loyal states.

The Confederacy also had designs on the U.S. territories and the Pacific coast, the latter, not only for the spread of slavery but also to curry favor of the Russians.

Neither North or South was prepared for all out war at this time, however the Southern Confederacy had a head start in assembling fighting units and materials of war. The Federal Government on March 1, 1861 had less than 21,000 regular soldiers, and these were treasonably scattered throughout inland waters and on the oceans.

No formidable U.S. army would be assembled and indeed no effective Union strategy for execution of the war by Federal armies would take shape for several months. Strategic campaigns by the U.S. armies came only after recruiting and training volunteers, and after much shifting of regiments, divisions, and command personnel forming armies to the satisfaction of commanding generals and Mr. Lincoln.

Southern states militia (men assembled in local military units to defend their homeland) did much of the early stage confiscation of U.S. property, and much of the fighting with U.S. regular army personnel, and with opposing state militia. [Militia of eastern Virginia moved into the western part of Virginia engaging militia of that same state in an unsuccessful attempt to persuade western Virginians to join the secession movement. The pro-Union stand of northwest Virginia citizens won statehood for residents of that area before war's end. West Virginia became the 35th state on June 20, 1863, at the expense of the State of Virginia which lost over 24,000 square miles in the formation of the new state.]

State militia of both loyal and secessionist states were gradually structured into Union and Confederate armies respectively.

In the assembly of command personnel, Mr. Lincoln as Commander in Chief had to contend with jealousy, petulance, incompetence, and insubordination of some of the high echelon army personnel. Political and public pressure played no small part in the shifting and release of generals in the field.

As the war progressed, both North and South called for more volunteers, and both sides finally resorted to the draft. By the end of the war approximately two million Union soldiers had been placed in the field of battle for the Union cause, and eight hundred thousand for the Confederacy. In most major battles the Federals were superior in number which speaks well for the valor of the rebel soldier.

With the obvious intent of the Confederacy to escalate the secession movement into a full-scale war, the Federal Government called for increased enlistments for its army and navy. The first major military strategy by the Union was to declare a blockade of southern ports. The blockade was known as the Anaconda Plan because of its snake-like action in choking life sustaining commerce through those ports. The blockade proclamation also had diplomatic advantage to the U.S. through international maritime rules; European nations were thus advised of the Southern Confederacy's status, that of a belligerent power. In the early war, the U.S. Navy did not have sufficient ships to guard all southern ports and harbors, and blockade running provided many necessities and luxuries to the Southern people.

Armies were assembled by the Federal Government to defend loyal states, to save border states for the Union, to retard the northern march of the Confederates, and to establish an offensive move into the Confederate states. New U.S. armies and army divisions were formed and new commanding generals and lesser officers appointed. Army divisions were shifted as were army commands, the latter, in many cases, to satisfy the press, the populace, or the politicians. Thus was the unstable U.S. military in the early war.

As Northern and Southern armies maneuvered to accomplish their missions, cities and towns were invaded by the respective armies and clashes between opposing forces occurred almost daily. Those clashes, variously described by history books as "light", "minor", "small", or as "skirmishes", were none the less just as serious and foreboding to the soldiers involved as were encounters in major battles.

Between the surrender of Fort Sumter on April 13, 1861 and August 25, 1862, the day Thomas Berry left family, home, and farm to join the Union army, hundreds of military encounters in as many locations had taken place in all rebelling states. Fighting also took place in the Territories, on Indian land, and as far west as the free state of California. The neutrality status of Kentucky was disregarded on September 3, 1861, when the town of Columbus, Kentucky, was occupied by a force of General Braxton Bragg's Confederate army under General Leonidas Polk against the published neutrality proclamation of that state. From that time on Union armies were compelled to enter Kentucky.

Major battles fought thus far included:

- The First Battle of Bull Run, July 21, 1861, in which the Federal army under General Irvin McDowell was routed in defeat by General Thomas J. Jackson's army. The Confederate general earned the title "Stonewall" Jackson because of his stand against the Union army in that battle which is also known as the Battle of Manassas a nearby town from which Confederate president Davis was observing the battle. The town of Manassas is located within 25 miles of Washington, D.C.

- The capture of Fort Henry on the Tennessee River by General U.S. Grant, February 6, 1862, and the capture of Fort Donelson on the Cumberland River by Grant ten days later. Both Union victories were won with the participation of the U.S. Navy under Commodore A.H. Foote. The capture of these forts in western Tennessee won strategic water-ways for the Union.

- Battle of Shiloh in western Tennessee, April 6 and 7, 1862, also known as Pittsburg Landing. Union losses were in excess of 13,000, the Confederates lost over 10,000. The Federal forces held ground as the Confederates retreated to Corinth, Mississippi, in this battle which saw Grant and Beauregard as adversaries.

- The battles of Fair Oaks and seven Pines, May 31, and June 1, 1862, within six miles of Richmond, Virginia. Confederate general Joseph E. Johnston was wounded at Fair Oaks, resulting in the promotion of Robert E. Lee to the position of commander of the army of Northern Virginia. The Confederates were successful in repelling the Union Army.

- The Seven Days battles June 25 – July 1, 1862, along with Fair Oaks and Seven Pines, proved victorious for Lee's army in staving the threat against the Confederate capitol at Richmond, Virginia by General McClellan's Army of the Potomac. McClellan's army had marched from fortress Monroe in an unsuccessful attempt to capture the Confederate capitol. That maneuver was known as the Peninsular Campaign, the brain-child of McClellan, having prevailed over Lincoln for its initiation. The failure of that campaign in spite of numerically superior Union forces proved Lincoln the better strategist.

With the threat against the Confederate capitol diminished, Lee was now able to move north and assume the offensive, threatening Washington and the northern states.

Naval encounters offshore and on inland seaways and rivers had taken their toll on both sides, and as the Confederate Armies were marching north into border and loyal states, an expanding naval blockade of Southern ports was crippling the Southern economy. The trend of the war in the summer of 1862 had not yet been determined.

The residents of Washington, D.C. were in turmoil over an uncertain defense of that city as Robert E. Lee's army threatened to advance on the United States Capitol. The 2nd Battle of Bull Run was under way, and with people tiring of war, the propaganda battle loomed against the war. Horace Greeley of the New York Tribune had in the past week criticized Lincoln's stand on pursuit of the war, and in defense of that stand Lincoln replied he would save the Union "in the shortest way under the Constitution...if without freeing any slave...or if by freeing all slaves". On the issue of preserving the Union there would be no compromise by President Lincoln. (That statement by Lincoln might well have been prompted by his need to move thought favorably for acceptance of the still secret Emancipation Proclamation. The Emancipation Proclamation would declare free, all slaves residing in rebelling states and counties. The Proclamation is a tactical maneuver planned by the President to divest the South of foreign sympathy, and to begin a program of manumission. Public announcement of the Proclamation would be made and its effective date revealed by Lincoln in timely manner.)

On August 27, 1862, Company G of the 89th Illinois infantry regiment was mustered into the United States Army. With Thomas in Company G were 92 others, 53 of whom were from Thomas' home town, Walnut Grove. Listed below are the men of Company G, mustered on August 27, 1862, with their attained rank and their town of residence given on enlisting. Thomas mentions most of them in his letters to Estelle.

MUSTER ROLL, 89TH ILLINOIS INFANTRY REGIMENT, COMPANY G, 1862

RANK	*NAME*	*HOMETOWN*
Captain	Whiting, Thomas	Walnut Grove
First Lieutenant	Copley, Isaac	Copley
2d Lieutenant	Howell, William H. (1)	Walnut Grove
First Sergeant	Tait, Peter G. (2)	Copley
Sergeants	Burneson, Richard J. (3)	Walnut Grove
	Smith, John B.	Lynn
	Swickard, John W. (4)	Walnut Grove
	Wales, Harrison G.O.	"

Above eventually promoted to:
(1) Captain; (2), (4) 1st Lieutenant; (3) 1st Sergeant.

Corporals	Allen, Squire D.	Walnut Grove
	Berry, Thomas	"
	Burneson, Nelson W. (5)	"
	Dayton, William O.	"
	Ferguson, A. Mart	"
	McLaughlin, John B.	"
	Wagoner, George H.	"
Privates	Atherton, Schyler	Walnut Grove
	Bainbridge, Charles V.	"
	Berry, George H.	"
	Berry, Isaac	Galva
	Bester, David H.	Walnut Grove
	Borkhart, Jacob	Walnut Grove
	Borkhart, Washington	"
	Brown, Christopher	Walnut Grove
	Campbell, John	Walnut Grove
	Chimberg, Nelson	Weller
	Codding, Jasper O.	Victoria
	Cole, Hiram	"
	Collinson, Charles	Walnut Grove
	Collinson, Henry G.	"
	Condrey, Edward P.	Weller
	Cragan, Jeffrey	Lynn
	Craig, Jacob F.	"
	Cramer, Jacob B.	Weller
	Dillworth, James H.	Lynn
	Dolye, Michael	Walnut Grove
	Elsworth, Albert W.	Lynn
	Ferman, William	Clover
	Fitch, William S.	Lynn
	Goddard, Henry	Lynn
	Hager, Levi	Lynn
	Hall, John L.	"
	Harris, Andrew J.	Victoria

(5) Eventually promoted to Sergeant Major.

Hester, Isaac	Walnut Grove
Hicks, William B.	Lynn
Higgims, Charles W.	Walnut Grove
Higgins, Washington L.	Walnut Grove
Hulich, John B.	Copley
Kerr, David	Lynn
Lamp, Peter	Copley
Livingston, James	Walnut Grove
Lyman, Richard H.	Lynn
McLaughlin, James W.	Walnut Grove
Mitchell, Joseph R.	"
Murphy, Benjamine F.	Walnut Grove
Murray, George W.	"
Nesbit, William H.	Walnut Grove
Newton, Winslow B.	"
Preston, Jacob	Walnut Grove
Reynolds, Andrew M.	Victoria
Reynolds, Frank	Walnut Grove
Riner, Benjamine F.	Walnut Grove
Rodgers, Needham	"
Roosa, Isaac	"
Rosenleaf, Hiram J.	Copley
Rowe, Charles	Henderson
Scagriff, Michael	Walnut Grove
Scott, William	"
Scudder, DeWitt C.	"
Smith, Herman P.	"
Smith, Russell M.	"
Spohr, Matern	Lynn
Sprouse, David E.	Weller
Sprouse, Isaac	"
Sprouse, Thomas	"
Starr, George B.	Walnut Grove
Stephens, Edward W.	"
Stoddard, Elliott M.	Weller

Stowell, Arad G.	Walnut Grove
Stroyan, William	"
Taggart, William D.	Weller
Tait, Horneston P.	Copley
Tait, John	"
Tait, William	"
Thompson, David	Walnut Grove
Topper, Andrew	"
Ulmbaugh, Jacob	Lynn
Ward, William E.	Walnut Grove
Wells, George H.	"
Whitney, Theodore F.	Knoxville
Whitney, Wilford H.	"
Wilson, Robert	Walnut Grove
Woolsey, David	"

Part 3

The First Letter

Three days after leaving home, Thomas Berry wrote his first letter to Estelle.

Camp Williams, August 28, 1862

Dear Wife,

    I thought I would write you a few lines to let you know how I am getting along. I am well and enjoy camp life very well so far. We arrived in camp Tuesday about noon. I did not get anything to eat from the time I left home until the middle of Tuesday afternoon, and we are not supplied with tents yet. Our Captain found tents for about a dozen the first night. I was one of that number and had a good nights rest. Last night I slept out in the open air, we had plenty of hay and our blankets. I am to day assistant cook. We have plenty to eat, we have good bread, coffee, sugar, fresh beef, potatoes, rice. We expect to have our tents and uniforms to day. We have drawn only our blanket. Our company have not yet been examined by the physician, but expect to be to day. Then we will draw our uniforms. Then I expect to get a furlough home but cannot say certain. Yesterday our company went down to lake Michigan and took a wash which is only about a half a mile off. I visited Douglas burying ground. Our camp is right south of camp Douglas. I saw some of the secesh as we passed along. Don't look for me for I cannot tell as yet what day I shall start. You had better have the threshers come on Monday if you can get them. I will be home by that time if I can come. I have not time to write anymore at this time, kiss Louella and Sylvester for me and tell them that their par would like to see them. I believe camp life will agree with me very well. I must close by sending my love to you and the children, from your husband

Thomas Berry

I cannot tell you as yet where to write, we talk some of changing our camp a few miles north.

Camp Douglas is a Union Army camp near Chicago providing temporary housing for rebel prisoners of war. Neither side has adequate facilities for holding all prisoners taken in the war and policy regarding treatment of prisoners varies as the war progresses. To relieve the burden of providing food, shelter, and medical aid to the enemy, prisoners are paroled to their respective governments. By means of a cartel between the Union and Confederate military councils, prisoners of war are detained no longer than ten days in enemy camps, and after release are to remain on parole until exchanged for paroled prisoners from the opposite camp. A paroled prisoner is honor bound to refrain from military duty until notified he is exchanged for a soldier of equivalent rank on parole from the opposing side. Such notification is the responsibility of the respective governments in respecting the cartel.

Under the parole system, it is not uncommon for entire companies of captured soldiers to be immediately released on the field of battle and sent back to their commanders with orders to report as paroled prisoners of war.

During the honorable parole, a soldier waiting exchange could be granted a furlough, or take leave of the parole camp as permitted by the commanding officer. Privates were exchanged on a one to one basis. Officers of like rank were also on a one to one basis. The exchange of officers for soldiers of lesser rank was based on a cartel of 1812 between the U.S. and Great Britain; for instance, "A lieutenant colonel, or commander in the navy, shall be exchanged for officers of equal rank, or for ten privates or common seamen." Such equations were established for all ranks. To the present time in Thomas Berry's military life, the above cartel is being honored.

The governments of both North and South were honor bound in respect to the cartel regarding exchange of prisoners. The cartel was honored until mid-1863 when the South could no longer wait for exchange candidates and immediately pressed into service those paroled in their care and not yet exchanged. That practice alone did not put an end to the exchange program, the exchange of prisoners ceased after the Confederacy refused to parole black prisoners. With the exchange program discontinued, prisons both north and south became overcrowded.

Thomas uses the colloquialism "secesh" to indicate a secessionist. In this case he refers to imprisoned rebel soldiers.

Sunday, Camp Williams, August 31, 1862

Dear Estelle,

I thought I must write and let you know of my adventures today. In the first place, George and myself got a pass to the city. We took a ramble through the principal streets and then went upon the Court house where we had a fine view of the whole city. It was about one hundred and eighty steps to the top, after we got through viewing the city we went to the Methodist Church and heard Bishop Jaynes preach, he preached a Missionary sermon. After the sermon was over we went to a public house and got our dinner. The best dinner I ever had away from home, they charged us three shillings apiece. Their usual fare is a half of a dollar, but they said they throwed off one shilling for soldiers, so much for being a soldier. After that we looked around a little and got in a street car and was off for our camp. The street cars come down opposite our camp, the fare on the cars was five cents, which I thought was cheap enough for about three miles ride.

I cannot tell when I can come home, we have not drawn our bounty yet but we expect to Tuesday and then I shall go if it is amongst the possibilities, 40 Dols we expect to get. I have drawn all my uniform except my cap and shoes, I have one overcoat, one dress coat, one blouse or fatigue coat, one pair of pants, two pair of drawers, two pair of shirts. I like the shirts first rate they do not prick me any, they are colored.

I have just heard that we expect to have marching orders by Thursday. It looks pretty squally about getting home. If I could come home and stay a day or two I would be satisfied, but if I cant I will make the best of it. If the threshers have not come on yet you had better get Ira to do the threshing. I keep well, I hope this will find you and the children well. You may write as soon as you get this and write how you get along. I want to hear very much, direct as follows,

Camp Williams
89 Regiments
c/o Capt Whiting
Chicago, Ills

From your affectionate husband,

Thos. Berry

P.S. They have appointed me Corporal, they are exempt from Guard duty.

Chicago, 1862

Corporal's uniform on an unidentified soldier

Conscription had not yet been introduced by the Union at the time of Thomas' enlistment. To expedite formation of an army Unit a bonus or "bounty" was offered to those who would volunteer to serve in the military. Bounty due to Thomas is one hundred dollars.

Military training was extremely brief as indicated by the "marching orders" after ten days of enlistment. As Thomas was writing on August 31, 1862, General Pope's Union army was losing the final encounter in the Second Battle of Bull Run.

A battle may be known by two or more names in the attempt to identify that battle with the general area at which it was fought. Major battles such as Bull Run engaged many army divisions and extended for several miles involving more than a single town or village. With few exceptions, the North named battles after geographical features on or near which the engagement took place, using the names of rivers, creeks, valleys, hills, or mountains; the South identified those same battles by using the names of nearby villages, towns, or cities.

The Second Bull Run Battle is also called Second Manassas, the Battle of Manassas Plains, the Battle of Groveton, the Battle of Chantilly, and the Battle of Ox Hill, all areas of the various encounters in that three-week campaign.

The Second Battle of Bull Run ended August 31, 1862, with retreat by the Union army to Alexandria. Pope's Army of Virginia ceases to exist as such, and that army is being absorbed into the Army of the Potomac under General McClellan's command.

With that Confederate victory, Lee has effectively removed the Federal army from the State of Virginia, and now he plans to move north into Maryland. Lee's objective in his next campaign is to draw Union troops to him and away from Washington. At the same time, he hopes to win the support of Maryland, one of the remaining slave states not claimed by the Confederacy.

Wednesday, 1 O'clock, September 3, 1862

Dear Wife,

This is to inform you that I have received twenty seven dollars and shall send twenty dollars to you by express, it will start from here this afternoon so you must go to Waldo's and get it. George is going to send twenty dollars to Harriet, it will be all in one envelope so you can give twenty dollars to Harriet. We have received our arms and expect to leave here by tomorrow night, our destination is not certain but we expect it will be Cincinnati or Louisville, Kentucky, but cannot tell for certain so I expect it will be along time before I shall see you again. My prayers is that the grace of God will be with you continually and may you rely on him for strength in times of trouble and if our lives should not be spared to meet together here on earth may we meet in that home where we never shall be parted. The Union army appears to

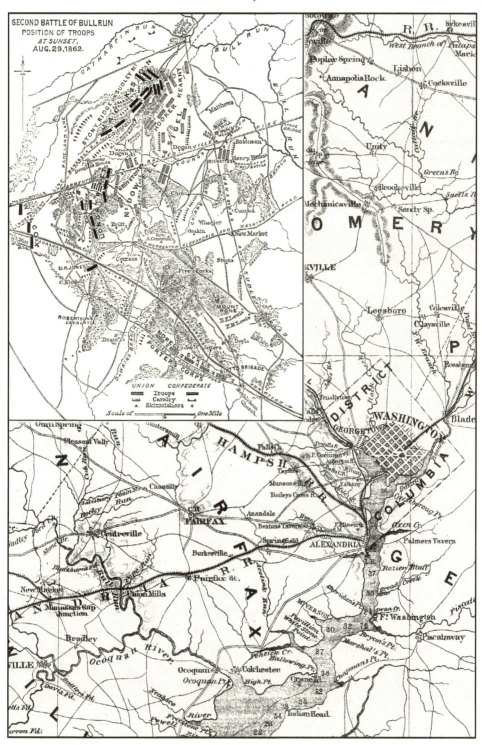

be losing ground. The rebels are doing all they can, they think this is their only chance before fresh troops get into the field.

Thomas received twenty-five dollars bounty money and a two dollars premium for having to wait payment of the remaining seventy five dollars.

He is correct in his assumption of Louisville as his destination since a Confederate army under the command of General Braxton Bragg is marching toward that city. At this same time a Confederate army under the command of General E.K. Smith is marching north from Tennessee and toward Cincinnati, Ohio.

Shortly after his retreat from Shiloh, Beauregard, due to ill health had placed temporary command of his army in the hands of General Bragg, intending to return to his duty following recovery from his brief illness. President Jefferson Davis having learned of that field operation, placed the command of Beauregard's army permanently under Bragg, taking that opportunity to undermine Beauregard who was growing in popularity with the Southern people. Such petulant and unmilitary administration is characteristic of Davis much to the frustration of his more brilliant generals. The manner of Beauregard's retreat from Shiloh bought precious time in which the Southern army was allowed to build. Now, five months later, the prospects for successful prosecution of the war by the rebels looks promising. The Confederate government has initiated conscription of all white males between the ages of 18 and 35, and munitions are starting to flow from southern factories as well as from foreign sources shipped through Confederate ports not yet effectively blocked by the Federal navy.

Camp Williams, September 4, 1862

Dear Wife,

I have just received your letter and portfolio that your Mother made me, tell her that I am very much obliged to her for it. It was just the thing I wanted. I was glad to hear that you had the threshing done. You say you had a dunning letter from Sterling, take no notice of it, they cannot sue while I am off to war. The receipt is in the stand draw, it was understood that the policy should be cancelled and the note given up with their agent at Oneida. You did not state how Prince was. I have got my likeness taken it will come wrapped up with my clothes, it will come by express. Don't forget to pay Mr. Brush 20 cts. for those bridal bits when you get the change. My likeness cost $1.50. We expect to leave to day or to morrow. From your husband

Thomas Berry

Direct as follows and it will follow the regiment wherever we go

Thomas Berry
c/o Capt. Whiting
Camp William's
89 Railroad Regiment
Chicago, Ills.

    Write often, I think the wheat turned out very well. I have not time to go and buy a stove, you had better get William to go with you to Oneida or Galesburg and get one to suit yourself. If you cannot drive Nelly you had better make that change you spoke of. I am sixth Corporal, they are designated by two stripes around the arm.
    There is a man in our company by the name of Isaac Berry. Our Colonels name is Christopher, your father is well. George has received a lot of things from home. I have just received the testament and letter and was pleased to receive it.

Prince, Nelly, and Fanny are horses used for farm work and transportation. Areas of military operations in the states and territories were generally defined as the Eastern, Western, and Trans-Mississippi Theaters. The Appalachian Mountain Range which runs northeast to southwest provided the broad center between the Eastern and Western Theaters. The Eastern Theater, defined as the land between the Appalachians and the Atlantic Coast, is the area in which Lee's Army of Northern Virginia is marching against General George B. McClellan's Union Army of the Potomac near Sharpsburg, Maryland, 250 miles northwest of Washington D. C.

In the Trans-Mississippi Theater, which includes the Mississippi River and the states and territories west of that river, the Union is at this time using one of its armies under General H. H. Sibley to put down a Sioux uprising in Minnesota. Other Union armies in the Trans-Mississippi Theater are at work in Missouri and the territories. Thomas' regiment is now ordered to Camp Manchester near Louisville, Kentucky. The 89th is assigned as an infantry regiment to the third brigade, second division, in the Army of Kentucky under Major General William Nelson.

General Nelson of the Unites States Army, holds also the rank of navy lieutenant. Entry into army life was a result of his observation while on navy leave in early 1861 of the plight of Union volunteers from his native state Kentucky, who were in short supply of firearms. Nelson advised President Lincoln of that situation and was in turn authorized by Lincoln to deliver Federal arms to those recruits; Nelson was further authorized to recruit cavalry and infantry to escort arms into eastern Tennessee. He assembled recruits on the Kentucky farm of Richard M. Robinson. That area became known as Camp Dick Robinson, birthplace of the Cumberland Army. He became brigadier general in the Army of the Ohio under General Don Carlos Buell at the approach of Bragg's Armies. He ordered the evacuation of non—

combatants from the city, directing them across the Ohio River into Indiana and Illinois. The terrified citizens fled northward with their valuable possessions, and Nelson declared martial law in effect in Louisville.

Confederate generals Bragg and Smith are marching their forces north toward the Ohio River in the Western Theater, the area of operation for the 89th Illinois regiment.

General Bragg with his Army of Mississippi is attempting to reach Louisville before the arrival of Union General Don C. Buell and his Army of the Ohio. Nelson's forces alone are not sufficient to defend Louisville against Bragg's large army.

Private Isaac Berry, unrelated to Thomas, is from Galva, Illinois.

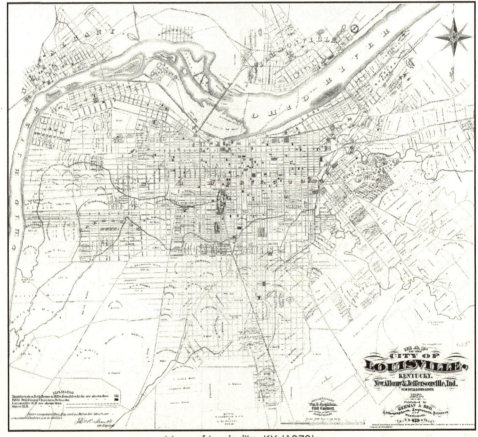

Map of Louisville, KY (1873);
Camp Manchester lay near Jeffersonville, IN, just across the Ohio River.

Camp Manchester, September 10, 1862

Dear Wife,

 I am at leisure at the present time, so I thought I would write to you that you may know how I am at the present time. I am well, I have not been sick a minute since I left home. I am getting pretty well use to camp life. I was out on duty from yesterday at eleven O'clock until today at nine. I had to place the guard around the camp. They detail so many men from each company to make three squads of fifteen men each. They are called reliefs, one corporal to each relief. Each relief is on four hours at a time for twenty four hours. My turn comes on once in eight days, when the corporals are all fit for duty.

 I had to sleep out under a tree with my blanket what time I had to sleep. Your Father has been quite sick. He has not been able to do anything since he came from Chicago. If he had been at home he would have been called a very sick man, but he has made the best of it. I was afraid it would go hard with him but he is improving very fast now. He is at the present time writing home. He told me day before yesterday that he would not write until he got better. I went out of camp last Sunday and bought a chicken and made him some chicken broth, he said it relished firstrate, and I have cooked him rice quite a number of times. Reynolds takes the principal care of him. He is a firstrate hand, he gets some milk every day. George is well he is out on guard duty today. It is very warm here, it has not rained here for four months. There is a large army concentrating here. How long we will stay here I cannot tell. I have learned more about war than I would in a year at home. We had preaching in our regiment last Sunday by one of our Captains, a methodist preacher. Wm. Dayton is well.

 We are using the army bread since we came here, it is about as hard as a brickbat. It is made in the shape of soda crackers and of the same color only they are about a third larger. They taste very good, but it requires good teeth to chew them. I think they are healthy, I have washed a shirt and one pair of stockings since we came here. I have drawn two pair of stockings. They told me that I had to draw them. They are firstrate socks I am well supplied with clothing. I bought me a pocket handkerchief yesterday. Most everything is sold around camp. Sell wheat enough to buy any thing that you need. See that it is well covered up. You had better get William to haul, five or six loads of coal before corn picking time and as much more as you think best. Have you got the beans pulled yet. Buy a good stove and enjoy yourself as well as you can. I have not received any letter from you since we came here. How do you like the likeness, I want you to get the childrens likeness taken. I wish I had yours and the children here. There is a Daguerrean gallery close to our camp he takes firstrate pictures better then they took them at Chicago. I should like to step in and see you and the children firstrate.

From your husband

Thos Berry

"George" is Thomas Berry's brother. A "Daguerrean gallery" is the earliest type photographic studio, named after Frenchman Louis J.M. Daguerre, inventor of the first process used for chemically developing pictures. Prior to Daguerre's discovery, pictures were produced by the use of the 'camera obscura', a box containing a lens focusing an image on a ground glass plate. After focusing, the plate was covered with translucent paper on which a picture was produced by tracing the image.

The Daguerrean process focused the image on a silver coated copper plate which had been treated with vapors of some halogen elements. After exposure, the plate was exposed to heated mercury for development, fixed, washed, and ornately encased behind glass. Daguerre was rewarded by the French government with a pension for revealing his process to the world. The Daguerrean process reached America immediately upon publication in 1839.

George Andrew Yocum, age 14, enlisted in the Confederate army at Springfield, Kentucky, on September 10, 1862. Yocum gave his age as eighteen when he mustered in as a private in Company K, 4th Regiment, Kentucky Cavalry. [He rode with the Morgan raiders, the deeds of which were the antithesis of Thomas Berry's political, social, and religious bearing. Thomas' daughter Louella married George Yocum in 1879.]

Camp Near Louisville, September 17, 1862

Dear Wife,

It is with pleasure that I spend these few moments in writing to you. I am well and in hopes that this will find you and the children in the enjoyment of good health. Our regiment has seen hard times since I have written to you. We had marching orders from Camp Manchester last Monday morning for a grand review. Our acting Colonel wanted us to show off to a good advantage so he told us to dress up in our best and then he marched us all through Louisville on a quick time. He did not rest the men until about a third of the men gave out and dropped by the side of the road. When they first begun to fall out the acting Colonel drew his revolver on some of the men, finally they fell out so fast that he halted the men for a rest. There was two or three men that came pretty nigh dying. Charles Collinson of our company came very near dying, he wilted right down and could not hardly move himself for an hour. He is now quite smart. After that we rested pretty often.

We kept marching until night, we marched some of the ground over twice. It was all by mismanagement, the Colonel says he had orders for all he had done but most of the men do not believe it. I have heard great many of the men say that they will shoot him in the first battle. When we got into our camp here at night there was not more then half the regiment in ranks. They was scattered all along the road and they all did not get here until the next morning. I did not leave the ranks, I stood it very well, but it was a hard days work. Your father and George stood it well. William Dayton came very near giving out, he is well and all right now. Your father is getting pretty well, he has lost good many pounds of flesh, the commissioned officers has the advantage of the rest of us they do not have to carry any load. I believe it was as warm a day as I ever experienced. I was out with a squad of men last night on picket duty. I had to see that they kept their places and bring around the relief once in two hours. There is not any easy place in the army. We all find enough to do. Our regiment is formed into a brigade. There is about one hundred thousand soldiers stationed around here about three thousand are on picket duty. It is so warm that I have bought me a cotton shirt. I wish I had mine here that I sent home. If you get this before Ben River starts for here I wish you would send me one of my cotton shirts, or Homer. Capt had a letter from him Sunday he said he was a coming. I received a letter from you Sunday and the postage stamps. It was the first letter that I received from you since I left Chicago. You did not write that you received any money. I sent twenty Dollars to you and George sent twenty to Harriet all in one envelop and directed to you. I sent it by Harriet Whiting the same day that we left Chicago. I sent home two pair of socks last Sunday and a lock of my hair. Lieut Howell sent home a trunk. I put it in the trunk. George sent home two pair also.

    I cannot tell how long we will stay here but I do not believe we will long. One of our regiment died last Monday morning of congestive chills. He was buried yesterday. I was to the funeral. A very good sermon was preached. I sent you three kinds of flower seed wrapped up together. I must close, write all the news, how is the corn coming on, give my love to all enquiring friends and a good share to your self.

Thos. Berry

The hard march forced upon the 89th regiment by the acting colonel, resulting in so many soldiers unfit for immediate duty, appears inconsistent with military preparations required to meet imminent attack by the enemy. On September 17, Bragg's army forced the surrender of the Union garrison at Munfordville, Kentucky, within 70 miles south of Louisville, and is now continuing its march to the north. On this same day, the armies of Lee and McClellan have met in the Battle of Antietam in what is termed the bloodiest one-day battle of the Civil War with over 12,000 dead and wounded on each side. Lee, with the smaller army, has suffered the greater loss in terms of percentage. Antietam is the name of a creek in Maryland flowing into the Potomac River. The Confederates name this battle after the town of Sharpsburg, Maryland.

The Battle of Antietam, which can hardly be called an overwhelming victory by the Union, causes Lee to halt his march to the north and forces his retreat into his home state of Virginia. McClellan does not pursue the retreating army to the dismay of Lincoln who plans to visit McClellan on the battlefield of Antietam to learn first-hand the reason for lack of pursuit of the rebels.

That battle and the retreat of Lee, however, gives Lincoln the opportunity he needs to publish his Emancipation Proclamation, since now with the defeat of the South's largest army, it will appear to both North and South and to the world at large, that the United States remains strong. The Proclamation which had been in preparation for several weeks by Lincoln, can now be put forth with conviction, and not as an appeal from a weak and diminishing nation.

The Emancipation Proclamation is to become effective January 1, 1863, and will declare to be free, all slaves in states and counties of states still in rebellion on that date. The Proclamation does not free slaves in those states and counties not in rebellion. [Such universal freedom will come about later with the thirteenth amendment to the Constitution. Official announcement of the Emancipation Proclamation will be made to the armed forces on September 24, 1862.]

"Homer" is Corporal George Homer Wagoner of Walnut Grove. A light brown "lock of hair" was found with this letter.

Camp Manchester, September 18, 1862

Dear Wife,

Enclosed you will find the order for fifty Dollars. I have heard that the money was ready, if you cant get the money now you can get a bounty order so you send this order to Knoxville by some responsible man and get the money or bounty order. I received your letter yesterday and was sorry to hear of so much sickness. I am well as usual. Your father is well, he has gone to the city this morning to buy him some things. We are under marching orders. Where we are going I cannot tell, if you think it is too hard for you to stay on the place you may try and get some goodman to come and take the place. I should rather have Barnes then anybody that I know of. I was in hopes that you could stay on the place until spring but you can do, just as you think best. You had better go and see Barnes and find out what share of the corn crop he wants for husking and cribbing the corn. If you leave the place you had better sell the hogs and the pigs if you can. Rent the place for one year and have a written contract. Get Becker to write it. If you think that Prince cant get well you had better get somebody to put him out of misery.

We have been digging trenches to protect the city for the last two days. There was one man shot in our regiment yesterday. He was shot by one of the guard for disobeying an order that was given by the Colonel. There was not one man in fifty that knew of such an order. He was sick at the time. The ball went through his arm and hip. It was a horrible affair. I think the Colonel and the guard will pay the penalty. There was good deal of excitement in the regiment. If our regimental officers are not changed before long, there will be an outbreak of some kind. I have heard as many as one hundred men say that they will shoot the acting Colonel, Colonel Christopher is not with us. I think when he comes things will go better. Homer Waggoner is here.

I think the prospects is pretty good for the war to close by spring. Write as you receive this.

Yours as ever

Thomas Berry

After learning of the surrender of the Union garrison at Munfordville, General Buell proceeded to that town to give battle. Upon arrival Buell found the Confederates had pulled out and are again heading north. A race to Louisville is now underway between Buell and Bragg.

The purpose for the "marching orders" is unclear, particularly for a force dedicated to the defense of a city facing an oncoming army.

Becker did not write the rent contract. Estelle traveled to Altona and had Herman Copley draw the lease, as she recorded in her diary.

"Homer Waggoner" is corporal George Homer Wagoner.

At the suburbs of the City of Louisville,
September 23, 1862

Dear Wife,

In my last letter I wrote that we was under marching orders, we started Friday about eleven Oclock, we marched about seven miles and stopped until yesterday forenoon, when we was ordered back to the city on account of the report of the advance of Braggs army on the city. His army is estimated at from fifty to eighty thousand. I think that they will meet with a warm reception if they attempt to take the city. We have in the neighborhood of one hundred thousand men stationed around the city and the city is pretty well fortified. We are at the present time close to our entrenchments. There has been great many colored men at work here, women and children have been ordered from the city. If Braggs army should come here there would be a great battle. I have just heard that General Buel was on the rear of Braggs army, if it is so Braggs army will likely to be captured with our force and Buels. Tuesday afternoon the news is that the enemy is approaching in force. We are getting ready as fast as possible. There was an order read to each company to be in readiness to meet the enemy at any time. We are in the 2nd division and 3rd brigade of Kentucky, under General Nelson, he is called a good officer. There is an artillery company about twenty rods from where I am writing, placing their artillery in position. I know not what is before me. I can only put my trust in God knowing that he ordereth all things, if I fall I feel to put my trust in him. Business of all kind is stopped in the city, everything is governed by military rule. We are ordered to fall in for drill so I must close. Tuesday evening, we have just got our tents pitched and I have washed and changed my shirt and I feel good deal better. I have one shirt and a pair of stockings to wash in the morning if the rebels do not come so I will close until morning by wishing you goodnight. Wednesday morning, our whole regiment was sent out on picket duty, we started out about ten Oclock. I had just got to sleep when we was aroused. Companies was placed around in different places to watch to see if the enemy was coming. We laid on a side hill with our blanket. This morning our company is divided up into squads placed along different roads not anybody is allowed to travel without a pass. I have the charge of ten men. We are about three miles from the city. The hospital is about half of a mile from here. A man just told me that there was about five hundred sick in the hospital. Troops are pouring in very fast, ten thousand came in this morning. I received a letter from Emeline last evening, she stated that Harriet was married and was going to Victoria to make you all a visit.

Thomas Berry

When the 89th Illinois regiment joined with Nelson there were 22,000 men for the defense of Louisville. Bragg was in the area bringing, according to Buell's June report, 56,706 men ready for duty.

(Any attempt by latter day writers to claim exact figures for the size of an army force in battle on any given day is presumptuous and leads to debate. For many reasons, the number of soldiers in an army ready for a specific battle may vary from the muster role tally used for calculating those figures. Between role tallies there occurs authorized leave, assignment of the army units to other areas, assignment to staff duty, sickness, desertion, and death. The army may also increase in the number ready for duty by those returning from leave, recruitment, and assignment of additional forces. In many cases records were not maintained nor did contemporary recorders of the Civil War always agree on the size of every army force either North or South.)

Buell did not gain the "rear" of Bragg's army. Instead, Buell's army entered Louisville directly on September 25, and continued for four days to pour into that city.

Bragg, with 68,000 Confederates, was at Bardstown on September 26, within 30 miles of Louisville issuing a proclamation to the people of that town and the state of Kentucky in general, in an attempt to endear the cause of dis-Union to the populace. His purpose, he stated, was not invasion of the territory, but "to secure peace, and the abandonment by the United States of their pretensions to govern a people who never have been their subjects, and who prefer self-government to a union with them." Bragg had hoped to gain volunteers for his army (a practice not inconsistent with invading armies). Kentucky, however, was not entirely dis-Union and on that score Bragg was disappointed.

Bragg went on with his proclamation to the point of ultimatum. "Here I am" he said "with an army which, including Smith's off to my right, numbers not less than sixty thousand men. I bring the olive branch which you refuse at your peril."

After feigning an attack upon Cincinnati, the army of O.K. Smith planned to meet that of Bragg's for a concentrated approach to Louisville. That meeting did not come about in time for the planned attack, nor could Bragg make a timely assault upon Louisville because of a destroyed bridge in his path at the Salt River. With Louisville fortified, and with an increasing number of Federal troops entering the city, Bragg withdrew from his plan of occupation.

Bragg and Smith met in early October at which time, notwithstanding the loss of Louisville, the two generals acted confident of holding the state of Kentucky for the Confederacy.

Sunday, September 23, 1862

Dear Wife,

>   I have just returned from church and I thought I would let you know that I am well and getting along very well. We had a very good sermon, the text was, what is man that thou art mindful of him or the son of man that thou fearest him. Our regiment do not care much about meetings, there was not more then seventy five out, seven from our company. Most of the soldiers appears to have lost all the restraints of home. We have a hard regiment as far as morality is concerned, most of the men go into vice of all kinds as far as they can. But still we have good many good upright men, a man requires good deal of stability to live as he should in camp. Everything around him tends to degrade

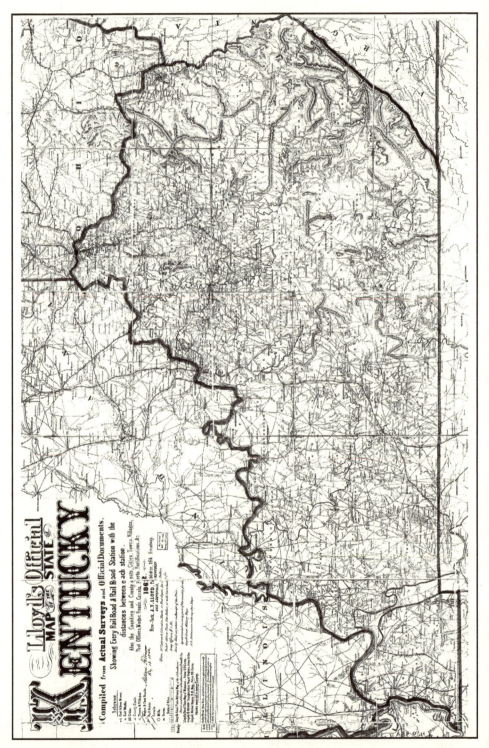

man in his own estimation and the estimation of others but I intend by the grace of God to live an upright life that if I should live to see the close of the war that I may have nothing to look back to regret. And I hope that you will aid me by your prayers that I may carry out these resolutions. Our chaplain is a congregationalist. We moved our camping yesterday in about a half of a mile of the Ohio river close to the city. The report is that we are agoing into another division. There will not be any battle here. The country around the city is swarming with troops. I heard someone say that there was about one hundred and fifty thousand. If all the soldiers in the field are commanded by the right kind of men I think rebellion will be used up in short time. There has been great many sick in our regiment. There is some in the hospital, Mr. Wales has been sick most of the time since we left Chicago, he has the ague all the old men do not stand it very well. I never enjoyed better health than I have since I left home. As long as a man keeps well he is all right but if he gets sick he is in a hard place. They have none of the comforts of home. Your father has had another drawback and been quite sick. Our regiment was all out on picket duty, I believe it was last Tuesday night and we all had to lay on the ground which is more than he can stand and the next morning he had the shake of the ague and has been quite feeble but is improving quite fast. I wish he could go home and stay about one month. I am afraid that he will not get well and rugged until he does. He cannot stand marching and sleeping on the ground with his present health and I am pretty well satisfied in my own mind that he will have to resign. His constitution will not bare such hard usage. Perhaps you had better keep this from your folks until they hear of it from some other source.

 I can sleep as sound on the ground as I could on a feather bed when I was at home. I should like soldiering very well if it was not that I had to be away from my family. I got those letters that you sent by Ben River and one a short time before. I have heard that Father Copleys is dead. Write and tell me all a bout the funeral, did he have his reason to the last and did he feel resigned, who preached the funeral sermon. You see that I have sent you another order the first one they say is not right. Joseph Copley can tell you how to get the money. Write as soon as you receive this and keep me posted in all that is going on. I must close for I have to go on dress parade in a few minutes.

 I shall number my letters after this and I want you to number yours and then we will know if we get them all.

 From your husband

Thomas Berry

No. 1

"Father Copley" is Estelle's grandfather.

September 29, 1862

Dear Estelle,

I have just received your letter dated Sept 22nd and was very sorry to hear that my Sylvester boy had been sick. There has not anything happened for a long time that has made me feel so bad. You must try and doctor him well if you can. I think you had better get some medicine from some doctor or get some advice from a doctor. When you write tell me just how he is. I sent you a letter yesterday with another order and they say that it is not right, we have received a form from Buffon so I guess this will be all right. You can find out by Joseph Copley how to get the money. Write as soon as you receive this. I will number my letters so you will know when you get all mine and you must number yours, this is no. 2.

William Dayton is going to send his order in this letter so you can hand it to Benjamin.

Thomas Berry

The talk is that we will soon leave here. It is getting cooler now and I will not need that cotton shirt. I have not time to write any more.

Louisville, Kentucky, September 30, 1862

Dear Wife,

I thought you would like to hear from me often so again I take this opportunity to write you a few lines. I am well as usual, your Fathers health is very poor. He tried to get a furlough home but the Colonel would not grant him one. He told me this morning that if he could not get home and did not get better pretty soon he would resign. I am sorry that he cannot stand it better for he would have made the best officer in the company. But as it is I think the best thing for him to do is to resign, for I am satisfied that he cannot stand the hardships of war. Gen. F. Nelson was shot yesterday. Brigadier General by the name of Davis had a dispute and Nelson slapped him in the face and Davis drew a revolver and shot him, he lived fifteen minutes and expired.

Our regiment is changed to another Division in McCooks, and to be in the reserve of Buels army, Buels army is here I suppose to reorganize. There is an immense army here at the present time. I do not think we will see any fighting very soon for we will have such an army that the rebels will have to skedaddle. It looks to me that the rebellion will be used up in three months, if our army is handled right, but still I may be misstaken, time will tell. There is four in the hospital from our company, Wales, Scott, Dilworth, and Hall. We have a sutler in our regiment but he charges about ten prices for everything cheese 25 cts a lb butter 40 cts and bread cakes in proportion. It would be fine thing if they would only sell reasonable. I have not bought much of him. I bought 5 cts worth of butter last night, I got just about enough for one meal. They keep crackers, tea pickles, herring, sardines, candies and great many other things that is needed if they would only sell for reasonable prices. I do not calculate to buy much as long as I keep well. I understand the manual of arms very well. We have to drill about four hours a day. When we are in camp, we have dress parade every evening just before sundown. The whole regiment is formed in two lines and the commissioned officers are called to the front and the Colonel gives them their orders and we go through the manual of arms. It is done for show more then anything else. A regiment looks splendid in that position. I suppose we will draw some more money in the course of two weeks. Our officers are making out the pay rolls. They are paid once in two months. What I send home after this I shall send by express. I wish you would send some more postage stamps they are getting very scarce here and it is a great place to beg stamps, I have lent six. I have just one left for this letter. I guess you think that I send orders enough. I guess the last one will be all right. Write and let me know and tell me all about Sylvester. I am anxious to hear about him often. Get his likeness by all means. Our company has been down to the river and taken a good wash and I washed one shirt. We had a good time.

    Yours as ever

                                          Thos. Berry

"F. Nelson" is the previously mentioned Major—General William Nelson. Nelson was killed in cold blood by his fellow officer, Union General Jefferson C. Davis, following an argument. Davis was immediately arrested and held for court martial, but that trial did not come about. Davis was released and returned to duty, much to General Buell's disgust. (Buell wrote later of the incident "Nothing but the law of violence could, under any circumstances, justify the manner of the killing for the alleged provocation, and no more merit of ordinary soldiership could ever atone for the sacrilege against discipline under the circumstances which existed".)

General Nelson was killed on the morning of September 29, 1862, one day before he was to march in pursuit of Bragg. Nelson's division was immediately assigned to General Charles C. Gilbert, the transfer of command resulting in delay of the proposed operation against Bragg's retreating army. On October 1, the 89th

Illinois regiment was assigned to the Sixth brigade under General Willich, Second division, General Sill, in General Alexander McCook's corps of Buell's Army of the Ohio.

Bragg left Bardstown and traveled east to Frankfort to combine his army with that of General E.K. Smith. A Confederate force remained at Bardstown to delay Buell's pursuit. Buell rested a large part of his army at Louisville for a week, in which time the Confederate army foraged and ransacked the countryside and destroyed supplies which would have been useful to the Union army.

Buell's delay in chasing Bragg is now the bone of contention chewed by many from the foot soldier on up the ranks to Washington and the political machinery. Buell later defended that delay by correctly stating the majority of his men needed rest, and the necessary reorganization of his large army at Louisville after the death of Nelson was time consuming. He ordered his army on the move in search of Bragg on October 1.

Part 4

The Chase After Bragg

Close to the town of Shelbyville,
Friday October 3, 1862

We left camp on Wednesday on a force march after the rebels. There was quite a force of them in ten miles of Louisville but when they heard that the federals was a comeing they skedaddled. They were cavalry. We took our lunch the first day where the rebels camped the night before and the rebels had possession of Shelbyville night before we came. They had the cession flag a floating in the town but when they heard of our advance they pulled it down in a hurry. The citizens of the town expressed a strong union sentiments as we passed through, men and women waved their handkerchiefs and appeared to be almost overjoyed at our appearance. Some of the women brought out pies and cakes and gave to the soldiers. I believe most of them was Union people. They said there was quite a contrast between our soldiers and the rebels. I heard a darkey say that they would draw themselves up in a line of battle and then they would break and run. Their officers could not control them. The colored people are good deal more intelligent then I supposed them to be. One of our boys asked one of them if he would not come along and fight the rebels, his answer was, I would if I thought you could not whip them. We are in about thirty miles of Louisville, two days march. My feet got pretty sore, we are not going to march to day. I suppose we will start again to morrow. We took three days rations in our haversacks. We left our knapsacks and tents and about 24 men in our company that was not able to march, back to Louisville. We have one blanket to a man so we have not a very big load to carry. I suppose we will go on to Lexington. There is a large force started out from Louisville, I believe it is about fifty miles from here to Lexington. The worst thing about marching is the scarceity of water, it is not very often that we get any water that is fit to drink. It has been so dry here that water is very scarce, the water is very good here. I think that the rebels will soon be scarce in Kentucky. We had quite a shower yesterday which makes it more pleasant travelling. No more to day.

Saturday morning. I received a letter from you last night dated Sept 28th and one this morning Sept 26th with the postage stamps. They came good I will send one back on this letter. I have not received the paper, yet, I should like to get the Advocate firstrate. I am sorry that you cannot get any help, do just as you think best and I will be satisfied. I cannot tell here what is the best for you to do. I think Thos McClum would be a good man to take the place. I spoke to Murry about it this morning. He said his father has never farmed it much but he thought he would do very well. I should think you had better go to Victoria if you rent. It will not cost near as much for fuel and you will be close to your folks. I think you might have part of Mothers house as well as not. I have just heard that the balance of our company was most here and your Father is to have a furlough home. I am getting along well if you and the children keep well.

From your husband Thos Berry

I think the war will not last long.

Bragg passed through Shelbyville on his march to Frankfort. As Buell is pressing to rid Kentucky of Bragg and his rebel army, the armies of General Grant and General William S. Rosecrans are fighting to hold Western Kentucky, Western Tennessee, and Northern Mississippi for the Union. General Rosecrans fought a major battle at Corinth, Mississippi, on October 3, 4, and 5, causing the Confederate army of General Earl Van Dorn to retreat with his army to the south. Rosecrans congratulated his troops for the victory at Corinth against a force "almost double your own numbers".

"Murry" is private George W. Murray from Walnut Grove. Thomas spoke to Murray about engaging Murray's father to assist Estelle with chores on the farm at Walnut Grove. Thomas refers to the elder Murray as "Murry" in later letters. The haversack is a shoulder bag issued by the army for carrying the soldier's rations. Commonly of canvas, the bag is approximately thirteen inches square, expandable to hold about the equivalent of a peck of oats (eight dry quarts). With tin cup attached, the bag is worn at hip length. Haversacks of leather with a separate pocket to hold a bottle of "medicine", sold by sutlers and generally purchased by officers, are more durable and water resistant as opposed to the canvas bag which, after a short time in the field, does little to protect its contents from rain damage.

In two miles of Frankfort, Kentucky
October 7, 1862

Dear Estelle,

We left Shelbyville yesterday about noon, the place where I last wrote. And arrived here last evening about ten O'clock, it is about twenty miles. We stopped about sundown about an hour and made some coffee. Our Company is divided up in messes now, six in a mess. George, Wm. Dayton, R. Wilson, Wm. Whitney and Theodore is with me. The rebels had possesion of Frankfort yesterday morning, but they evacuated it some time yesterday and crossed the river and destroyed the bridge. They formed in line of battle across the river but our boys throwed over a few shells and they left in a hurry, killed some of them. I have not heard how large a force they had but I suppose it was the rear guard. They are repairing the bridge now and I suppose we will cross the river in the course of the day. I heard that your father was a little better. I believe Reynolds is going home with him. If he does I want you to send me yours and the childrens likeness, have them taken in one case if you can.

George wants you to tell Harriet to send him a silk handkerchief by him. We are in a nice grove of maple trees. The roads in this state are hard to march on, they are turnpikes and as hard as plank roads which makes it very hard on the feet. I am well, George is well, William Dayton has been quite sick but is better now. I have no doubt but your father will resign, I think it is the best thing that he can do. We have our beans cooking for dinner, we have firstrate water here best we have had since I have left home. Afternoon I dont think we will leave here to day. We are in McCooks Division the 6th brigade and 2nd division. I think Kentucky will soon be rid of the rebels, the people appear to be tired of the war. Our Capt and Lieutenant has a darkey apiece to wait on them, they are a couple of pretty smart boys, they ran away from their masters. I should like to see your new stove and have some good baked potatoes. I hope that this unholy Rebellion will soon be brought to a close, that I may again return to my home and family. No one knows the endearments of home and the comforts of life as well as the soldier. I went to another regiment last Sunday that was camped close by us to meeting, and heard a good sermon preached. The Chaplain of our regiment was not with us. There is not many sick in our company, Wales is still in the hospital. Give my love to mother and all the rest of the folks and a good share to yourself. Write all the news tell Louella and Sylvester that their par thinks of them often.

Yours affectionably

Thos. Berry

I received two letters from you at Shelbyville dated 26th and 28th. Sunday, October 12.

I calculated to have finished this letter the next morning and sent it off but we had to start one O'clock in the morning and have been on a march almost night and day since, we are having busy times here. We camped last night on the battle ground, we came a little late to see the fight. It was in one mile of Perryville, I suppose you have heard the particulars before this time. They had a great battle, the Union force was 12,000 and the rebels about 40,000 and they was completely routed. They left their dead unburied on the field. Our loss in killed and wounded was about 1,000 and the rebels 2,000. McCook rode through our lines last night he said if he had our division at the battle he would have recaptured the whole of Braggs army. It was a hard looking place, our killed is all buried and many of the rebels are still unburied. I saw a mans foot and hand lieing on the ground which was a pretty hard sight. Our division had two skirmishes while we was marching here. I have heard the booming of the cannon and the noise of the musketing, it was in the advance of our division. Our regiment was formed in line of battle twice but we had no chance to shoot. The first skirmish was at Laurenceberg it was a calvary skirmish, quite a number of our calvary was wounded. They soon run and the next morning there was another skirmish, it was done by the rebels to keep us back. They hindered us about half a day. We arrived here about three Oclock and will stop here until morning and then I suppose we will be pushed on after Bragg. There is a large force after him now I suppose he will soon be captured. Your father came up with us this morning he looks quite smart. We have fighting material in our division if they get into a fight they will make their mark. I received your letter to day dated Sept 29th about the renting the farm I think you have done first rate. I am well satisfied. I went into a hospital at Perryville and seen some of the wounded. Some of them was pretty badly wounded. Mr. Wales is with us now and Scott. I have not time to write anymore.

From your husband Thomas Berry

No. 5

The rebels "destroyed the bridge" which crossed the Kentucky River at Frankfort, Kentucky.

Bragg's rear guard gave battle to the pursuing Federals at Perryville, Kentucky, on October 8. The casualties suffered by the Union were much greater than that of the Confederates who claimed victory after the day's battle and slept that night on the battlefield. Buell's main army was still marching toward the field of battle with what appeared to Bragg as an overwhelming force. Bragg held a council of war at which it was decided retreat was the better part of valor, and at midnight following the battle, Bragg withdrew his army from the battlefield retreating in darkness. On the basis of Bragg's withdrawal, the Union was able to claim victory. The decision to quit the battlefield at Perrysville brought criticism upon the confederate general not unlike that heaped upon Buell earlier for his failure to capture Bragg near Louisville.

Bragg's army continued in retreat to Harrodsville where it met with that of Confederate General E.K. Smith. Bragg assigned cavalry to the Perryville area to impede the Union army which he assumed would soon follow. The expected attack by Buell did not come about, and after two days at Harrodsville, the two Confederate armies marched through Camp Dick Robinson and are now heading southeast for Knoxville, Tennessee, by way of Cumberland Gap. Confederate cavalry under the command of General Joseph Wheeler is protecting the rebel troops and army trains in retreat, successfully fighting off Federal pursuers.

"Mr. Wales", Sergeant H.G.O. Wales, is not physically able to perform his military duties. [Wales will be assigned to hospital work as a private, serving out his enlistment with that rank to war's end.]

The fleeing Confederate armies of Bragg and Smith are still in Eastern Kentucky as Thomas writes his next letter.

No. 6

Dear Wife

Monday Oct 13th we marched to day about four miles, arrived here about nine Oclock and we are not going any further to day which seems good after such long marching. We are in a pretty place, any quantity of walnuts here. I wish you had some of them, also good water. I am well and getting fat, your father looks pretty well to day, he may stand it now if we dont have to hard marching before he gets recruited up. George is well and stands it firstrate. William Dayton is in the hospital at Bardstown he has been quite sick for two weeks but would not give up as long as he could possibly stand it. He was sent to the hospital last Thursday. There is troops camped here on all sides almost as far as I can see. I went to a house to day to get some water, and the man that lived there was ninety two years old, he said he was teamster in General Washingtons army, he said he was a union man. The report is that Braggs army is in about fifteen miles and that he is going to make another stand. If he does I suppose our division will be in the fight, if we capture his army it will close the war in Kentucky.

I sent you a letter this morning. I am well satisfied the way you have rented the farm and hope you will get along well. We are camped in about four miles of Danville.

Wednesday Oct 15th. We marched about ten miles yesterday and passed through Danville, it is a very pretty place, finest section of country I have seen in Kentucky. We are after Bragg and he is a leaving as fast as he can. I dont think he will make another stand in Kentucky. The people along the road says he has a hard looking army some of them are almost naked. It is just about sunrise and we have had our breakfast, we have to get up at 4 Oclock. Our Lieutenant Colonel is getting to be a firstrate man. He has learned a good deal since he has been here, he is not half as strict as he was. We are getting along very well, our skirmishers are thrown out every night and they bring in chickens, turkeys, pigs and everything that is palateable. There is not much guarding property, the fences have to suffer when we want fire, which is quite a change from the beginning of the war.

They were not allowed then to touch a rail. I wish you could see the soldiers that is camped around here. They say that our train is about twenty miles long, men and wagons.

Thursday Oct. 16th. We marched yesterday about sixteen miles, we camped about one mile south of a town by the name of Crab Orchard, we passed through after dark. The Union forces had skirmished here yesterday morning. The rear of Braggs army about twenty of the rebels were killed and good many taken prisoners, the report is that we took 1,000. I saw some of them. I saw one he said he lived in Georgia and he was tired of the war. I suppose Bragg is making for Cumberland gap, nothing more this morning.

Write

T. Berry

Friday October 17, 1862

Dear Wife,

I again take this opportunity to write to you. I am well and in hopes that this will find you and the children in the enjoyment of the same blessing. This will connect with the last letter that I have written to you. We did not march any yesterday. I saw about thirty prisoners and one deserter from Braggs army. He said he belonged to the Louisiana Regulars. He said he had fought long enough. One of the above prisoners was a paymaster, he had $9000 Dols in gold with him. Saturday 28th, we are still here, we are getting to be a self sustaining army. Great many of us grind our own corn meal. I have made a grater with my plate and have made some good meal and some good corn dodgers which goes good for a change. Corn cakes taste good deal better here then they would at home. Our captain has been manufacturing meal also. I received your letter No. 1 last evening. I should like to come and give you a call after you get things settled. I think you will get along good deal better now then you would on the farm. One of Goffs boys was here last night. He belongs to the 59th Ills he had a brother killed at the battle near Perryville. Their regiment was cut all to pieces, a young man by the name of Hawk was killed, he lived south of Victoria.

Sunday morning 19th. I see no signs of leaving yet. About seventy prisoners passed through here yesterday, they are going to Louisville. There is a report in camp this morning that Braggs army is cut all to pieces but cannot tell how true it is and have taken 20,000 prisoners, I hope it is so and the rumer is that General Halleck is going to take Buels place. Most all the soldiers are down on Buel, they say he is a traitor and Buel and Bragg are brother-in-laws. They are enlisting men for the regular service, some talk of enlisting from our company. They offer to give them thirty days furlough as soon as they enlist. There must be some important move going on or else they would not keep so many soldiers here being on the ground without tents and doing nothing. We have very pleasant weather for camping out and a very good place for studying astronomy. We have nothing over us but the canopy of heaven save our blankets. After dinner. I have heard our chaplain preach this morning, a very good sermon and have had a very good dinner which consisted of coffee some corn cakes, hard biscuit, meat and sugar. So you see that we fare sumptuously. Your father does not improve in health as fast as I wish he would but I think he is gaining slowly. I have not heard from Wm. Dayton since he left us. I have nothing more of importance to write. Write often as you can for it does me good to hear from you and the children, take good care of them and may God's richest blessing rest upon you.

Yours as ever,

Thomas Berry

The 89th Illinois regiment remained several days near Crab Orchard while the Union army ahead and to the rear encounter Confederate cavalry. Bragg's strategy in delaying the Union army pursuit by means of harassment with rebel cavalry was working. The Confederate armies completed their escape into the state of Tennessee on October 22, with a huge wagon train of supplies, plundered goods, and captured artillery.

Skirmishing and guerilla warfare continue to menace Union troops in Kentucky. In addition to Braggs cavalry commanders Wheeler and Forrest who are directing attacks upon the Federals, destroying wagon trains, taking prisoners and seizing arms, is the well known and feared General John Hunt Morgan and his band of rebel cavalry.

Following the Battle of Corinth, General Grant, on October 16, was assigned commander of the Department of Tennessee which included all of Kentucky and Tennessee west of the Tennessee river. His new command is now the 13th Army Corps.

Rosecrans, on October 25, was ordered to command the Department of the Cumberland which includes Tennessee east of the Tennessee River, and parts of

Georgia and northern Alabama, all of which are considered to be in the Western Theater. His command is now the 14th Army Corps. In his new assignment, Rosecrans, on October 30, officially replaced Buell who had been in command of the Army of the Ohio. With change of commanders, that army is now revised, forming the Army of the Cumberland. The 89th Illinois regiment is once again in a different army, the Army of the Cumberland under Major General William S. Rosecrans, and will remain in that army until mustered out at the end of the war.

Thomas alludes to Estelle's burden of moving her household goods from the farm to her rented house. As Estelle recorded in her diary on October 2, she rented one—half of Mr. and Mrs. Leet's house in Altona, a short distance from Walnut Grove, for two dollars a month. Thomas continues addressing his letters for Estelle to Walnut Grove.

October 30th within 16 miles of Bowling Green

Dear Estelle

I have a few leisure moments this afternoon so I thought I would let you know how I get along. I am well and hearty and can eat my full rations. I can stand soldiers life very well. We left the camp where I last wrote last Monday morning and have been on a march since.

We march from 10 to 20 miles a day. I believe we are bound for Nashville. We stopped to day about two Oclock so we will get some rest. We will go as far as Bowling Green tomorrow. We do not see anything of rebels through here. I received that paper that you sent me last night. I was glad to get it for we dont often see a paper here. We are shut up from the news of the day, I would give most anything if I could get a paper once a week. I wish you would send me one often. I have not heard from your father since he left us for Lebanon. I should like to hear how he is. George is well and stands well. Dick Burnerson has been sick for the last two weeks, he rides all the time. George received a letter last night and one to day from Harriet. The last letter that I have received from you was dated Oct 8th. I am well pleased with the way that you have rented the farm. Have you taken any honey from the bees, eat a good piece for me. Our Company has three darkeys now. There was one boy taken from our regiment this morning. There was three or four men that tried to take one of our boys a few days ago but they could not take him. Our boys hid him in the waggon, they said that they had an order from headquarters but our chaplain told him to show the order but he could not do it. Its getting dark so I must close. Give my love to enquiring friends and a good share to yourself, I think of you and the children often.

From your husband Thos. Berry

Direct your letters as follows
    89th Railroad Regiment
    Illinois Volunteers
    Louisville Kentucky
    Care of Capt. Whiting

The letter of Monday, October 27, is missing. It was not uncommon for letters to and from soldiers to be lost or stolen in transit.

Estelle's father, First Lieutenant Isaac Copley, is on disability leave. Lebanon is a terminal of one railroad line to Louisville where Isaac is hospitalized. Ill health forced him to resign from the army on May 3, 1863.

Bowling Green
November 1st 1862

Dear Wife,

This is to inform you that we arrived here last night we are camped about two miles from the town, we passed through it, it is quite a good sized place and some very good buildings. Kentucky cannot compare with the free states for improvements, which is on account of slavery for they have good natural advantages, any quantity of timber and stone. I have not seen a barn in Kentucky. They have log stables and sheds, and have not seen more then two school houses. The negroes appear to know about as much as the geneality of the whites. I think all that keeps the Southern army together is the ignorance of the soldiers. Their officers know that they are whipped but they mean to hold out as long as they can. I think if they are wise they will come back to the old Union before the first of January. We are camped in a half of a mile of one of the best springs I ever saw. I suppose it would afford water for a hundred thousand men. It is about twenty feet wide and the water rushes with a perfect stream, and empties in a cave about twenty rods from the spring. I went in the cave about thirty feet it is quite a sight. I have a chance to see good many sights. We passed within 9 miles of the Mamoth cave I should have liked to have seen that.

I have heard to day that General Buell has been superceded by Gen Rosecrans, I think it is a good thing, for I believe that Buell is a traitor. He just as well captured Braggs army in Kentucky as not. The old soldiers denounce him as a traitor, that is what is going to prolong the war the lack of proper officers, but I hope they will soon be found out and proper one's put in their places.

Have you seen or heard of any deserters from our company. There has three left us, Homer Waggoner, Brad Stowell and Livingston. They have been amongst the missing quite a spell. Homer was awful sick of soldiering, but I do not envy his place as a deserter.

I have just finished my dinner we have had a good bean soup. We have plenty of sugar and coffee and crackers. We have coffee most of the time three times a day. If we only had milk it would be quite an improvement. The coffee is of a firstrate quality. We draw it ready browned and each company has a coffee mill. I have not went hungry much since I left home, the greatest trouble is one thing over to much. It keeps very dry here, we have warm days and cool nights. The roads are very dusty which makes disagreeable marching.

I will put in all the things that we draw, pork and ham and fresh beef and beans, the pork and smoked meat is the thing for soldiers. Great many gets sick when we have fresh beef. They do not get it properly cooked, I think is the reason. The main cause of so much sickness in the army is the irregularity of their victuals, eat is upper most in most of the soldiers minds. They eat a good deal of trash which makes them sick. If a person is regular in what he eats he will be apt to keep well. I have never enjoyed better health then I have since I have been in the army. Dick Burnerson and Ellsworth have gone to the hospital to day. I think Dick is not dangerous all he wants is rest.

Sunday morning Nov 2d.

My dear Estelle

Another Sabbath has come and through God's Blessing my life and health has been preserved and I hope that this will find you and our dear little ones the same. It seems hard to be away from our loved one's so long. But our Country needs the service of all and I have one thing to console me, that I am not the only one that have left their friends and home to defend our Country. I hope it will not be very long before we all can return to our homes where we can be blest with the society of our families and friends.

John Smith came here last night from Lebanon. He was one of the sick that went ill there when your father did. He said your father has gone to Louisville and was going home. He said he was not any better. He has a hard time of it. I hope he will get home safe.

I should not be surprised if we should stay here quite a spell, but cannot tell certain. I have just returned from church. Our Chaplain preached a very good sermon he preaches again at two Oclock for the brigade. There has been one man in our regiment carrying a rail. It was for getting drunk, its called the Lincoln Drill. I must close by wishing you good bye, kiss Luella and Sylvester for me for their par thinks of them often. Write often for it does me good to hear from home give my love to all enquiring friends. I did not number the last letter which was No. 9 this is No. 10.

Yours as ever

Thomas Berry

Thomas was not above coining a word: "geneality" in his lexicon means "general average."'

"Homer Waggoner" is Corporal George H. Wagoner. "Ed Stowell" is Private Arad G. Stowell. Both remained in the service as did Private James Livingston. (Livingston was given a disability discharge February 10, 1863.)

Company F. joined the regiment at this time making the tenth company in the 89th Illinois Railroad Infantry regiment.

No. 11

November 9th Saturday
Tarry Springs

Dear Wife

We left Bowling Green last Tuesday morning and arrived here Wednesday night. It is about twenty miles to Nashville. Our regiment is stationed here for the present, there is a tremendous large building here. It was a public house before the war broke out and a noted place amongst the rich nabobos of the south. There is some splendid springs and bathing houses. It is all secesh through here and there have to be kept out a strong guard of pickets. There is cavalry skulking about here. Our whole company was out on picket night before last. There was quite a number of prisoners brought in yesterday. The above house is used for headquarters and for the sick. The owner of the house belongs to Morgans Cavalry. Tennessee shows the effects of the war very plainly, most of the houses along the road are left without any occupants. Some are burned down. We passed through one small village where I did not see but two families remaining. It is a rough timbered country. I would not give our little farm for the whole of Kentucky and Tennessee for me to live on. Dick Burnerson is with us, his health is improving. The general health of the regiment is good. We have pretty cold weather here. It snowed some yesterday. There is great many chestnuts, walnuts, and hickory nuts here and we pass good deal of our leisure time in cracking. Tell Louella and Sylvester if they was here their par would give them some good chestnuts and fill their little pockets full.

Monday 11th Our company went out on picket yesterday morning and was relieved this morning. Our regiment is all the troops that is left here so we have to go out on picket duty every other day. Our division has gone on to Nashville. Troops and trains are passing here every day. We are kept here to keep the way open. We have not got any mail for a long time. I have not received only two letters from you since you have commenced numbering No. 1 and 2. I feel very anxious to hear how you are. I presumed I will get quite a number when the mail does come.

I wish you would send me the Presidents Message. When you get it, cut it out of a paper and send it in a letter. A letter will come quicker then a paper. I suppose our mail all goes to Nashville to the division. We will be apt to go there before a great while. How much corn has Murry got picked. Write all the news. Give my love to all and a good share to yourself. Take good care of the children.

Thomas Berry

Thomas corrects the spelling of his location to Tyre Springs in his next letter. He was one day off on the dates for Saturday and Monday in his letter of Saturday November 8. Since he keeps a close watch for Sundays, the days of the week are accepted as correct. The envelope containing this letter and the next traveled from Tennessee through Kentucky before postmarked at Louisville.

"Nabobos," another coined word. His meaning is evident, and is probably a take—off from the word "nabob" meaning any European who has made a fortune in another country.

The "President's Message" is the announcement of the Emancipation Proclamation.

After a few days of preparedness at Knoxville, Bragg had his army on the move westward toward Murfreesborough, Tennessee. He was once again seeking to do battle with the same Union army. His cavalry was continuously menacing General Rosencrans' line of communication (supply line), and hampering Union foraging. Foraging was a necessity for an army extended from its base of supply.

No. 12
Tyre Springs Nov 15, 1862
I wrote Tarry springs before

Dear Estelle,

This is to inform you that I received two letters from you last night, no 4 and 5 and was very glad to hear that my little family was well. No. 4 two stamps. No. 5 two stamps and one dollar bill which comes very acceptable. I have not received letter No. 3 yet. I keep well yet. We have had firstrate times since we have been here, foraging parties are sent out every day for provisions and we get quite a variety of eatables. They bring in flour, meal, apples, sweet potatoes, so you see we have some change in our food which makes it go good deal better. The foraging parties takes every thing that they can get hold of if the owners comes and takes the oath they can get their pay. I believe most of them does. The country through here will soon be cleaned out of provisions and there must be good deal of suffering amongst the women and children. Their chickens are all taken from them. Some of them begs them to leave a few chickens but they generally take all. It seems hard but such is war, they brought it on themselves and they will have to suffer the consequences. Andrew Reynolds is one of the provost guards, he has been on to Nashville with the division, he came back here last night. I enquired of him if he had seen the 42nd regiment that George Copely was in. He said he did not, do you know what company he is in. If we go there I will try and find him, he returns back to day. I think we will stay here quite a spell. General Rosecrans was here a few days ago, he told some of our officers that we would stay here until we was discharged. We have a very pleasant and healthy location, good spring water. We have splendid weather, we had a fine shower a few days ago which laid the dust. Our duty is not very hard, one hundred men from our regiment goes out on picket a day now. Our company has to furnish from ten to twenty men a day. Today our Captain and one sergeant and eleven men was called for, Corporals has as about as easy a time as any of the officers. You say you would like to take the Headlight. The paper is stopped, it is not printed any more. I presume you had a pleasant time down to the wedding. I have received two letters from Emeline since I have been in the war. I am glad to hear that your Mother is getting better. How does Mother and that Missourian make it. I have heard that some thought they would get married. I hope she will not disgrace herself and family.

 I was glad to hear that you had received the bounty money. When I get my pay I want to keep enough to take me home. If we go into winter quarters I may get a furlough home. I was glad to hear that my Sylvester boy was getting fat and hearty. I wish my birdie could come and see me. John Hulice received a letter from his wife last night it stated that you had made her a call. John Hulice is getting pretty well now, he has been quite feeble. George received two letters from Harriet last night. He is well, he received one from George Cumming's, their regiment was at Bowling Green. I guess that regiment has seen hard marching. Dick Burnerson is improving very fast. I have not heard from father since we left Bowling Green. I feel very anxious to hear how he is getting along.

 I hope the shrubbery will do well. I heard this morning that

Illinois has gone Democratic, I suppose it makes Sam feel pretty good. I presume he carries a pretty high head when he rides in that buggy. I have written one letter to Mother. I think if the Northern states sustains the President in his Proclimation the war cannot last many months, but if they dont it looks as if it would prolong the war. It would save an immense amount of suffering in the south if the war was closed. I think they must see their folly before long and come back to the stars and stripes. I must close give my love to all and you need not be afraid that you will write too often.

From your husband

Thomas Berry

Does Louella and Sylvester learn their letters pretty fast?

George Copley is Estelle's brother. He is in Rosecrans' Right Wing, Third Division, General Phillip H. Sheridan, Third Brigade, Colonel George H. Roberts, 42nd Regiment under Colonel Nathan N. Walsorth.

"John Hulice" is Thomas' spelling for John Hulich, (he later spells it "Hulie" and "Hulin").

Illinois was not the only state to go "Democratic." At best the Republican party held a tenuous edge in the elections of 1860. Now, two years later, the majority vote of all northern states is clearly in opposition to Lincoln's party. Had the war been concluded at this time with the capture of Lee's army by McClellan, and that of Bragg's by Buell, the ardor of the North with which it entered the war would have been maintained, supporting Lincoln at the polls. (That fickleness will be demonstrated in the 1864 national elections.)

Burden of the drawn-out war and the announcement of the Emancipation Proclamation caused reversion of northern sympathies to prewar factions as expressed at the poles. Further, Lincoln was being subverted by many in his own administration and the military because of his adamant stand on maintaining the Union, and the administration of the war to that end. From that subversion, both clandestine and overt, the domestic and foreign press censored Lincoln.

McClellan's hesitation in moving against Lee as Lincoln urged, finally brought the President's patience to an end. On November 5, 1862, Lincoln replaced McClellan with General Ambrose Burnside as commander of the Army of the Potomac. McClellan and Buell were now both relieved of army commands. McClellan accepted other official military duties under Lincoln. Buell, after sitting out an investigative commission on his military performance, refused further assignment which was offered by General Grant.

Bragg's forces were at Tullahoma, heading for Murfreesborough, Tennessee when Thomas wrote this letter of November 15, 1862.

The information "we would stay here until we was discharged" was intended more for Bragg's ear than that of the Union army. Rosecrans was determined to do battle with the rebel army near Murfreesborough.

George Cummings is the brother of Harriet, George Berry's wife.

No. 13

Seven miles south of Nashville
November 19th

Dear Wife,

We left Tyre Springs Monday morning and arrived here last night. We passed through Nashville yesterday about noon. Nashville is quite a city, some splendid buildings. The state house is a good building. The streets are very narrow which is the greatest objection. The 42nd is camped close to the city. I saw good many boys that I knew, I saw George Copley just as we was coming out of town. He was up on a high bank and I could not fall out to have a talk with him. I asked him how he was, he said firstrate. He looked very natural and was quite fleshy. I understand that their regiment will be with army so I presume I will get to see him again. I saw Wm. Whiting, Pap Reynolds and that Scotchman that used to clerk for Champers and quite a number of others that I knew by sight.

I received your letter no. 7 dated Nov 12th last night and was glad to hear from you. You say that I need not be surprised if I should have a stepfather before long. I am very sorry that Mother should be so foolish. Capt Whiting had a letter from Father he is at Louisville in a hospital, a hospital purpose for officers and has good treatment.

Our Capt has been quite sick for the last two days. He had to ride in the ambulance waggon, but is better now, George is well, my health is good, most of the boys feel pretty well.

We are with our division now, how long we will remain here I cannot tell. There is skirmishing not far from here most every day. I have heard the report of some big guns this morning.

I am glad to hear that prince is getting well. I have not time to write any more for we have to go out on drill so I will close by sending my love to all enquiring friends.

Yours as ever

Thomas Berry

I bought two loaves of bakers bread and one peach pie as we passed through the city yesterday which went pretty fair for a change.

Thomas hears the gunfire between Union artillery and Confederate cavalry. Confederate General John C. Breckenridge is stationed with his army at

Murfreesboro, within 25 miles of Thomas' camp. He will soon be joined by Bragg. Breckenridge was vice president of the United States under James Buchanan.

Six miles from Nashville
Nov 23rd

Dear Estelle

This is to inform you that I received letter dated Nov 16th last night and was very glad to hear that you and the children was so well. You say they are romping while you are a writing, I wish I could see them romping and playing. You cannot imagine how I long to see them. I have not been very well for the last two or three days, I have not had any apetite to eat anything but I will be all right in a few days; its the first sick spell that I have had its a hard place to keep well there is very few in our company but has had a sick spell. If I get home by the first of January, I want one of those turkeys well baked and stuffed but I guess there will not be any such good luck. I hope that this war will not last many months longer, I do not see how it can.

Our whole regiment was out on picket last Thursday night, its getting pretty cold here now to do picket duty. Our regiment will have to go out on picket about once a week while we stay here. The rebel pickets are not very far from our's. How large a force they have here I have not learned so you see that we are in the face of the enemy. We no not how soon we will be called into action. A forage train was attacked a few day's ago by rebel cavalry. 49th Ohio went out on double quick and they soon skedaddled. Quite an accident happened to Isaac Berry of our company since we have been here. He shot himself through the hand. He had to have his hand amputated close to the thumb which will end his soldiering, its doing firstrate. Our captain had a letter from Homer last night he is in Kentucky and has been sick, he says he will soon be with us, he has been gone thirty days, I hope he will come back all right.

Since writing the above I have found out what is the matter with me. I have a touch of the jaunders. My eyes and skin is turning yellow, it appears to be a common complaint amongst the soldiers, quite a number of our company has had it. I am going to the doctors and get some medicine if I get sick I shall be awful homesick, I will miss you to take care of me.

There is no regard paid to the Sabbath here. We have to be out and drill Sundays as much as any other day, which I think is very wrong. There is an immense sight of wickedness and corruption carried on in the army. I think sometimes its no wonder that this war does not close, when there is so much wickedness, it appears as if some of our high officers thought more of their pay than they do their country, but I hope for the best knowing that He that ruleth all things will do right. I do not see any signs of pay yet. I hope we will get some before long. I think we have earned our money I presume we have traveled five hundred miles. Our camp is within a mile of a lunatic asylum. It is a nice brick building. I guess we will not go into winter quarters I hope not I want to see the war closed before any more stopping. I was sorry to learn that Uncle Clint was so feeble, I was in hopes that he was getting well. Give my love to him and Aunt Mary, tell them I will be back and eat a square meal with them sometime or at least I hope I will.

Give my love to all your folks, if any of them will write to me I will answer it. Give my love to Mother I have not heard from Wm. Dayton for a long time, if you have heard let me know in your next letter. I gave John Hulie that letter that was enclosed in mine. He is getting pretty well now. I hope I will see those likeness of my loved ones before long. I do not know how long we will stay here but I suppose our next move will be down in Alabama. George is well and hearty. Tell Hellen that Theodore is well and that he is a firstrate fellow. Its a good place here to find out a person, I must close from yours until death.

Thomas Berry

Direct as follows:
Thomas Berry
C.O. G. 89th Ills 6 Brig 2 Div.
Army Cumberland
Via Nashville Tenn
Care of Capt. Whiting

I guess you will not have to change the direction again, make the figures plain. You did not No. your letter that I received last night. I suppose it is No. 7. You will have to write plenty often to keep up with me for you are considerable way behind now. Write all about Mother and what she is doing, keep all my letters.

Isaac Berry from Galva, Illinois. He was discharged January 7, 1863, due to disability.
"Jaunders" is Thomas' spelling for "jaundice".
"Theodore" is Private Theodore Whitney, Hellen is his wife.
Rosecrans at this time has located his headquarters at Nashville. By repelling attacks against the railroad and posting guards along the line, he brought to Nashville ammunition and supplies by rail from Louisville. His supply line will

thereby be shortened for the anticipated battle with Bragg at Murfreesborough, 30 miles southeast of Nashville.

Camp near Nashville
December 1st

Dear Estelle,

I thought you would be anxious to hear how I am at the present time, so I thought I would improve these few leisure moments in writing to you. In my last letter I wrote that I had the jaunder's. I had them quite bad I reported to the surgeon and he gave me medicine which helped me very fast. I reported to him four mornings and I am now about as well as ever. I was exempt from duty only five days, I believe we have a good doctor. Yesterday our regiment was ordered out to guard a foraging train we went out about five miles, and whilst our teams was loading with corn and hay we were attacked by a small force of Cavalry. I presume there was about forty of them, they fired at us quite a number of times and we gave them some in return. Some of the boys says that some of the rebels was dismounted, but we was to far apart to do much damage. There was only two or three of our company that had a chance to fire at them, most of us was kept back as a reserve, those that fired was thrown out ahead. Some of the other companies gave them quite a number of rounds, the rebels dont like to see their grain taken away from them. As soon as the wagons was loaded they started for camp and we brought up the rear. We was prepared for a pretty good fight there was one other regiment and two pieces of artillery. Our regiment done what fighting there was, it's the first time that the 89th has had a chance to fire at the rebels. We arrived back to camp about sundown. This is a good country for Guerrilla fighting its a very rough timbered country. I have heard some of the boys say that it is very much like New York State. We have moved our camp about two miles from where I last wrote, some nearer Nashville, we are camped in the timber and a very good place.

I received your letter last night dated Nov 23rd and was very glad to hear that you and the children was well and inhopes that you will continue the same. I have received the Tribune and Advocate which furnished me with good deal of reading. I want you to send me some every week. You had better subscribe for the Tribune and Advocate.

I suppose Father is at home before this time. Our captain had a letter from him dated the 23rd he stated that he was going to start the next morning. Mr. Scott is dead he died of the Typhoid fever, poor old man he had a hard time of it, he is the only one that has died from our Company. Homer is not with us yet, his name has been dropped from the list and has been reported as a deserter. I don't see any signs of leaving here yet. Some thinks we will stay here this winter, there will have to be a large force kept here to protect the city. We had a very heavy rain last night, we keep very comfortable in our tents. We have a good lot of straw and with our blankets we are all right, straw is prized very highly amongst the soldiers. I have seen some carry a armful of straw three miles to sleep on. I have carried some quite a piece. When I am sleeping on the ground it makes me think of the good bed at home. I dont know as I have anything more to write at this time so I will close by sending my love to all enquiring friends and a good share to your self. Yours as ever

Thos. Berry

(Enclosed Note)

My dear Estelle,

You cannot imagine how I long to see you and our loved ones. There is not many hours that pass away but I think of you. I did not consider what a trial it would be to be seperated from my loved ones so long. I hope that I have your prayer's daily that I may have Gods assisting grace to assist me in my trials. You have my prayer's I hope if it is consistent with our heavenly Father's will that our lives may be spared, and we maybe blessed with each others society again, but if it is ordered otherwise I hope we will prepared for the change for in that good world that is prepared for the righteous, there will be no seperation of friends and if we are not spared to meet again on earth may we meet each other in heaven, where there will be no seperation.

Yours in love

T.B.

William Scott died at Jefferson, Indiana, November 23, 1862. Bragg arrived with his army at Murfreesborough on November 23.

Camp near Nashville
Dec. 5

Dear Wife

This is to inform you that I received your letter dated Nov 28th night before last while we was out on picket duty and was glad to learn that Father had arrived home. I hope he will soon get well, if he does get as well as he was when he enlisted I should not advise him to come back again if he can get discharged because its no place for a man in the army that has had his constitution impaired any for they cannot stand the exposure. We have some now in our company that ought to be at home. Mr. Lamb has not been able to do any duty for two months, he has been trying to get discharged but they will not grant him one. He never will be of any account here, also John Smith, a person ought to be sent home when they get sick and not fit for duty. Homer arrived here last night, he does not look very sick. Our Captain reported him to the Colonel, what punishment he will receive I do not know yet. He will either get his stripes taken off or else he will loose his pay from the time of enlistment until now, that is if he has not a pretty strait story to tell. We have not received any money yet and I do not see any signs of getting any. Uncle Sam is rather a poor paymaster so you must not depend on me for any money, but I guess I will have to look to you for some. That is if you can spare it. I suppose the taxes will be pretty high. I want three dollars to buy me a pair of buckskin gloves which will cost me two dollars and fifty cents. Gloves is the only thing that I need in shape of clothing.

I am getting about as well as ever now. I do not see any signs of leaving here yet. We have had very pleasant weather here until to day. Its snowing quite brisk, they do not have such sudden changes here as there is in Illinois. I think the grain and fodder will soon be scarce in Tennessee. There is sent out about one hundred wagons a day a foraging, they generally have a little skirmish. I am glad to learn that Prince is getting all right for I expect to be at home by spring and I will want him and Nelly. Let Murry keep Fanny. Nothing more at present,
Yours as ever,

Thos Berry

If you send that money send it as soon as you receive this. I guess it will come all right.

"Mr. Lamb" is Peter Lamp, discharged February 10, 1863 due to disability.

Dec. 10th

Dear Estelle,

This is to inform you that I received your letter dated Nov 30th in due time and was glad to learn that you and the children was well. I am well and hearty again. Our regiment is out on picket. We came out yesterday at one Oclock and will return this afternoon to camp, or rather our homes for it seems like that camp was our homes. I am writing in a log house that has been forsaken, it is the headquarters for our company and a very comfortable place. There is a good fire place in it and there is plenty of chestnut rails close by so we have a good fire. Fourteen of our company is on duty at a time and they are relieved once every two hours. This is a beautiful day, it seems almost like spring, the nights are pretty cold. We have had some pretty cold weather and some snow. The picket lines is about two miles from camp. They have moved our camp one mile and a half nearer Nashville, since we have been out. I cannot tell what it is for. It may be that they expect an attack or else go into winter quarters. A soldier does not know what will happen one hour ahead. You wanted to know what you should do if Mother and that old Missourian should get married, it is a pretty hard question. Sometimes I think that I should not go nigh them and then again I think she is so old and childish it is the best way to make the best of it. I am very sorry that she should act so foolish, that old scape grace ought to be tarred and feathered, I always thought that he was a nobody and have told her so, but she will not take notice of any advice that is given her so if she gets into another MacReady scrape there will not be anybody to blame. I guess you had better go and see her. I should not take any notice of him if I was home. I do not believe that he has any relation in Ottawa or Kaperwell. Our regiment has had quite a present from the ladies of Chicago, they have furnished each man in the regiment one pair of mittens, which comes very acceptable. Wm. Dayton is with us now, he is quite smart. Winslow Newton is in the hospital at Nashville. I heard a few days ago that he was getting better. He was taken sick at Tyree Springs. Tell Harriet that she need not worry about George getting sick, soldiering agrees with him firstrate, I never saw him look so rugged before. Mr. Rogers has been quite feeble for a long time but I think he looks better now. I do not think of anything more of any importance to write so I will close by sending my love to all enquiring friends and a good share to yourself. Kiss the children for me for their par would like to see them.

Thomas Berry

"Mr. Rogers" is Private Needham Rogers. (Rogers was discharged February 10, 1863, due to disability.)

Bragg's army is 40,000 strong. This week at Murfreesboro he was visited by the president of the Confederacy, Jefferson Davis.

Chain of command for the 89th Illinois regiment in the Army of the Cumberland is now organized

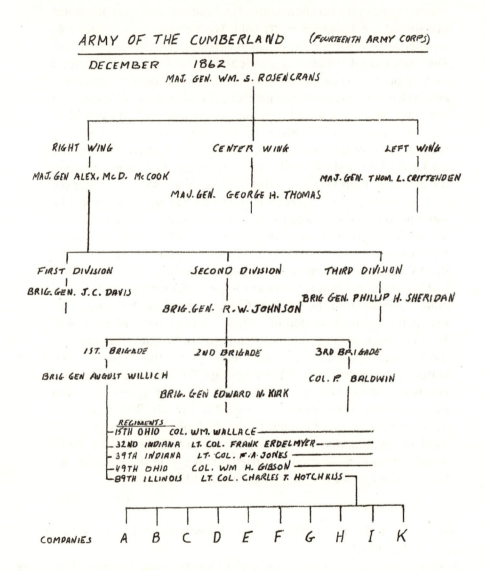

PART 5

BATTLE OF STONE'S RIVER

Camp near Nashville
Dec 20th 1862

Dear Wife

This is to inform you that I received your letter with the three dollars and two postage stamps last night. I will not need it to buy mittens as I have a pair, but it will come good to buy other things that I will need. I have bought twenty five cents worth of letter paper and a diary book for next year for fifty cents. I am going to write down what transpires everyday. It would be interesting to look over if I should ever get home.

I am sorry to hear that the children was sick but I hope they will be better the next time that I hear from you. It seems hard to hear of sickness of my loved ones and cannot go and see them. We have been out on a Brigade drill this forenoon. It is a very pretty drill. There is five regiments in our brigade, commanded by Brigadier General Willick. He is a splendid man, he does not feel too big to talk with the soldiers. I saw two men drummed out of their camps yesterday for stealing. They was marked thief on their backs and was drummed around the camp by the tune of the rogues march. George Copley has been here since I last wrote and made us a visit, he took dinner with our mess, he looks very healthy. I have heard that Burnside has had a big battle and has to retreat, but I hope he will be successful and whip them out for if we get Richmond in our possession I think the Rebellion will be about used up. I think this army will have some big fighting to do before many weeks if they do not come to terms.

I think you got a very good price for those hogs. I am glad that you are getting along so well, write often. I have lost track of the No. of my letters. I will write once a week when I can, from your true and affectionate husband

Thomas Berry

Send me some stamps I have three now.

Thomas refers to General Burnside's Army of the Potomac in the Eastern Theater. At the Battle of Fredericksburg, Virginia, which culminated on December 13th, the unsuitable leadership by Burnside caused the Union to suffer overwhelming defeat in the ratio of 12,000 Federals to 5,000 rebels in killed and wounded. Lincoln is once again dissatisfied with the command of the Army of the Potomac.

Confederate cavalry in the Western Theater, including that of J. H. Morgan, continue to harass Union troops in Tennessee and Kentucky, capturing Federal garrisons, taking prisoners, and destroying property to impede Union armies.

The ruse spread earlier, that Rosecrans was reluctant to move his army and that "we would stay here till we was discharged", worked to the extent that Bragg reduced the size of his army by sending a formidable cavalry force to harass Grant in Mississippi. Rosecrans saw this as his opportunity to move the Army of the Cumberland on December 26, from Nashville for the encounter with Bragg at Murfreesboro.

Thomas did not wait until "next year" to use his new diary. He started on the 24th making the following entries:

> Dec. 24th 1862
>
> Our division was ordered out. Marched about two miles stacked arms laid there about two hours and then orders came for us to go back to camp. We went back to our camp and pitched our tents.
>
> Dec. 25th
>
> We spent Christmas out on a foraging expedition, went out about 8 miles. Drove in the rebel pickets. There was cavalry skirmishing most all day. The rebs had small pieces of artillery. Arrived back to camp about sundown.
>
> Dec. 26th
>
> Forward move of the army of the Cumberland. Marched about 12 miles to Nolansville. The rebs had quite a force there but they had to skedaddle. There was skirmishing most all day and artillery and cavalry. Received my wife's likeness by mail while we was a marching. It rained most of the forenoon. Our shelter tents kept up quite dry.
>
> Dec. 27th
>
> Continual fighting and skirmishing all day. Our artillery was used pretty freely. We took some prisoners. We took possession of Triune and camped close to the place. We have marched ten miles. It has been very rainy today.
>
> Dec 28th
>
> Our brigade was sent out to make a reconnaisance. Went out about four miles but could not find the enemy so we returned back to camp. Arrived back about one Oclock.
>
> Dec 29th

Marched about six miles on a crop road to the Murfreesboro Pike. A very bad road through a cedar swamp. Splendid cedar timber, camped about ten Oclock. Was not allowed any fire. About six miles from Murfreesboro. A battle is expected to come off near that place. The Penn. cavalry had a fight with the rebel cavalry here today.

Dec 29th

Fighting all day. We was kept in line of battle most of the day.

Bragg, by dispatches from his cavalry, was made aware of Union forces approaching Murfreesboro, and therefore set his army in position for the encounter.

From the initial Federal movement out of Nashville on December 26, to nightfall on December 30, when the Union line was formed in front of Murfreesboro, McCook's corps was continuously skirmishing with Confederate cavalry. On the evening of the 30th, his 1st brigade under General August Willich, bedded down (bivouacked) on the right of the Union line within site of the enemy. Rosecrans was not in accord with that position of his right wing but left final judgment to McCook.

Rebels made the initial attack early on December 31, to open the Battle of Stone's River, also called the Battle of Murfreesboro. The Union right was overrun by the enemy, suffering great loss in killed, wounded, and missing in the first hours of battle. Among the missing was Corporal Thomas Berry.

The Federals were pushed back to ground which permitted an effective defense to stem the tide of onrushing Confederates. The battle continued through the day with the Federals holding to their defensive position.

New Year's day brought a lull to the battle with some skirmishing while both armies replenished supplies of food and ammunition, and maneuvered their armies for continued fighting.

On that New Year's day, 1863, the Emancipation Proclamation was placed in operation. The Proclamation declared free, all slaves residing in rebelling states and counties. Note that slavery was still permitted in loyal areas of the United States.

The battle of Stone's River was resumed January 2, with heavy losses on both sides. Rosecrans was relentless in pursuit of his goal, Murfreesboro, which he won the following day by the withdrawal of the Confederate Army of Tennessee under General Bragg.

Estelle made the following entry to her diary January 2, 1863:

> Still at home. It has rained all day. We heard today that they were fighting at or near Murfreesborough. Oh what an anxiety it creates to hear such news.

When letters were no longer forthcoming from Thomas following the Battle of Stone's River, Estelle's fears rose to new heights. She received no further word from or about Thomas until her diary entry two weeks later on January 16:

> Got a daily tonight with a list of casualties of the 89th in it. As I glanced my eye down its columns it fell upon this Thomas Berry missing. Oh such feelings.

Estelle was painfully aware of the various consequences suffered by a soldier listed as missing in action. Her diary reveals her distress:

> Sunday January 18
> Another Sabbath morning has dawned on us here and am I prepared to spend this day as I ought? I fear not. I cannot set my mind centered upon divine things. It's far from here upon the battlefield of Murfreesborough.

> Friday January 23
> Had a good deal work on hand today. The teacher's mother came down here tonight...I'm living on suspense yet. Oh it's hard to bear.

> Saturday January 24
> It is a little colder. This evening brought me a letter from George stating he never had seen Thomas since the action on the morning of 31 of December. Oh! The anguish of my heart none can tell except those placed in the same circumstances. If I only new if he is living or not. This terrible war...

> Monday January 26
> Washed today but I do not feel very well. Such awful suspense is enough to make anyone sick...

> Friday January 30
> It is very pleasant today. Have been home all day but had several callers. Still I cannot hear from that dear one away from home. It is wearing upon me. What shall I do?...

> Saturday January 31
> Went to see Aunt Kate today. It is so beautiful today, warm and pleasant, but I am so lonely. I fear all is not right. If I could be placed where I was six months ago how happy I'd be, but alas. That home will

not be a home to me without him. Can I endure it? I must stop writing for tears blind me.

After a month near despair, Estelle made the following entry:

>Tuesday February 3
>
>It is very cold weather at present. William hauled me a load of coal today. He says father is getting quite smart. Mrs. Livingston got a letter from her husband tonight dated January 30, stating that himself, the captain, Thomas, and several others were at Annapolis and were paroled. How thankful ought I to be that he is still alive. My heart is lighter tonight than it has been for one month.

Two days later Estelle received a letter from Thomas dated January 31, postmarked February 2, 1863.

Thomas had written a letter December 28, 1863, but was unable to post it before the battle at Stone's River. He carried that letter throughout his captivity until he reached Annapolis where it was finally mailed, postmarked February 7. Even though Estelle received the letter of January 31, before that of December 28, the latter appears next so that we may follow Thomas' letters in the intended chronological order.

>Dec 28, 1862
>
>(I thought I would send this letter if it was old, I had no chance to send it when it was written)
>
>Dear Wife
>
>We have had stirring times since the 25th, the Army of the Cumberland is on a move, we spent Christmas a foraging and the next day the army commenced a forward movement. The first day we marched about 12 miles to Nolensville, the rebels had quite a force there but they skedaddled. There was skirmishing most all the way long with artillery and cavalry. I received your letter while we was marching, with your likeness. I opened the letter and found something wrapped up in a paper and it said How you do sir and I opened it and found it was birdie and I had to kiss her. I am very much pleased with it. I think it looks very natural, it had come one day one day sooner it would have been a good Christmas present. I have to look at it pretty often. We have to carry our own tents now, two of us carries one tent, its not very heavy, I like them very well. They are a good thing when we are out in the rain. It rained almost all day yesterday, I have half of one wrapped around me and it kept me as dry as you please. We marched

about 8 miles yesterday. There was a continual firing all day mostly with artillery. We expected they would give us battle, but they kept falling back towards Mumfordboro. I suppose they have a large force there, its about 16 miles from here I believe, but I presume they will leave before we get there. It dont look as if anything that the rebels can raise can stand at Chatanooga. We took about 149 prisoners yesterday so we was pretty close to the skirmishing. Our brigade was drawn up in battle line two three times today, the army is not moving, our brigade was sent out to reconnoiter. We went out about five miles but could not see a rebel so we returned back where we was camped last night, got back about noon. I am now writing in our shelter tent George and me has one together. What or where we'll be the next move I cannot tell. If we keep a moving I will not have time to write very often, this is first time that I have to write since the 24th. So if you should not hear from me sometimes you must not think it strange. Mr. Condra has not arrived yet. For fear that you have not received my last letter I will write that I received the letter with the three dollars and two postage stamps. I want you to send me some more stamps in your next letter. The number of our brigade is changed now it is 1st Brigade now. George wants you to tell Harriet of the change. There is not but three brigades in a division and they are numbered one, two, and three. Enclosed is a ring for Louella, it is a New Years present, I made it myself. I must close, my love to you.

Thos. Berry

The 89th Illinois regiment was marching in Rosecrans' army toward Murfreesboro, the stronghold of the enemy, when Thomas Wrote this letter of December 28.

The letter of December 24 is missing.

"Condra" is Edward Condrey, an absentee from the Company G since December 1, 1862.

Annapolis Maryland
January 21, 1863

Dear Estelle

I hasten to write you a few lines to let you know that I am still in the land of the living. I have been in the hands of the rebels for the past month. I was taken prisoner the last day of December. Johnson sold our Division and we was taken by surprise. We was attacked before all our boys was up and some was getting their breakfast and some after water, I had just got through eating my breakfast when the enemy opened fire upon us and the balls soon came as thick as hail and we was thrown all in confusion. Good many was shot while they was getting up. Our Colonel ordered us to lay down and the rebels commenced closing in upon us, and he ordered us to retreat great many was shot while we was on the retreat and the cavalry came around and took any quantity of prisoners. I among the rest. If our division had been in battle line the way it ought to have been, Rosecrans army would have been in Mourfresboro before night. Our division was on the right when it gave away, it affected the whole line. I think we have just as good a division as there is in Rosecrans army but it was not of much service that day. I suppose they took about three thousand prisoners, I have seen about that many. The rebels have taken us almost all over the Confederacy since then and we have seen pretty hard times. After they took up prisoners they took up to Mumfordsboro and we took the oath not to fight against the Confederates until we was legally exchanged and they kept us in the court house yard until Friday morning when they started us off in the cars for Vicksburg to our lines. Went as far as Chatanooga that day, 100 miles from Murfresboro. Sat the 4th we went as far as Atlanta Georgia, 138 miles from Chatanooga. 5th went as far as Westpoint 90 miles. Tuesday the 6th went as far as Montgommery Alabama 90 miles. Wednesday we had orders back because they was a fighting at Vicksburg and they are going to send us to Richmond, arrived back at Atlanta Thursday morning. Left Atlanta Friday the 9th and went as far as Dalton 100 miles from Atlanta. Left Dalton Sat 10th and arrived in Knoxville Tenn Sunday. 11th 110 miles from Dalton. Tell Harriet that there is a man living here by the name of David E Cumming about 40 yrs of age has a wife and 4 or 5 children has been a colonel in the rebel army, has been wounded and is at home now.

Monday the 12th left Knoxville on the east Tenn and Va. R.R. and went as far as the place where the bridges was burned 400 miles from Knoxville to Richmond. Great many Union people in east Tenn.

Tuesday 13th had to cross the river in a boat the bridges that was burned is about nine miles apart, so far we had to foot it. Went as far as Bristol on the line between Tenn and Va. Started from here the 14th and arrived in Lynchburg Thursday the 15th. Arrived in Richmond the 16th and kept in houses and very much crowded. They did not give us half enough to eat. We left Richmond the 27th for City point about 32 miles from Richmond and found our boats waiting for us, we stopped at Fortress Monroe Tuesday night the 27th. The fort is quite a sight 600 guns is on the fort. I saw the Union and Lincoln gun, they are large fellows. I have seen the wreck of the Congress and Cumberland and we arrived here the 29th. So you see that they have moved us around considerable. I do not know but we will have to stay here until we are exchanged. Some says we will be sent to our own states. I hope we will, if we are there will be some chance of getting home. I am very anxious to hear from our regiment and company I have not heard how many was shot and killed. Write and let me know who is killed and wounded. I want to hear how George is. We are going to draw a new suit of clothes here. Homer Wagner is here, Cole Ferman, Livingston, Hopper, Geo. Welles, of our company. I want to hear from you and the little ones very much, it seems a great while since I have heard from you and I hope this will find you well.

I never expected to be taken prisoner, they treated us very well, only they almost starved us. They are pretty hard up for provisions. They fed us as much as their own soldiers get. If we could only get Richmond the rebellion would soon be used up, but it is a hard place to take. I do not think it can be taken. They will have to cut off their supplies and starve them out and it would not take very long. I must close for the present write as soon as you receive this, from your affectionate husband

Thos. Berry

Direct as follows
Camp Parole
Annapolis, Md.

Thomas told Estelle of his month-long experience as a prisoner of war. Fortunately, the rebels did not confiscate Thomas' writing material, so he also told his diary of that adventure. At risk is the boredom of redundancy in presenting here his diary covering those same days, but when we realize the conditions under which he wrote, and we read of the less savory experiences which he withheld from Estelle, the risk appears worthwhile.

From Thomas Berry's diary:

Dec 31st

Our division was taken by surprise. The rebels attacked us before we had any orders. Some of our boys was not up. Others was getting breakfast. The bullets came whizzing into our camp pretty thick. The first order that we had from our colonel was to lie down. The bullets began to come thicker and faster and the rebels was marching nearer and nearer in heavy columns. We laid there about five minutes when we had orders to retreat. Good many was shot on the retreat. The rebels had flanked us. The rebel cavalry came around and captured great many prisoners. I was one of the unfortunate ones to be taken.

About a dozen was with me when I was taken. A large squad of cavalry rode up to us and demanded us to surrender. So we concluded that we had better acquiece to overpowering numbers. A resistance would have been useless. They took us to Murfreesboro and put us in the courthouse yard and I found here quite an army of our men in the same predicament that I was, prisoners. The following members of our company was also taken, Captain Whiting, David Sprouse, Wilford Whitney, they are both wounded. Jay Livingston, A. Topper, H. Wagner, G. Welles, W. Ferman. They have captured over 5,000 of our men today. They are bringing in small squads most of the time. They treat us very civally. They feel very confident that they will whip us in the evening. They gave us some raw beef and flour. We have nothing to cook it in and have no fires. Its very cold. There is some very heavy fighting today.

Thursday, January 1st, 1864.
New Years Day has found me a prisoner of war. The rebel commander here has required us to take the oath not to fight again against the confederate forces until we are legally exchanged. We are going to be sent to Vicksburg and pass through our lines. I do not hear any musketeering or cannonading today. The rebels tell us that our forces are falling back to Nashville.

Friday 2nd
We was put aboard on the cars about sunrise. Every town and road bridge is guarded that we pass by.

Saturday 3rd
Arrived in Chattanooga about 12 Oclock last night. We are going to remain here today. They gave us some rations here. About 100 miles from here to Murfreesboro.

Sunday 4th
Left Chattanooga one Oclock this morning and arrived at Atlanta before sundown. We are going to stay here until morning. They have given us some soft bread and pork. We are well treated by the citizens and soldiers. They have good many of our officers here among them is Captain Whiting. 138 miles from here to Chattanooga.

Monday 5th
Went as far as Westpoint. 90 miles. We have passed through some

very pleasant places. Very rough country. There is quite a large amount of cotton here.

Tuesday 6th

Went as far as Montgomery. They gave us some hardtack and boiled beef. Colored people are plowing here with one horse one drives and one holds the plow. Quite a good looking city.

Wednesday 7th

We are going to be sent back to Atlanta. Started in the fore noon. We have rough passage in stock cars and they are very filthy. The nights are very cold. We cannot get much sleep. There is no chance to lie down. About 75 in a car.

Thursday 8th

Arrived at Atlanta about five Oclock this evening. We are going to stay here today. They have given us rations to last three days.

Friday 9th

Left Atlanta at eight Oclock last night. Stopped at Dalton a little while. We are going to be sent to Richmond going through Knoxville 110 miles from here. There is two trains of us prisoners.

Saturday 10th

Left Dalton this morning. There is some fine country through here.

Sunday 11th

Arrived in Knoxville this morning about an hour before light. They have given us some crackers and meat.

Monday 12th

Left Knoxville on the East Tenn and Va RR this morning about four Oclock. Its called 400 miles to Richmond. Passed through Greenville the home of governor Johnson. A fine view of the mountains covered with snow. We went 80 miles where the bridges was burned by our men a short since.

Tuesday 13th

Crossed the river in a small boat, then we had to march nine miles a foot. Then we took cars. Most all Union people through here. Went as far as Bristol on the lines between Tenn. and Va.

Wednesday 14th
Started from Bristol this morning about four Oclock.

Thursday 15th
Arrived at Lynchborg this forenoon, one hundred and forty miles from Richmond, a good sized place. They gave us four crackers apiece and a small piece of meat.

Friday 16th
Arrived in Richmond at five Oclock this morning. We was marched up in town about two miles, and put in tobacco warehouses that they use to put prisoners in. There is about one hundred and fifty in the room that I am in. They have given us some rations.

Saturday 17th
They have taken our names down also our regiment and companies. Governor Lactcher's son came in the prison to see the Yankee boys. Our rations are very small and we are very hungry. The bread that they give us is good but the meat is awful. We got soup once a day. Sometimes the soup is covered with maggots. They would not be very palatable to a person that does not know anything about hunger. I have not as yet taken any of the soup when I see the creepers.

Sunday 18th
The rebel officers tells us today that our government will not receive us until they give up our officers.

Monday 19th
We are close to the James River. There is three small gunboats here.

Tuesday 20th
It's very unpleasant to be a prisoner of war and to be guarded here by these rebels, and to be excluded from the outside world. We cannot hear anything that we can rely on. It makes one think of sweet home that I left where I have a plenty. I hope and pray that this rebellion will soon be crushed out and law and order returned.

Wednesday 21st
Nothing new has transpired today. My mind wanders far away where my loved ones is. It is hard to be thus separated from them but I put my trust in my heavenly father for I know that he will do for me

what is best.

> Thursday 22nd

The officer that has charge of the prison told us that we will be sent to our lines Saturday, which is joyful news. I think that we will be at liberty again.

> Friday 23rd

I finished a ring for my wife today.

> Saturday 24th

Nothing worth notice.

> Sunday 25th

Ditto.

> Monday 26th

They have moved us to another jail or prison, a very foul and filthy place. This is called Libby Prison. There has been great many of our boys shut up in this awful place for months. They say we will leave tomorrow morning at four Oclock for our lines. Glorious news to be released from rebel rule.

> Tuesday 27th

Goodby to Richmond. We was started about four Oclock this morning. Marched about three miles afoot. We had to cross a canal on an iron bridge. Soon after leaving it, the bridge broke down, and over a hundred fell in the canal. I heard that there was some drowned, some badly wounded. The rebel officer that had charge of us said that he would not had the bridge broke down for five hundred dollars. We took the cars, went to Petersburg, 22 miles from Richmond. We changed cars here for City Point on the James River. Arrived at that place about eleven Oclock, ten miles from Petersburg, and found three of our boats waiting for us with the stars and stripes in full view. When the boys saw the good old flag they gave three rousing cheers. The old flag never looked so good to me before. I hope to see the time when she will wave over every inch of ground in these United States. The rebel flag with the stars and bars is hoisted on an eminence close by. There is a great contrast between the two. One is for liberty and elevation of the human race, the other is for slavery and for aristocracy of a few and degredation of the masses.

We soon got aboard and commenced sailing northward. We had a very pleasant ride. They gave us good rations of bread, meat, and coffee. We arrived at Fortress Monroe about dusk, eighty miles from City Point. I saw the wreck of the Cumberland and Congress. There is a large blockading fleet in front of the fort. We are going to Annapolis, 220 miles from here.

Wednesday 28th

The boat that I was in stopped at the fort. last night. Started this morning as soon as light. The fort has 600 guns mounted on it. There is two very large guns mounted close to the water's edge. One is called the Lincoln and the other the Union gun. I heard one of the boat hands say that they would carry six miles. We are sailing on the waters of Chesepeake Bay today. Our boat was anchored just before night on account of the waters being so rough. The boat leaks very bad. They keep three pumps a going all the time. Some of the boys on board appear to be quite alarmed and the captain appears quite uneasy.

Thursday 29th

The wind blows very hard this forenoon, boat leaks very bad, passengers getting uneasy. We will not start today without it calms down. There is about 400 soldiers aboard. At two Oclock we again started as it has calmed down quite still. Six hours ride will bring us to Annapolis. We are going to remain on the boat here until morning.

Friday 30th

We was taken out the boat this morning and went in barraks in the navy yard. It's very cold and we are not allowed any fire on account of there being a magazine close by. We are going to draw a new suit of clothes and then go to the parole camp, one mile and a half from here. They have given us one blanket apiece.

Saturday 31st

The clothing has not come yet. Very cold.

McCook's corps, particularly the 1st Brigade, of his 2nd Division under Brigadier General R.W. Johnson, paid the price for his unwillingness to act on Rosecrans' apprehension regarding the position of the right wing. The whole of Rosecrans' plan depended on a favorable position of the right wing to hold the rebels in check for only a few hours while the Union left moved forward across Stone's River and into Murfreesboro.

At first light on December 31, the army of Confederate General William J. Hardee attacked the Union right wing. Pickets of General Johnson's 1st Brigade were driven back, unable to give timely warning. Close proximity with the enemy's lines did not allow the 1st Brigade opportunity to prepare a defense against the charging rebels. The 1st Brigade was just rising and in the act of preparing breakfast.

Thomas' hasty estimate of 3,000 prisoners taken by the Confederates is not too far off from the 3,717 missing, a number given at that time as official, suffered by the Army of the Cumberland in the Battle of Stone's River. Johnson's 1st Brigade alone lost one half of its men in killed, wounded, and missing (which included those taken prisoner); 90 killed, 373 wounded, and 701 missing.

Rosecrans won the Battle of Stone's River but suffered the greater loss with over 13,000 casualties in killed, wounded, and missing in action. Bragg's loss was 10,300. Thomas made the following entry in his diary: "The battle of Stone river was fought with 43,400 men according to general Rosecrans report...The rebel general Bragg had a force of 62,000".

Rebel cavalry gathered the prisoners for transport, and after enrollment, Thomas Berry was an honor bound prisoner of war. Brigadier General August Willich was also taken prisoner in that battle.

Three of the men from Company G were killed in the surprise attack on December 31; privates David H. Bester, George W. Murry, and DeWitt C. Scudder, all from Walnut Grove.

Estelle's brother, George Copley of the 42nd Illinois regiment was wounded in that battle. His brigade commander Colonel George W. Roberts was killed.

Thomas was one day off on his date for Saturday the 3rd.

The *Cumberland* and *Congress* were sailing vessels, warships of the United States Navy destroyed in the naval battle at Hampton Roads on March 8, 1862, by the frigate *Merrimack*. Hampton Roads is a body of water (a sound) connecting the James River and lesser tributaries with Chesapeake Bay.

When Lincoln took office the United States Navy was deplorably outdated as a bulwark against invasion or as an aggressive military tool. Previous secretaries of the navy did not bring the navy fully abreast of marine science, leaving a navy fleet to Lincoln's administration which consisted predominantly of sailing vessels dependent upon the vagaries of air currents for propulsion rather than controlled steam power. Of the 90 vessels in the navy, only 40 were equipped with steam power. Of that forty, less than half were effective for immediate defense of the country, the rest being in foreign service, in disrepair, and in ordinary, a term used by the navy to indicate a vessel out of service for an indeterminate length of time to undergo scheduled overhaul and refitting.

Lincoln's Secretary of the Navy, Gideon Welles, was pressured to provide iron clad and steam powered vessels of various paddle and screw propeller design which could be used to enforce the Anaconda Plan. Welles was slow to act and with advisors who clung to outdated designs, yielding reluctantly to naval science, delayed for six months the start of construction of ships so badly needed for off shore and inland water maneuvering. Romance with the contemporary, tolerated by those entrusted with defense of the coasts, leads to military stagnation and a

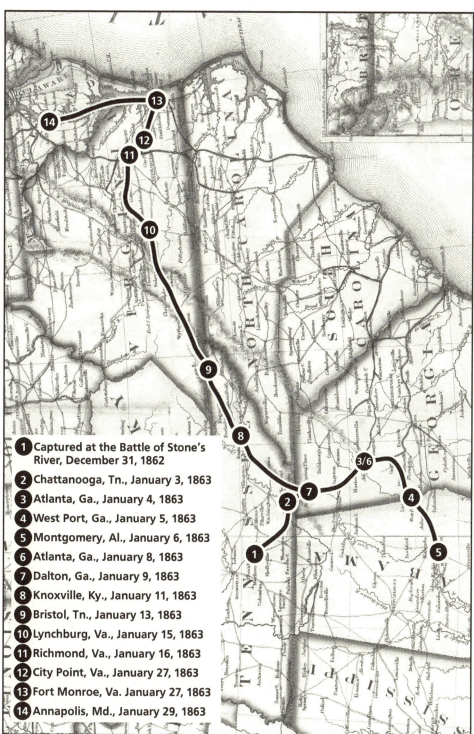

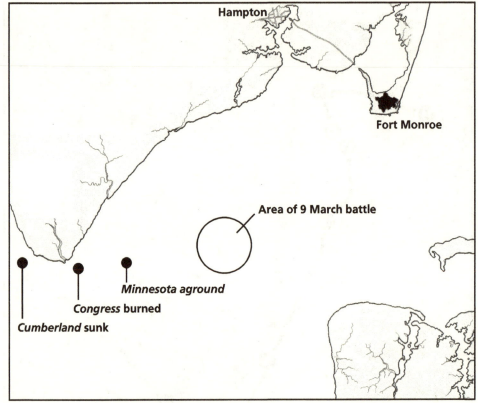

Map of Hampton Roads, James River, VA (1862)

vulnerable nation. Such was demonstrated by 1861, not only through lack of naval flotilla strength but also by lack of trained and experienced naval officers.

The *Merrimac* was one of six U.S. steam powered screw propeller sail augmented frigates which were built in 1855. Those six ships were considered the best of the fleet which Lincoln inherited in 1861. The *Merrimac* fell into Confederates hands following a needless abandonment of the Gosport Navy Yard at Norfolk, Virginia, April 19, 1861, by the Federal commandant of that U.S. facility. The navy yard was set afire at the hands of Federal men, and abandoned, for no compelling military reason. Many U.S. navy ships including the *Merrimac* were fired and scuttled.

As swiftly as the Federals fled the Gosport navy yard, the Confederates moved in. The partially damaged navy yard yielded a treasure chest of armament to the Confederate government which distributed the much-needed heavy armament to several locations in southern states.

Abandonment of Gosport Navy Yard was later attributed to traitorous Union officers of Southern sympathy who ill advised the Federal commandant, Commodore John McCauley, of imminent peril by overwhelming rebel forces at the gates of the navy yard. In truth, there were no large unified forces at the gates, and Federal troops at the yard, and those a short distance away at Fort Monroe, were more than adequate to withstand the inferior enemy scattered throughout the immediate area of Gosport. By means of minor sabotage the rebels only pretended a threat to the naval installation. Willful action of the rebellious citizens orchestrated with betrayal of the commandant caused the latter's hasty retreat and allowed time for organization of a Confederate occupation force. The determination of ill advice and betrayal by U.S. naval officers is supported by the defection of those officers who led the Federal commandant astray.

The Confederates raised the *Merrimac*, removed the masts which had provided auxiliary propulsion by sail, and covered her deck with an iron shield. The *Merrimac* was then fitted with an iron ram to become the most formidable navy ship in the world entering combat on March 8, 1862.

The *Congress*, a frigate with 50 guns and a crew of 434 men was of little or no contention against the *Merrimac* in the inland sea battle at Hampton Roads. Nor was the sloop *Cumberland*, with 30 guns and a crew of 376. Gunfire from neither ship could penetrate the armor of the ironclad even at close range. The *Cumberland* was rammed leaving a huge hole below the waterline, and both Federal ships were fatally damaged, sunk in shallow waters, by gunfire from the *Merrimac*, or *Virginia*, as it was renamed by the Confederates.

That battle which saw the sinking in shallow water of the *Congress* and the *Cumberland*, opened the eyes of naval military strategists at home and around the world, concluding a centuries old system of naval warship architecture and combat tactics.

One of the first vessels completed after contracts were issued for construction by secretary Welles' navy department was the iron clad *Monitor*. Its radical design included a gun mounted within a revolving turret. The turret was constructed of iron plate to a thickness of eight inches for 360-degree protection of gunners and gun. Its low freeboard, that distance between the waterline and the watertight deck, gave the ship the appearance of a barge with minimum exposure to enemy gunfire. Its narrow draft, the distance between waterline and keel, permitted maneuver in shallow water.

The *Monitor* entered Hampton Roads on the night of March 8, 1862, too late to defend the *Congress* or *Cumberland*. The *Monitor* engaged the *Merrimac* in battle the following day. Neither ship could destroy the other in two days of battle, and both withdrew from the encounter. Success of the *Monitor* in that two-day battle was measured by her ability to halt further destruction to other Federal ships in Hampton Roads, a staging area for the U.S. fleet.

The *Merrimac* was scuttled by its own commander in the James River, a premature and rash action for which that commander (the latest in a series) was censured.

The *Monitor* foundered in an Atlantic storm off Cape Hatteras in December 1862, as it was heading for Charleston, South Carolina. The ship did not break up, sea water had found its way through seams around the turret, sinking the ship intact. The *Monitor* had by then proven itself as an effective ship of war and was first of many of its class.

Note enclosed with old letter dated Dec. 28, 1862

We are in barracks now and have a good place, plenty to eat and to wear and nothing to do. We are not in the regular parole camp, there is one hundred and twenty in the building that I am in. There is not but one of my company here the rest are out to the regular camp and that is Wm. Ferman, the Drummer. We bunk together. I heard a good sermon last Sunday, remember me in your prayers. May our prayers commingle together at the throne of our heavenly father for each others protection and guidance,

Yours as ever,

T.B.

Direct as follows
    Camp Parole
    Annapolis
    Maryland
I will commence again to number. No. 2

This note enclosed with the letter of December 28, was written after Thomas made the following observations for his diary:

Sunday Feb. 1st

We have good deal of reading matter distributed amongst us. The post chaplain preached us a good serman.

Monday 2nd

There is splendid hospitals here. The sick and wounded is well cared for. There is a soldier's library here.

Tuesday 3rd

Very cold.

Wednesday 4th

Good many are getting sick for want of good quarters.

Thursday 5th

We have drawn a new suit of clothes and moved us in good barracks where we can have a fire which makes us feel much better in body and mind.

Part 6

Soldier on Parole

Camp Parole, Annapolis MD.
Feb 6th, 1863

Dear Wife

I take this opportunity to write to you a few lines so that you may know how I am at the present time. I am well and hearty and have been well and healthy with the exceptions of a cold since I was taken prisoner, but I have seen hard times. We had a long and tedious ride in rebeldom, in box cars without any seats and crowded full. Sometimes as high as seventy five in a car. Some of the cars was very filthy with dirt and cesesh lice. I have had plenty of body guards since I have been a prisoner of war. I was never honored with any before. Uncle Sam has given me a new suit of clothes. So I concluded that I would give them a discharge as I have no further use for them. I am dressed in my new suit and feel as clean and as slick as a ribbon. I should like to come home and stay until we are exchanged, but I guess I will not have the privilege. I think we ought to be sent to our own states. If I had money, I dont think they would keep me very long for I am not any benefit to the Government here. Good many has left for home already, but if I have to stay here I shall try and make the best of it. I do not know how soon we will be exchanged. But I hope it will not be very long for I had rather be with my regiment. I have rather poor opinion of the Southern Confederacy, I think that they are pretty near played out, in eatables especially, for they gave us just enough to keep body and soul together and their soldiers told us that we got as much as they did. I heard an officer say that he could live on one meal a week. But I guess he would not like to try it. Their soldiers are awful sick of the war. I have had a chance to see good many of them. The war would soon close if they had their say about it, the citizens are the most rabid. They say they will fight until the last man is killed, but I think if they could be put in one or two battles it would cool them down very materially. I dont think they have provision enough to last them until they raise another crop, but I may be mistaken. I could not see much along the railroad, and we had a pretty good chance to see as we came very slow and stopped almost to every town. I hear that Jef is going to keep all the officers, it will go pretty hard with Capt Whiting. He was at Atlanta the fourth of Jan. Some of the boys saw him. I do not know where he is now. I have not heard from my regiment since I was taken. I long to hear for they have had some big fighting since after I was taken prisoner.

I long to hear how George has come out. John Hulin was wounded very bad. He said the night before that if he was shot he hoped that it would kill him immediately. I am afraid that I shall hear of his death. Scudder was killed, there was some that fell close by me. Wolford Whitney was wounded slightly he is a prisoner and Chas Bainbridge was wounded and a prisoner. Time passed off slowly while we was in prison at Richmond. We heard all kinds of reports there. One was that we was going to be kept until the close of the war, I begun to get the blues, you may guess. When the news came that we was going to the land of freedom, there was quite a change in our looks and feelings. I hope when I go to Richmond again it will be with a gun on my back headed by Gen. Rosecrans. We started from Richmond at four Oclock in the morning. We had to foot it about two miles through the city to the cars. There was about one thousand of us and there was quite an accident happened while we was going to the cars. We had to cross a canal on a wire bridge, while we was going over the bridge broke down and about one hundred was plunged in the canal, five was drowned and quite a number was injured. I had got across before it broke down. Little did I think that danger was so nigh when I was passing over it. One of the rebel officers said that he would not had the bridge broke down for five hundred dollars. So you can see how much they value federal lives. When we got City point we found three steamers with a flag of truce and the Stars Stripes a floating in the breeze. When the boys saw the old flag they gave a good hurrah. The rebels stars and bars was hoisted on the bank. City point is on James river, they have three gunboats there. I must close this letter I have a great deal more to write. I made you a ring while I was in Richmond jail. I made it for a relic to remember my imprisonment by. And I have made one for Luella. I wanted to make one for my darling boy but could not get the material. I shall send them by mail before long. This is the second letter that I have written since I have been here.

T Berry

Write as soon as you receive this and put in two postage stamps. Write all the news give my love to mother and your folks and all enquiring friends. Kiss the children for me from your husband

T. Berry

The 89th Illinois regiment lost 142 men in killed, wounded, and missing in the Battle of Stone's River.

Private John B. Hulich, from Copley, Illinois, was mortally wounded in the battle but did not get his wish, he died of his wounds sixteen days later. Private Benjamin F. Murphy, from Walnut Grove, was also mortally wounded.

Discharged from Company G due to disability following the battle were Private Isaac Berry, Galva, Illinois, and from Walnut Grove, Privates Hiram Cole, William O. Dayton, A.M. Ferguson, and Charles W. Higgins.
"Wolford" Whitney is Wilford H. Whitney.

Parole Camp Annapolis MD.
Feb 13, 1863

Dear Estelle

This is to inform you that I received your kind letter the 11th and was very glad to hear from sweet home and loved ones and that you and the children was blessed with health. It has seemed a long time since I have heard from you. I feel that I have great reasons to thank my heavenly father for his protecting care that has been over me through the dangers that I have passed through on the battle field in prison and on the waters. I can say with the poet that 'dangers stand thick through all the ground to push us to the tomb'. The boat that we was on came very near sinking. They had too many passengers on aboard for the size of the boat and it racked her so that it leaked very bad. They had to keep three pumps at work all the time and then at one time there was three feet of water in the boat. The captain was considerable worried and the Chesepeak bay was very rough so we had to lay over one day. There was about four hundred prisoners on the boat when we arrived at Annapolis. They had no place for us to go but an old shed in the navy yard and it was very cold and we was not allowed any fire on account of the magazine being close by. They kept us there about a week and we suffered a great deal. I should have thought if they calculated to have this a general parole camp the Government would have a comfortable place for the men that are sent here. Its a disgrace to the Government the way that we have been used when we first came here. Those that came first about one thousand had to lodge on the ground without any tents or covering of any kind and it has been very cold good deal like Illinois weather, quite a contrast from the weather down in Georgia and Alabama. They was ploughing there, but there is no use to complain, we have to take things as they come and inhopes it will end all right. If the war was closed I would not grumble at the hardships that I have passed through but I have about made up my mind that it is in the far distance if we cannot starve them out, it will take good many years to conquer them by fighting. Their leaders are bound to fight as long as they can keep an army together but I believe our Government has the means and men to put down the rebellion but it will take a good while without we have better Generals. Now for something else, when we left Richmond they took our blankets, canteens, knives and all the old tin cups we had, pocket knives will sell for most any price and they would pay most any price for our clothing. Great many of the boys sold their dress coats and overcoats to get money to buy something to eat. They would pay as high as seventy dollars for the dress coats and other things in proportion, in confederate money. Every little boy has a pocket full of money. They would give two dollars of their money for one of the greenbacks. They said that they wanted it when they run the blockade.

Some of the Murfreesboro prisoners took the oath of allegiance to the southern confederacy at Richmond and they conscript them right off which served them right. I saw in one of the Richmond papers that there was about fifty that took the oath, and they think that Vallandingham and a few others is helping their cause a great deal in the north.

I am down in the regular Parole camp now, came down last Monday. I am now in the same tent with the rest of our boys, in a sybil tent. We have a stove in it and it is a very comfortable place for a paroled prisoner. I went to the methodist church last Sunday in the city and heard a very smart man preach. It seemed good to go in a church once more. There is going to be a quarterly meeting there in two weeks. I calculate to go. While we was in the barracks they let us go to town when we pleased. This is a great place for oysters. You can buy them for a shilling a bushel in the shells. I have had one good mess cooked up in good style for one shilling I liked them firstrate and they do not go very bad raw. We could live firstrate if we had plenty of money, they have all kinds of good things to eat here and at reasonable prices. Annapolis is a very pleasant place, and I should judge a very healthy place.

Quite a number of the prisoners caught the small pox in Richmond and there is good many cases of it here in the hospitals now. It was reported that there was one case of it in the same building that I was in at Richmond. I was vaccinated last Sunday but I do not see any signs of it taking any effect yet.

I have written a letter to George and told him to send my dress coat home and send my letters here and to keep my childrens likeness. I have a very nice dress coat there and should like to get it home. I wish I had my portfolio here. I had about twenty five sheets of paper in it, I told him to keep it with his. I also sent for my descriptive list so that I can get some money. I am very glad that you are getting along so well. I believe I could enjoy home now with my loved ones. This sheet of paper and two stamps came very good. I wish you would send an extra sheet and some stamps every time that you write, write often and all the news.

> T. Berry
>
> You can imagine how proud I am of my step-father. The prisoners are all awfully dissatisfied here and they are running off home every day. Kiss Louella and Vessy for me I think you will see me home before I go back to the regiment.

The Federal Government's disdain for the welfare of its soldiers during parole was inexcusable. Such treatment as described by Thomas may have been rationalized by commanders of U.S. prison camps with knowledge that some soldiers made little or no attempt to escape capture, even inviting capture in the early part of the war to escape further battle action. Capture by the enemy was a nobler choice than desertion. An estimated 100 thousand Union soldiers were listed in the latter category. Notwithstanding a few soldiers volunteering capture, contempt for the health and safety of Union soldiers held in captivity by the Federals, soldiers who would be returned to duty upon exchange, was militarily unwise. Many in such captivity were unable to return to duty following the severe treatment; moreover, disrespect for those unable to escape capture caused many to desert the army which treated them so shabbily.

"Vallandingham" is Clement L. Vallandigham, a former member of the 37th Congress from Ohio, and a leader of the Peace Democrats of that state. He was defeated in his bid for reelection to congress in the fall elections of 1862. Peace party members, also known as Copperheads, were in sympathy with the South. Vallandigham was an outspoken critic of the Civil War and would have hostilities cease at any price, even to the point of giving the Confederacy all for which it was fighting, a separate nation and restoration of the slavery oligarchy.

Lincoln had suspended the writ of habeas corpus in September 1861, leaving to his field commanders discretion in application of that act of martial law. Union General Ambrose E. Burnside, commanding the Department of the Ohio, issued a proclamation of the following April which threatened Southern sympathizers with arrest and indefinite confinement, and death to those convicted of treason. Vallandigham boldly defied Burnside's orders and was promptly placed under arrest and sentenced to confinement. He was spared the death penalty.

Vallandigham's loss of privilege by suspension of the writ was not an isolated case. Burnside also suppressed distribution of the Chicago *Times* and the New York *Press* in the area of his command.

Vallandigham's arrest gave rise to hard questions regarding Lincoln's use of executive powers in time of war. However, Congress and the courts supported Lincoln and the president's action was not without precedent. In the War of 1812, at the Battle of New Orleans Andrew Jackson imprisoned several men including a judge for violating Jackson's wartime orders under martial law, which considers foremost the safety of the nation and its citizens. If as a result of martial law action certain individuals suffer restraint, no recourse or recompense can or should be pursued against those so protected; such are the unwritten rules of war.

Compassion may be exercised by the military following an agreement with the accused to act in accord with rules of conduct within the borders of the aggrieved nation. Lincoln did in fact exercise such compassion with the press and with Vallandigham. An active press to keep citizens abreast of national affairs was more important than the repression of editors, whom, by the action of Burnside, were forewarned to restraint in their editorials.

Vallandigham was released to the Confederacy, passed through the lines by Rosencrans to Bragg, with sanctuary in Richmond where the firebrand was coldly welcomed. Vallandigham eventually sought refuge in Canada where he was groomed by the Copperheads for the gubernatorial race of Ohio in 1863. In that contest he was overwhelmingly defeated.

It is of interest that Horace Greeley, editor of the New York *Tribune*, gainsayer of Lincoln, was not too far off the outskirts of the Copperheads. His negativism regarding determination of U.S. citizens to pursue their goals dates back to 1851 when an American citizen, John C. Stevens, challenged the British in a sporting marine event. Stevens sailed his two-masted schooner to England, taking on all challengers (at a wager) in a sailing race off England's shores.

Greeley predicted the American would disgrace the U.S. by losing the sailing event. In that prediction as in his doubt of Lincoln's successful prosecution of the Civil War, he was wrong. Literate Americans would not let Greeley with his newspaper direct their minds nor will they let his successors, in whichever media chosen.

Stevens' entry, the *America*, won the cup for the U.S., the America's Cup [vied for but never leaving the shores of the U.S. for 132 years, until 1983 when it was placed in temporary custody of Australia).

The Sibley tent (Thomas spells the name 'sybil') was patented by Henry H. Sibley in 1857. Sibley got the idea for his tent from observing the Indian teepee while traveling in the west with explorer John Charles Fremont. The center of the twelve foot-high tent was supported by a single pole, the covering was spread at the base teepee fashion. An opening at the top provided ventilation and allowed space for a chimney.

The Federal Government paid Sibley a royalty for each tent purchased by the military. Thirteen of thirty-five tent manufacturers under Federal contract provided poles for the Sibley tent. Royalty payments to Sibley were stopped after Sibley joined the Confederacy.

Fremont, the first Republican presidential candidate, losing in 1856 to Buchanan, became a general in the Union army.

Fremont was dissatisfied with Lincoln's administration and made a bid for the Republican nomination against Lincoln in 1864 but withdrew from the race. He withdrew not to help Lincoln but to work against the election of the Democratic candidate General George B. McClellan.

Thomas once again mentions the shilling. Common U.S. coins in circulation at that time were the one cent, three cent, half dime, dime, quarter dollar, half dollar, and silver dollar. Gold coins ranging in value from one to twenty dollars were also in circulation. Circulation of U.S. paper money (greenbacks) used for legal tender was first authorized by the 37th Congress in December 1861.

The confederate government issued paper money in the form of notes ranging in value from fifty cents to one thousand dollars. A few Confederate coins of one cent and fifty cents were struck but were not of sufficient quantity for circulation by the general public. Confederate notes were issued in the years 1861 through 1864, the coins in 1861 only.

None of the prisoners from Company G took the oath of allegiance to the Confederacy.

Parole Camp
February 18th, 1863

Dear Estelle,

This is to inform that I am not very well. I have the mumps on both sides of my face but I am getting better now. My face commenced swelling last Friday. I supposed it was a cold. I did not know for certain that it was the mumps until Monday. I went to the doctors and he pronounced it mumps. My face is swelled up pretty good size, looks so that I had pretty good keeping. I do not like them for I cannot eat my rations, the swelling has commenced going down on one side. I think I will get along with them well if I do not catch any cold. I sent for some money in my last letter. If you have not sent it when you receive this you need not. The mumps have knocked my calculations in the head for it would be quiet a spell before I should dare to start out. And I heard today from pretty good authority that we was going to have two months pay the 10th of next month. So I will try and take it easy as I can. Write often for if I cannot get home it does me good to hear from home. Send me two Dollars in your next letter, that is if you have not sent any.

From your affectionate husband,

Thos. Berry

Wednesday morning
February 25th, 1863

Dear Estelle,

This is to inform you that I received the letter with the fifteen Dollars yesterday afternoon and the two stamps. Expect to get the balance this afternoon. In my last letter I wrote that I had the mumps. I got along with them finaly. I am almost well now. I did not doctor much for them. The doctor gave me two pills. I took one and lost the other.

I have good news to write this time. We are going to be sent to our respective states. We are going as soon as transportation can be got for us. That will be this week or the first of next. I heard it from headquarters and I consider it reliable.

So you need not write again until you hear from me again. I hope that the next time that you hear from me will be in person. I was afraid the money would not came until we was gone, if you had not received the countermanding order. I shall send this letter as soon as I get the balance of the money.

From your husband

Thomas Berry

Wednesday afternoon. I have just received the other letter with the ten Dollars. Good Luck. I hope I shall soon see you and our dear little ones so good bye for the present.

Yours as ever,

T.B.

Parole Camp March 1st 1863

My loving Wife,

I thought I would embrace the present opportunity in writing to you a few lines so that you may know how I am getting along. I am well and hearty and in hopes that this will find you and the children the same. You see that I am still here. We are going to be sent west this week. It is not definitely known amongst us what place we are going to be sent to, rumor has it at different places, one is Benton Barracks Missouri, Chicago, and Springfield. I presume we will get some pay before we leave, the officers in command here are pretty near through mustering us. I cannot tell what time you may look for me but I can insure you that I intend to see home if it is amongst the possibilities, but my dear Estelle you must not put too much dependence on seeing me home, for I know not how strongly we will be guarded when we get to our destination. I have made calculations to see home before I go back to the regiment and if I cant I shall be greatly disappointed, and I shall think that Uncle Sam is a hard master. If all of the parole prisoners had been sent to their homes it would have been great deal better for them and the Government, and I dont think there would have been as many deserters as there will now. For most of them say that they intend to go home, if they have to go on their own hook, they intend to stay. I am glad that you are getting along so well. I hear of great many soldiers wifes and children are suffering on account of the Government not paying them, which I think is a shame. If I thought my dear ones was suffering for the necessities of life I do not know what I should do, but if we had to depend on Uncle Sam I think it would be pretty hard. I presume we will get two months pay, if I do I will bring you a pretty good sum with the twenty five dollars that you sent me. I received a letter from George this last week, with the letters that was sent to me at the regiment. There was four from my loving birdie and one from your mother and one from Arthur Taber. I calculated to have written to Arthur, but I never got at it. If you see him before I do tell him that he must excuse me. George was quite sick he said he had a pretty hard time through the battle and he caught cold and it settled in his head. I have missed him a great deal and I guess he has me for we was always together. If he was not in the army I should not want to go back on account of the way the war is carried on. Its a speculative concern from General down to quartermaster. The officers dont care how long the war last so long as they get their large salary. Their pay ought to be cut down about two thirds then we would have generals that would work from principle.

I have Rosecran official report of the battle of Murfreesboro. He does not blame Johnson for not having the 2nd Division in line Wednesday morning. I think he ought to be shot, for not having us in position. While we was at Nashville he had us up two hours before light and in line and stacked guns, but when we was in the face of the enemy we was allowed to sleep until all light and some was building fires some getting breakfast and a good many was not up when the bullets begun to come amongst us as thick as hail. Some was shot while they was getting up. I was considerable suprised that Rosy did not censure somebody for there must be some one to blame.

I calculated to have gone down to town to church to day but it is a rainy day therefore I shall have to content myself here. But I can get good instruction from that book of books, that you sent me while I was in Chicago. I read it often and derive good deal of consolation from it in my troubles and hardships that I have to pass through and I feel that I have an enduring friend that I can go to at all times. As long as I am faithful he will never forsake me. I feel that he is precious to my soul, and that he has protected my life in answer to prayer. My dear Wife let us go often to the throne of divine grace and pray that our heavenly father may give us grace according to our day and trial. And if it is consistent to his holy and righteous will that our lives may be spared that we may enjoy each others society around our own fireside, but if otherwise ordered may we make full preparations that we may meet in that better land, where there will be no more parting of friends. I hope I shall soon see you love,

From your true and affectionate husband

Thomas Berry

(Note enclosed)

My dear Estelle, you cannot imagine how I long to see you, my thoughts are continually about you. You know that I always did love and it seems that I could love you better then I ever did before if I could return home. I try to hope that this war will not last a great while longer but the war clouds looks pretty dark and discouraging at the present time, but we must put our trust in God for he will do for us what is best. May we go to him for help when troubles and darkness come before us and he will aid us by his spirit for prayer is the christians hope. May we throw our cares and troubles on Jesus for he is willing to help at all times if we will only come to him with a humble spirit. May God bless you and preserve your life and those little ones that he has given us, and may we train them up for the kingdom, and may we ever have on the wedding garment that we maybe in readiness for the change that awaits all mankind that we may enjoy the sunshine of Gods presence world without end is my prayer. Pray for me, you have my prayers. I guess I will write again just before we leave here. When we get to our stopping place if I cant get away I will write for you and the children to come and see me.

You must look for a good loving if I get home, home sweet home.

For good reason Thomas tells Estelle the war clouds look pretty dark and discouraging at this time. Not only Union soldiers, but also Northern citizens are still discouraged and demoralized by the defeat of the Army of the Potomac at Fredericksburg and by the indecisive Battle of Stone's River, General William Tecumseh Sherman and General Grant are meeting stubborn opposition in the Vicksburg Campaign adding further to the gloom surrounding the Federal cause. The Confederacy is gaining European support and the copperheads are becoming more vocal.

With General Bragg building his army to meet that of General Rosecrans and Lee planning a march into loyal states and posing a threat to the Federal capitol it appears at this time the war can go either way and the possibility exists for the states to remain divided.

Lincoln, dissatisfied with leadership of the huge Army of the Potomac at the Battle of Fredericksburg, once again selected a new commander. Burnside was replaced by General Joseph Hooker on January 25, as commander in chief of that Eastern Theater army. Hooker immediately reorganized his army, as did Rosecrans in the Western Theater with the Army of the Cumberland following the Battle of Stone's River. Destiny of the United States now rests heavily on the shoulders of Generals Grant, Rosecrans, and Hooker.

Camp Parole
March 9th, 1863

Dear Estelle

I thought I would commence a letter this morning so that my loved one may know how I am at the present time and to let you know that I still think of you. I am well and inhopes that this will find you and the children in the enjoyment of the same blessing. I try to enjoy myself as well as I can under the circumstances that I am placed, but I must say that I have not found any place like home, around my own fireside, with the society of my own dear wife and children. If my life is spared to return home, I think I could fully appreciate home and the comforts that surrounds a pleasant home. I live inhopes of seeing better days if our lives are spared to return home, I think we will love each other better then ever before. Let us put our trust in our heavenly father for I feel that he will do for us what is best. When I last wrote to you I did not think that I would be here now, but so it is and I have to make the best of it. But I think we will leave sometime this week. I shall send this when we have orders to start. I should have started for home as soon as I received that money if I had not heard that we was going west. I presume we will be sent to St. Louis. We may be exchanged before long, but I hope not until I see home. I suppose the farmers begins to think about sowing wheat. Murry ought to sow our wheat where there was corn last year. You had better tell him so if you have a chance to see him for he would raise a better crop. There has been three crops raised on the wheat stubble land. I think that you had better sell prince if you can. Perhaps your father can sell him for you. If you can get anything near what he is worth I would let him go, let Murry have Fanny to use. I should like to have Nelly put in some good pasture this spring, perhaps you could get Samuel to pasture her. I would rather she would not be worked.

(Note enclosed)

March 10 We are going to leave here today. What place we are going to I cannot find out. Some place at the west. I hope I shall have the privilege of seeing home and my loved ones, but I cannot tell what I will do. So you need not look for me until I come. If I do not come home it will not be my fault. Since writing the above there has been sent off of about two thousand of the paroled prisoners of the States of Pennsylvania, Indiana, Ohio, and Michigan. I guess they will be sent to Camp Chase, Ohio. I suppose we will be sent off tomorrow. I will close by wishing you goodnight.

March 11th We are going to leave for the west in a half of an hour. We have had orders to get ready, I think we will be sent to Benton Barracks.

Yours in love

T. Berry

From Thomas' diary:

Wen. 11th

Left camp about two oclock, arrived at Baltimore about eleven oclock. We sleep in the cars tonight. 30 miles to Annapolis. We was furnished with a good supper at the Union relief association, a grand institution. They can feed three thousand soldiers at a time. It's kept up by the Union people of Baltimore.

Thur. 12th

We took breakfast and dinner at the above institution. Baltimore is a splendid looking city on a high eminence. We started at two oclock on the Ohio and Baltimore R. Road.

Fri. 13th

Sun about an hour high at the Ohio and Chesepeake canal, 123 miles from Baltimore. Stopped at Cumberland a few minutes. Present place.

Sat. 14th

We travelled all last night. We took our breakfast little after sunrise. Sixty miles from Wheeling. Went as far as Balair in four miles of Wheeling and crossed the Ohio river in a boat. They call it four hundred miles to Baltimore. Took the cars at six oclock.

Sun 15th

Arrived at Columbus this morning before light. Arrived at Richmond, Ind. about noon, sixty two miles from Indianapolis. Very liberal people here. They brought us any quantity of of provisions and gave us, and it was very thankfully received by the boys.

Mon. 16th

I concluded that I would start for home this morning and leave the balance of the boys. I went and bought a ticket to Indianapolis, and got aboard of the passenger train, and arrived in Indianapolis about ten oclock, left here for Chicago at one oclock, 218 miles. Arrived at Chicago at ten in the evening, bought a ticket for Altona at eleven, jumped aboard the cars on the Chicago B & Q R.R. for home.

Tues. 17th

Arrived at Altona about light, stepped from the cars and started for the house where my family lives, went to the door and knocked. Presently Mr. Leet came to the door and informed me that my wife was down to Burnerson he thought. I went in our part of the house, found everything looking neat and in order, but my loved ones was not here, so I soon started for the Burnerson's. As I got opposite of Capt. Whiting house I saw my loved wife sitting by the window. I was very soon by her side. I found her very well, also Louella and Sylvester. We have great reasons to thank our heavenly father for his goodness towards in sparing our lives and having the priviliege (sic) of seeing each other again. Stopped here about an hour and then started down to our farm. I harnessed up Fanny and we went back to Altona.

Sat. 21st

We went down to Victoria and found all the folks well.

Tues. 24th

Started back to Altona this afternoon.

Mon. 30th

I thought that I had better report to the Parole Camp at St. Louis, so I started this morning. It was very hard for me to go away and leave my loved ones again. Went to Quincy on the cars. There I took a boat.

Tues. 31st

Arrived at St. Louis about sunrise. About three miles to the barracks. We soon arrived at the camp. They have very comfortable quarters. The soldiers are divided off in companies, one hundred in a company, and have company cooks.

Thomas' comrade, Private Benjamin F. Murphy of Walnut Grove, died the day Thomas reached home, March 17, of wounds received at the Battle of Stone's River.

Benton Barracks Missouri
April 1st, 1863

Dear Estelle

I thought I must drop a few lines to you so that you may know when I arrived here and how I am getting along. We took the boat at Quincy Monday afternoon and arrived at St. Louis yesterday morning about sunrise. The camp is about three miles from where the boat landed. We took it foot the balance of the way. We might have taken the street car which would have taken us to the Barracks but we concluded that we would foot it. My fare to Quincy was $3.75cts and from there to St. Louis $1.50. I paid full fare clear through. Mr. Waldo would not give us soldiers tickets, the balance of the boys paid their fare to Galesbury and there they got soldiers tickets to Quincy. So they got through some cheaper then I did. I do not see why Mr. Waldo could not give us soldiers tickets as well as they could at Galesbury. We took deck passage on the boat, we reported at headquarters and they told us that we had just saved ourselves, and that the Presidents order included the paroled prisoners. The Major is going to send for our descriptive rolls and we will be paid all that is due us the first of May. I went to see him this morning to find out if I could get a furlough home, but I could not. He said he could not give furloughs except in extreme cases where our families was in a suffering condition and those that go home with out a pass will be treated as deserters. So you see that I am in a pretty tight place. The only way is to try and make the best of it. I guess you will have to come and see me after a while when you get some money. It will cost you $3.75 to Quincy and from there here I believe it is $4.00 to go in good style.

We have very comfortable quarters (for soldiers) the soldiers are comeing in yesterday and to day with a perfect rush. There is great many paroled prisoners here, I do not believe we will be exchanged very soon by the way things is looking. I am well and hope this will find you and the children the same. Tell Luella and Sylvester that their par says they must be good children and may the Lord bless us and preserve our lives that we may again enjoy each others society, I will close by wishing you good bye for the present.

From your affectionate husband

Thomas Berry

Write as soon as you receive this and direct as follow
    5th Company 4th Battallion
    Benton Barracks
    Missouri Compay G 89 Ill.

P.S. When you get out of money you had better sell that hog, Sam Whiting will buy it. You know birdie that I miss you but I hope we will not be seperated long.

The "presidents order" was the proclamation issued by Lincoln on March 10, 1863, offering amnesty to all soldiers absent without authority. Such soldiers returning to active duty by April 1, 1863, would suffer no punishment. Those not returning to the army by that date would be classified as deserters.

Benton Barracks, St. Louis Mo.
April 5th

My Dear Wife

I thought I must drop you a few lines this pleasant Sabbath morning so that you may know that my health is good and trying to content myself as well as I can under the circumstances that I am placed, and in hopes that this will find you and the children blest with health. We have great deal more comfortable quarters here than we did at Annapolis, I am well satisfied with the change. I am sorry that I cannot have the privliege of going home until we are exchanged but it is otherwise. The order from the commanding officer is all those that leave without a pass from their superior officers will subject themselves to a court martial, if I had my pay that is due me I would not stay here long. If I should leave they would be apt to keep back some of our pay which would be all they could do with us, I am not certain that they could do that but it is best to be on the safe side. So I had better remain. I feel thankful that I had the privliege of staying with my loved ones as long as I did, I had a good visit and a pleasant time and inhopes that the time is not far distant when I can go home to stay. Homer and myself got a pass down to the city yesterday, we went all through the main part of the city. There is great deal of business done here. We went into a museum and saw different kinds of wild animals, and birds the admittance 15 cents, I thought we got well paid for our money. When you come to see me I will have to take you there. What do you think about comeing down here. I should like to have you come firstrate if you can bring plenty of money, we can have a good time. When you arrive here enquire for Fourth Street and there you can take the street car which will take you to Benton Barracks. When you get here enquire for the 4th battallion 5th company the number of our company room is 65. You may think that it would be quite an undertaking but I do not think you would have any trouble. I should like to have Louella and Sylvester come and see their par but they would be to much trouble to you. When you write let me know what you think of the plan.

We are divided off in companies, one hundred in a company and have company cooks, I have not done any cooking since I have been here.

The Methodist are holding a protracted meeting here in the barracks in a hospital building and are having quite a revival. Quite a number comes forward most every night for prayers and some have experienced religion. There is a good state of religious feeling manifested in the meetings. O that the lord would pour out his spirit more abundantly here amongst the soldiers. There will be meeting this afternoon and to night. Enclosed you will find a card at the close of one of the meetings a lot of these was distributed amongst the soldiers and we was requested to commit it to memory and then send them to our wives and friends. The rest of the boys that came here with me are well, Mr. Bainbridge came here yesterday, he is going to try and get a furlough for Charley. There has good many left for home since I have been here without any furlough.

I do not know as I have anything more of great importance to write so I will close by asking you to remember me in your prayers that we may grow in grace and in the love of God. Write all the news, so good bye for the present.

From your husband

T. Berry

There are no letters from Thomas between the 5th and 14th of April, nor did he make entries in his diary between those dates. It is assumed Thomas took French leave to visit Estelle again, however no reference to such visit is made in either his letter of the 14th or in his diary for that date which reads:

Tues. 14th

There is about six thousand paroled men here. Signed the muster roll for our rations in money while I was a prisoner. 27 days, 30 cts. per day.

Barrack St. Louis
April 14th, 1863

My loving Wife

This is to inform you that I received your second letter containing one from George yesterday. I am well as usual, but not very contented. This laying around in a Parole Camp does not suit my taste very well, I prefer being at home with my dear family and be a free man until we are exchanged. I do not think we will be exchanged before July, if we are not exchanged before that time I think there will be no trouble in getting a furlough next month. We will be mustered for pay the last of this month and paid the first of next month and then if I should not get a furlough I intend to go on my own hook. There is some leaving for home most everyday and there is great many that have not reported yet and I think it would have been just as well if we had not reported, only we would not get any pay if we was not here pay day. If I have the privilege of going home again before I am exchanged when I return I want you to come as far as St. Louis with me and we will go by the way of Peoria and have a good time. I have received those two papers that you sent me and one St. Louis paper. I sent them by Jeffry Craigin he belongs to my company he was captured the same day that I was, but was paroled and sent to our lines at Murfreesboro. All those that was not sent around by the way of Richmond have to return to their regiments. We are going to have extra pay whilst we was in the rebels hands. We are going to have our rations that was due us in money which is thirty cents per day, we was prisoners twenty seven days which will amount to eight dollars and ten cents. We have signed the roll to day for the above. There is about six thousand paroled men here at the present time. If I thought I should not get home again I should want you to come down with out fail. But I think I will. I have not done any duty yet. There is some paroled men on guard every day they stand guard with clubs. They dont dare to give them guns. I should like to be there and hear those temperance lectures, liquor is destroying men by the thousands in the army. I can see the evil effects of drinking every day here in camp. I will close for the present by hoping that this will find you and the children well.

Yours as ever

Thos. Berry

(Enclosed Pamphlet "The Great Warfare")

Benton Barracks
April 21st, 1863

Dear Estelle

I thought I must drop you a few lines this pleasant afternoon to let you know that I am well. I received your letter dated the 15th last Saturday and was sorry to hear that you was not very well and inhopes this will find you in the enjoyment of better health for good health is one of the greatest blessings that can be bestowed on us. I received your third paper that you sent me yesterday. I received a letter from Arthur Taber last Friday.

Nathaniel Shurtleff was here to see me last Tuesday, he is going to get up a colored regiment if he can get the authority to do so, he has a recommend from the Colonel that he was under and Govenor Yates and General Curtiss. If he gets authorized to raise a regiment he will be Colonel and he said he would give me a chance as one of the officers if I wished to. The regiment will be officered by whites. I gave him some encouragement, if I do I will be Captain. I should not be surprised if he should succeed for I have seen in the papers since then that negro regiments was being raised. What do you think of it, would you like to see your man at the head of a company of curly heads. It suits my views well to arm the blacks, they are the cause of the Rebellion and they are to be benefitted by it so I think they ought to help fight for their freedom. Nat was in the battle at Shiloh, he was wounded twice, he lost seventeen men out of his company there. He was discharged on account of wounds received there. He said he wanted to raise a company at Galesburg and one at Chicago and the balance south. What do you think of the above arrangement. Write and let me know. He learned by Emeline that I was here. We had a fine rain here last night for the first time since I have been here.

There was a little excitement in camp to day. A Missouri Battery has been here quite a spell and they had orders to leave today and they refused to go so the commander here called out the 34th Iowa that is here and brought them out in battle line with loaded guns and fixed bayonets and told them to obey orders or suffer the consequence which made them cool down. They arrested the leaders and put them under guard and marched them down to the city to General Curtiss headquarters. What he will do with them I do not know. I cannot find out what they refused to obey orders for. Some say their pay before they leave. There is no signs of being exchanged very soon that I can hear of. I have not heard anything about Captain Whiting yet. I dont believe that he is exchanged yet. There was one hundred and ten rebel prisoners brought here Sunday and one Lieutenant Colonel and one Captain. The officer that had them in charge had to bring them here to report. They was captured near Memphis. Most of them was guerrillas. They was a good looking lot of men well clothed for rebels. Making paroled prisoners stand guard is played out I guess for there has not been any detailed for that purpose for quite a number of days.

I calculate to start for home as soon as I get my pay. I will close by sending my best respects to all enquiring friends.

From your husband

Thos. Berry

Tell Louella and Sylvester that their par says that they must be good children, so good bye. Write.

The names dropped by Thomas Berry's nephew, Captain Nathaniel Shurtleff, are those of Richard Yates, Governor of Illinois, and that of General Samuel R. Curtis, a commander of Federal armies in the West and Southwest. General Curtis is well known for his victory at the Battle of Pea Ridge, or Elkhorn Tavern, Arkansas, which took place March 6 through March 8, 1862. General Curtis is commander of the Department of Missouri. [Captain Shurtleff did not raise a colored regiment. He resigned from the army as quartermaster, 17th Regiment Veteran Reserve Corps, on November 28, 1865.]

Three black regiments had been recruited in the Spring of 1862 under Union General Benjamin F. Butler's command after he occupied New Orleans. These are thought to be the first such recruits. [An entire division of black troops was enlisted in the Army of the Potomac in 1864, in the Fourth Division of the Ninth Corps. General H. G. Thomas, commander of the Second Brigade of that division, praised his command for its gallantry in the battle near Petersburg, Virginia, July 30, 1864, and further stated "a colored deserter was a thing unknown".]

Thomas' view of the slavery issue reflects that of Lincoln. In his message to the second session of the 37th Congress in December 1862, the President said 'Without slavery the rebellion could never have existed; without slavery it could not continue'. That statement was in support of his Emancipation Proclamation announced to the world on September 23, 1862.

Benton Barracks, St. Louis

Dear Estelle,

I have to call on you for more help, for when I get in trouble you are the only one that I can look to for aid. Well I suppose you would like to know what I want. I want you to send me a citizens dress, send it by express. I want coat, vest, pants, white shirt and those gaiters. Send them in that box that we brought from Victoria. I guess you can get them all in the box and nail it up solid and put the same directions on it that you put on the letters. The express charges will not be a great deal. Get a receipt from Waldo for the box. I do not calculate to try and get a furlough for I do not calculate to come back until I am exchanged. I do not know weather I will get any pay or not, my descriptive roll has not come yet and I do not know as it will. I cannot get any pay without it. The major sent for them when we first came here and I have written for it. I shall wait until the first of May and then if it is not here I will leave for home and wait for the money when I go back to the regiment. I do not know but I could go home with my soldiers clothes but I want to be on the safe side. I hope this will find you well, you need not tell anybody what you are going to send, if the box holds any more then the clothes, you can put in something good to eat.

Yours in love,

Thos. Berry

After requesting Estelle to send civilian clothes, there are no further letters from Thomas until May 12. However, some communication must have taken place (unless Estelle paid her husband a surprise visit) since Thomas made the following entry in his diary:

Wed. 29th

My wife has come to see me. I have found a place for her to board.

Thomas then made a few entries during Estelle's stay:

Thursday 30

We went to meeting today and took quite a ramble through the city. Visited the museum, went to a tavern and got our dinner, went to the institution for the blind and had a pleasant time. We arrived back to camp a little before sundown, some tired.

Sat. 9th

We took a walk around the camp this morning.

Sun. 10th

We attended church twice today. The ordinance of baptism was administered to five soldiers by immersion. Estelle has received a letter from Mrs. Leet stating the unwelcome news that Sylvester was very sick, which will make it necessary for my wife to go home.

Mon. 11th

My wife started for home at four oclock on the steamer Die Vernon.

Benton Barracks
May 12th, 1863

Dear Estelle

I thought I would drop you a few lines this forenoon so that you may know that we are exchanged, the order came out in the morning paper. It was an order sent from Washington to General Curtiss, stating that all paroled men that was reported to City Point up to the 6th of May was exchanged, which somewhat disappoints me for I wanted to make a visit home again before I was sent back to the regiment, but we are living in a world of disappointments. I know not when I shall have the happy privilege of again seeing you and the children. But we know that if we live faithful to the requirements of our heavenly father, if we should never see each other again here on earth, we will meet where seperation and disappointments never come. I am very lonesome without you, it was hard to see you go off in that boat, I hope you will find Sylvester good deal better when you arrive home. I long to hear how he is. I do not know how long we will be kept here. I am afraid we will not get any pay. I will write again as soon as I hear from you and

keep you posted. So good bye for the present.
From your husband,

Thos. Berry

Benton Barracks
May 15th, 1863

I have just received your letter and was very glad to hear that you had arrived home safe, and was glad to hear that Sylvester was on the gain. It is very hard to have my dear ones sick and be deprived of the priviliege of going to see them, but such is war.

My health is good. I miss you very much, I wish you could have stayed here until we was sent away but its otherwise and I will have to make the best of it. I suppose you have received the letter that I wrote to you stating that we are exchanged. The order has not been read to us yet but I do not think there is any doubt but we are exchanged. Its reported that we will have to be mustered over again before we get any pay. The muster rolls that was made out while you was here was not made out right, on account of the officers here trying to cheat the boys out of their pay while they was at home. They have found out that they cannot make that work. The captain of my company told me that he did not think we would be sent away before the first of June and he thought we would get paid, which is good as far as it goes. If I knew we would not be sent away before the first of June I do not know but I would take a french furlough for a few days. The rest of the boys are talking about it pretty strong. I should like to see you and the children once more before I started for Tennessee. I should like to see Emeline very much. I received a letter from George to day. He was well. He said that your father talked of starting for home the next day. The letter was written on the ninth, if so he must be at home by this time. I have not called at the old lady's where you boarded yet but have understood that she and Mr and Mrs Crane liked to have had a knock down. Crane went to the Barracks Master and rented the house that she lives in which caused the old lady's anger to rise, and she gave them fits, for you know she has the gift to do it. She swore at them and called them almost everything. She is determined not to leave the house. The old lady told Mrs Crane all she wanted of the house was to flirt around amongst the officers in the Barracks. The cook told me of the above. Mrs Basset has come since you left, she is boarding at the old lady's. I saw that soldier that could not talk aloud to day he said his wife started for home yesterday. When you think the corn gets as high as it will you had better sell it. You can find out by Mr. Chambers. I have attended meetings two evenings since you left. I hope this will find you and Luella well and Sylvesters health greatly improved. I will close by sending my best respects to all enquiring friends

From your affectionate husband

Thos. Berry

I have not any stamps to put on this letter.
(Envelope marked "postage Due 3" also "from a soldier")

Thomas took "French furlough" (unauthorized leave) as we learn from his diary:

Mon. 18th

I started for home at four oclock this afternoon on the Die Vernon.

He arrived at Estelle's house the following evening at eleven o'clock and stayed with his family through June 2, when he made the following entry:

Tues. 2nd

I have received a letter from Homer Wagner stating that the paroled men are all exchanged. I shall start for St. Louis this afternoon. My wife and children are going with me as far as Galesburg. Arrived at Uncle Tabor's middle of the afternoon. We went to a Daguerrean gallery and got our likeness taken together.

Wed. 3rd

Estelle went with me down to the depot to see me off and wish good bye. It's hard parting with my loved ones. I know not when I shall see their lovely faces again. I feel to put my trust in my saviour believing that he will do for us what is best and right. Arrived at Quincy before noon. I have taken passage on the Die Vernon.

Thur. 4th

Arrived at Benton Barracks about ten oclock and found the Fourth Battallion gone that I belonged. I reported to the Post Commander and was sent to Schoefield Barracks to wait for transportation to my regiment.

Apparently Thomas addressed a letter to Estelle at uncle Tabor's residence in Galesburg immediately upon arrival at Schofield Barracks. That letter is missing. His next letter, sections of which have been torn away, makes reference to the Galesburg letter.

Schofield Barracks
June 4th 1863

My dear Estelle,

When I wrote that letter that I directed to Galesburg we thought that we was going to be sent to our regiments today, we was sent down in the city to the transportation officer. But he could not furnish us transportation to day, but he thinks he can tomorrow. He sent us to the above barracks, there is about fifty that belonged to the same battalion that I did in Benton Barracks. (Piece torn from letter.)

Those that was here got their pay, I suppose Homer has expressed my things home. I wish that they had not left until I had arrived here for I need the blanket but I can draw one when I get to the regiment. My testament is with the things also. I wish you would send that to me by mail when you get it, if it dont cost too much. I have expressed my citizens clothes home.

I came down on the Die Vernon. I took cabin passage and had good fare, I had three meals, the boat did not arrive at St. Louis before nine Oclock. I have bought me one pair of blue pants and a pair of boots, two pair of cotton socks which left me ten dollars so I have not much money. I have had a pretty good nights rest, I got to sleep but it took me a good while to go to sleep for I had to think so much about home and my loved ones. It seems harder than ever now to be seperated from you its getting dark and I will close until tomorrow morning. Write as soon as you get this and direct to the regiment.

Friday morning 5th, this morning finds me well, we are in the same kind of barracks that they have at Benton Barracks. I should think there was about one hundred here this morning, if they continue to come in we may be kept here two or three days so that they can send off as many as they can together, but I hope we will have leave today for I want to get to my company. I have not my silk handkerchief here with me I must have left it at home. I hope this will find you and the children well I suppose they have good many questions to ask about their par.

From your loving husband,

Thomas Berry

Friday 9 Oclock A.M. We are going to be sent to our regiments right off so good bye, I will write as soon as I get to the regiment. Write, put in a stamp and a sheet of paper, write once a week and I will do the same.

During Thomas' confinement as prisoner and parolee, the 89th Regiment remained in and around Murfreesboro with Rosecrans' army. The Union army based at Murfreesboro was constantly in contention with that of Bragg's, preventing

Bragg from sending troops to the west in defense of Vicksburg and against Grant who was waging a campaign for the seige of that city.

In the Eastern Theater Burnside was replaced as commander of the Army of the Potomac by General Joseph Hooker on January 25. Burnside then became commander of the Department of Ohio where his martial law edict resulted in the arrest of Valladigham. After Lincoln commuted Valladigham's sentence of confinement to exile, Burnside in disgust of that action submitted his resignation which Lincoln refused to accept.

Hooker engaged General Lee at Chancellorsville, Virginia, but was defeated in his attempts to subdue the enemy. The Confederates were dealt a stunning blow at Chancelorsville by the loss of General Stonewall Jackson who was mortally wounded on May 2, by his own soldiers. Jackson with his aides had ridden to the front to survey the field of battle and while there he and his party were fired upon by confederate soldiers who mistook them for the enemy. Two of his men, Captain Boswell and Sergent Cunliffe, were killed on the spot, Jackson was hit in the left hand and arm and died of his wounds eight days later in a Confederate hospital.

The Union suffered over 17,000 men killed, wounded and missing in the Chancellorsville Campaign between April 29 and May 6, 1863; the Confederates lost over 12,000.

Bolstered by his successes in the Chancellorsville Campaign against the Army of the Potomac, Lee is now heading his army to the north through Virginia. The South needs victories to secure support of foreign governments and to bolster Southern morale. Furthermore, the preponderance of industrial resources, stuff that wins wars, is in the north. If Lee is victorious in the northern states, gaining northern sympathy for his cause with the help of Copperheads, the Confederate outlook will be much brighter.

Lee's northern march beyond the Confederate border is being made in desperation. The South is feeling the effects of inflation due to loss of agricultural and industrial resources inflicted by the Federals. A loaf of bread in the South at this time costs twenty Confederate dollars, the South is being drained of its white males, and women are replacing men in Southern factories and other workplaces.

Both North and South have enacted conscription acts to bolster ranks of their respective armies.

Part 7

Return to the Army of the Cumberland

Murfreesboro, Tenn.
June 16th, 1863

Dear Wife,

This is to inform you that I arrived here today, after so long a time, I did not get transportation from St. Louis before last Friday afternoon. When I wrote that last letter at Schoefield Barracks, we thought that we was going to be sent off immediately but it proved to be a mistake, and we was kept there until the above time. We had pretty good times there we had the privliege of going around town most every day. We came all the way by Railroad, we was taken on the Ohio and Mississippi road as far as Mitchel Junction in Indiana, there we changed cars for New Albany, close to the Ohio river, arrived in Louisville on Sunday, stopped there until Monday morning, when we started for Nashville. Arrived at Nashville last night about sundown one hundred and eighty-five miles from Louisville, we left Nashville this morning, and arrived at our regimental head quarters, about noon and the boy's all appeared glad to see me. Murfreesboro looks very natural, especially the old Court house yard. The boy's are all pretty well that is here, Theodore Whitney and Houstin Tate was sent north sick yesterday to some hospital, Mr.Newtons health is not very good, George is well. Our Brigade is going to be mounted, so we will not have to foot it much more, that is the order now. We will be furnished with horses sometime next month. I found my knapsack all right two shirts, one pair of drawers two towels and my portfolio. There is no signs of having a fight here very soon. The fortifications here are worth seeing, and I guess the rebels dont like the looks of them very well. I think they had better keep of good distance. I will close this letter, and write again in a few days.

From your husband,

Thomas Berry

I send my love to all enquiring friends.

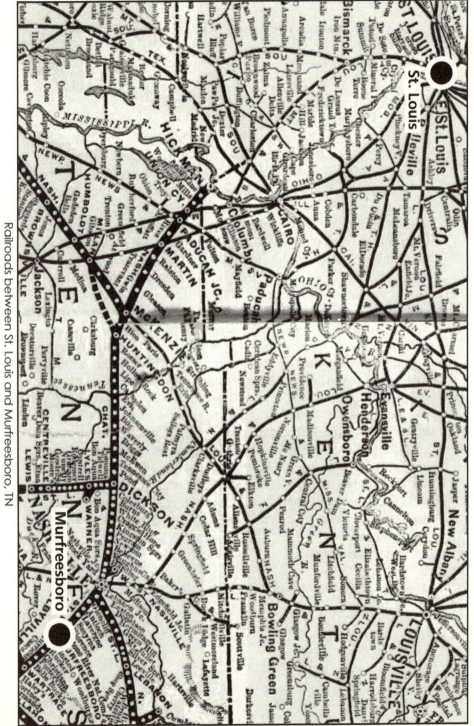

Railroads between St. Louis and Murfreesboro, TN

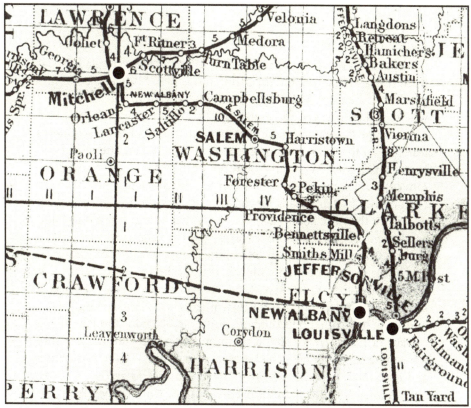

Map of southeastern Indiana showing Mitchell, New Albany, and Louisville, KY.

Thomas is now with his regiment in the Army of the Cumberland.

Following the Battle of Stone's River, Rosecrans reorganized the Army of the Cumberland by dividing his army into three corps. A corps is a completely independent and tactical unit commanded by a general whose responsibilities include strategy for meeting an ordered objective, and the maintenance of a communication line for supplies and medical needs of his command.

Rosecrans reorganized Army of the Cumberland now consists of the Fourteenth Corps under General Thomas, the Twentieth Corps under General McCook, and the Twenty First commanded by General David S. Stanley. Rosecrans petitioned Secretary of War Stanton for a larger cavalry force, but to little avail. (At the Battle of Stone's River, the Confederate's 10,000 cavalry outnumbered the Federals by more than two to one.) With continued appeals to augment his cavalry, Rosecrans requested 5,000 horses and saddles on which he would mount as many foot soldiers. His urgent requests resulted in the mounting of only 2,000 additional men in the spring of 1863.

Murfreesboro, Tennessee
June 19th, 1863

Dear Estelle

I have just received your welcomed letter and was very glad to hear from you, and that you and the children was well. My health continues good with the exceptions of the toothache. I went to a dentist while I was at St. Louis to get one pulled but he made rather bad work of it or rather he had poor sucess in pulling at it. He got his instruments fastened on the tooth and commenced rasing on it and he pulled and kept a pulling but Mr tooth would not yield to his efforts to extricate him from his long habitation. When he found out that he could not capture him by fair means he commenced jerking it sideways which was more than Mr. tooth could stand on the account of old age and crack went the tooth. It broke most even with the gums. He took a short rest and then made another attack on it and it broke again. It broke this time most even with the forks of the roots, by this time it was getting to be a pretty sore thing. He said he never saw such a hard tooth to pull and finally after the instruments had slipped off pulled out one of the roots other but could not pull it out he said without breaking my jaw or pulling out a sound tooth next to it. He said that it would not trouble me but it has ached every day until today it stopped aching and I am inhopes it will not any more. So you see I have had a pretty serious time. Now for something else, General Willick looks about the same as he did last fall. He had us out on brigade drill this morning, we went out at five Oclock and drilled three hours. We have to drill greater portion of the time now. The programme for the day is generally about as follows, roll call at sunrise, company drill before breakfast, after breakfast squad drill, in the afternoon company, battalion, or brigade drill, which keeps us pretty busy. We are camped in a very good place. We have the shelter tents, they are raised up from the ground about two feet with boards and bark which makes them quite comfortable for soldiers. Our sleeping apartments are elevated about one foot from the ground which makes it healthier then it would be to sleep on the ground. The tents are covered by a shed made by setting crotches in the ground, and covered over with brush. Our company is not very large now or at least those that are fit for duty. There is only twenty seven able for duty now. Peter Tait is sick in the hospital, Allen is quite sick, Sam Ward started back before I arrived here. The whole company does not look as well as they did last fall. They show the effects of the wear and tare of war. Mr Newton is with the company and keeps around all the time but is not able to do any duty. Captain Whiting has been quite sick for a couple of days. The weather is very warm here now. I was sorry to learn that Mary was sick. George Cumming came here yesterday to see George and went away to day. He looks as if he stood soldiering very well, his company is stationed five miles from here on the railroad between here and Nashville. The rest of the boys have not arrived here yet, if Homer had come to see me when he came through we would have went to Peoria, but those days are in the past tense and there is no use to complain. There is a great difference in the order here than what there is in parole camp. There is not much drinking and carousing carried on here. There was about ten that came with me from St. Louis that was drunk all the way through. They just poured the poison stuff down, which was perfectly sickening to me, poor fellows, I pitied their condition for I am satisfied that they will come to an awful end. I saw the effects of drinking and the untimely end that awaits a man that indulges in the poisonous draught as we was passing over the Cumberland river by Nashville. The cars went across the bridge very slow when we was about half way cross, a man came on the bridge from the opposite side a staggering. I thought he would fall down front of the locomotive but he staggered towards the side of the bridge and went headlong over in the river. It must have been thirty feet down to the water. I did not see him after he fell from the bridge but I suppose he never got out alive. He was a good looking man and well dressed, such was his end. I saw some splendid fields of wheat in the southern part of Illinois as we passed through, it was ripening for the harvest. I saw one or two pieces harvested and in the shock. All along the road showed thrift and plenty, and we could see improvements going on in almost every town. After we left Louisville there was quite a change in the appearance of things. In the place of peace and quietude we see that the strong arm of military power has to be used to secure order and protection to justice. I hope the day is not far distant when we shall have law and order through out the whole land and military law done away with.

    I bought me a good blanket at St. Louis for one dollar which came very good while I was there. The childrens likeness looks very natural but I can see that they have grown a great deal since last fall. I wish I could see them now. Kiss them for par. I must close this time, from your loving husband

T. Berry

During Thomas' absence the Army of the Cumberland had built fortifications at Murfreesboro, as did the Army of Tennessee at Tullahoma, Shelbyville, and the surrounding area. Except for clashes to maintain communications lines, Rosecrans and Bragg were both content to remain on the defensive while building their respective commands for the inevitable battles ahead. Furthermore, the presence of each antagonist assured the confinement of both armies to the area, preventing the sending of aid to their respective comrades doing battle in the area near Vicksburg, Mississippi. Such aid would weaken the army from which forces were sent, leaving that army vulnerable to attack.

Grant is maneuvering in the final stage for the siege of Vicksburg, attacking the forces of Confederate General Pemberton. Pemberton's superior officer, General Johnston, is attempting to bring an army to reinforce Pemberton and prevent the siege but is confronted by Union General Sherman near Jackson, Mississippi. Rosecrans was concerned an aggressive move against Bragg, made too soon, would cause Bragg to retreat to the aid of Johnston. Yet, such move by the Army of Tennessee would have been to the Union's advantage since the State of Tennessee would then no longer be occupied by a major Confederate force. The fear of Bragg sending significant aid to generals Johnston and Pemberton was the ostensible excuse for Rosecrans to hold the Army of the Cumberland for six months at Murfreesboro, the same period of time in which Grant was moving his army toward Vicksburg.

A military objective set by President Lincoln is the occupation of Chattanooga, Tennessee, by Union forces. That town is a rail center providing a transportation lifeline throughout the Confederacy. Lincoln considered the occupation of Chattanooga more important to the demise of the rebellion than would be the occupation of the Confederate capitol at Richmond, Virginia. Chattanooga is now the long-range goal of Rosecrans, and Bragg at Tullahoma is in his way.

With no significant Confederate victories to attract foreign support, by June 20, 1863, the tide is slowly turning against the rebellion. On that date President Lincoln issued a proclamation declaring West Virginia the 35th state to join the Union. West Virginia was split from the original State of Virginia, because of the loyalty of citizens in the northwestern region of that state.

Rosecrans is no longer concerned over Bragg's sending aid to General Johnston since by now it is too late for the Confederates to save Vicksburg. The Army of the Cumberland which had not moved since the Battle of Stone's River in which Thomas was taken prisoner, is now beginning to stir, preparing to move against Bragg's forces. Thomas writes in his diary:

Wed. 23rd

The order has come to move tomorrow.

The Tullahoma campaign is about to begin. Southward from Murfreesboro, within 30 and 36 miles respectively, are the towns of Shelbyville and Tullahoma. The former is with Confederate General William J. Hardee and his army, the latter is with the entrenched army of Confederate General Leonidas Polk. Rebel forces are also posted at the base of Cumberland Mountain, including Liberty Gap and Hoover's Gap, about ten miles southeast of Murfreesboro.

From Thomas' diary:

Tues. 24th

Forward movement of the Army of the Cumberland. Our Division left Murfreesboro at five oclock. Marched about ten miles when skirmishing and the rebs was upon a high hill and it fell to our Brigade to drive them off. The 32nd done most of the skirmishing and the rebs was finally routed. Quite a number of our men was wounded. Our regiment was kept in line of battle all the time. The balls would come a whizzing over our heads. There was one of our regiment wounded. The rebs was drove quite a piece by our Brigade. We camped where the rebels camped last night.

Thomas is in the skirmish for Liberty Gap.

Thurs. 25th

Our regiment has been under pretty heavy fire all the afternoon. We was on pickets. The rebs tried to drive in the picket line. They came down on some of the Companies with a pretty heavy force but was repulsed every time. Some of the companies suffered pretty bad. There was no one hurt in Company G, but there was some very narrow escapes, Capt. Blake was mortally wounded. The bullets patted the ground most all around. We had a pretty good cover, trees and a rail fence. It has rained most of the time since we left Murfreesboro. We was relieved about sundown and went about a mile and camped. After we got in camp General Willich rode through the regiment and stopped and told the boys that they had done well and said boys you're baptized now. Then the regiment gave him three rousing cheers.

"Captain Blake" is Captain Herbert M. Blake of Chicago. He was in Company K of the 89th Illinois regiment.

Frid. 26

We have not moved today. All quiet along lines with an exception of an occasional picker shot. After dark orders came for us to march, also to build big fires to deceive the enemy before we started. Marched about six miles through mud and water. We had an awful march. Some places the mud and water was knee deep. It was about 12 oclock when we stopped for the night. The order is to march at five in the morning.

Heavy, unseasonal rains began with, and are continuing throughout the Tullahoma Campaign, turning the ground to deep mud and bottomless bogs of quicksand. Non-essential material is jettisoned to lighten the wagons, mules unable to free themselves are lost in the quagmire. Troop movement is slowed, and the element of surprise is lost by the Federals in the plan to capture Bragg's elusive armies. Piecemeal engagements are fought on the drive south.

The rebels were driven from Liberty Gap on June 24 and 25 by General McCook's Second Division including General Willich's First Brigade and the 89th Illinois Regiment. The Federals occupied Shelbyville on the 24th and pushed the rebel army toward Tullahoma.

Sat 27th

We struck the Manchester pike, marched through Hoover's Gap. Rousseau's Division drove the rebels from this gap. They had a strong position here. We have marched 12 miles. Went in camp at five. The 89th goes on picket tonight.

Sun 28th

Commenced marching about nine oclock. Marched about five miles and stopped and made coffee and then commenced marching. Marched until dark when we again stopped and made coffee and then started. It rained most of the forenoon and the roads are awful.

Mon 29th

We marched until three oclock this morning, through rain and mud. A hard march. We marched across Duck Creek. Camped close to Manchester. It rains and rains.

Tues 30

We have not moved yet. It has finally cleared at present. We had inspection of arms at nine.

Wen July 1st

Commenced marching about eleven oclock. When we got within six miles of Tullahoma the news came that the rebs had evacuated the place. Arrived at Tullahoma eleven oclock in the evening.

Thurs 2nd

We are gone into camp about a half of a mile from the town. The rebs had one pretty strong fort here. They left three siege guns in it. They was dismounted.

Skirmishing continued through July 3 as the Union army occupied Tullahoma. Bragg retreated the following day, taking his remaining army to the defense of Chattanooga.

Sat 4th

Spent the fourth on picket. Rainy day.

Sun 5th

Received a letter from my wife, stating that Louella was attacked with the croup.

Mon 6th

News has come that Vicksburg has fallen. The whole force was surrendered to Grant on the fourth, also that Lee's army was badly whipped and on the retreat. There was a general hurrahing in camp over the news.

Tullahoma
July 6th, 1863

Dear Estelle,

It has not been long since I wrote to you but I thought you would like to hear from me often, so I concluded to commence a letter this morning. This is the fifth letter that I have written to you since my arrival at Murfreesboro, including this one. If you do not get all the above letters I wish you would let me know in your next letter as I want you to know all about our march to this place. I received a letter from you last night dated 28th which makes four in all. Enclosed in the same was fifty cts which will come very handy as I was perfectly strapped. I am well and hearty and inhopes this will find you and the children in the enjoyment of the same blessing. Tell Sylvester that his Par was glad to hear that he went to Sunday School and kept still and was a good boy. His par wants him always to be a good boy when he goes to meetings or Sunday School. I am sorry to hear that Louella was taken sick, but I hope she is well before this time. I presume you would like to know how I spent the fourth, we celebrated that day out on picket. Little did I think last fourth when we was down to Victoria that I would be away down in Dixie this fourth doing picket duty and watching for the rebels. We know not what a day may bring forth. I wondered to myself where you was, when I was out on duty that day, I hoped you was enjoying yourself if I did not have the privlilege of spending the fourth very pleasantly. Everything is quiet around this place. There is not many rebs near hear, all the rebels we see here are prisoners and they are bringing them in from the front every day. They have about one thousand here now. Great many comes in our lines and gives themselves up, they say that they are tired of fighting. Our forces are still pushing on after Bragg. Its reported that his army will he soon broken up and scattered among the mountains or captured. I think Bragg is about used up.

Rosecrans has frustrated all his plans and if it had been good weather Rosy would have captured his whole force here. I think we will be left here to guard this place but cannot tell certain for we may have marching orders at any time, for soldiers have no abiding place.

Gen Willich rode up to our camp yesterday and said boys, come out here I want to tell you some news; and it was not more than a minute before the whole regiment was flocked around him, then he stated that General Lee and Meade, had a great battle and that General Meade had drove Lee back four miles and his communication was cut off from Richmond and there was fifty thousand men under General Dix marching on Richmond. He thought Lees army would soon be broken up and all we would have to fight would be guerrillas and robbers which is good news and l hope it will turn out to be true.

It still continues to rain most every day, if you could have some of the rain up there that we have here it would come very acceptable.

Bragg had this place pretty well fortified but it did not do him any good. Most of the boys are well. Mr Newton is pretty well at the present time. Reynolds has been quite sick since we left Murfreesboro, but is improving some now.

There is a running stream close to our camp which makes it handy for washing but the water is not very good it has a bad taste. The rebels camping grounds are awful filthy. I dont think they pay any regard to cleanliness. George and me has a shelter tent by ourselves. They are just right for two. We have company cooks, we have been pretty short of rations since we have been here on account of the bad roads. They will soon have the cars running here.

From your loving husband

Thos. Berry

Write often

General Willich was referring to the Battle of Gettysburg which took place on the 1st, 2nd, and 3rd of July. Lee had taken his Army of Northern Virginia into the loyal State of Pennsylvania where he was defeated by the Army of the Potomac under General George G. Mead. Meade had replaced General Hooker as commander of that army on June 28, just three days before the Gettysburg battle.

Official records referenced place Federal losses at 3,072 killed, 14,497 wounded, and 5,434 missing for a total of 23,003 Union casualties suffered in the Battle of Gettysburg. The Confederate's loss is estimated near that number; however, exact numbers are not found since generals are reluctant to elaborate regarding a lost battle.

The great drama of this battle, as with other battles mentioned in this work, is lost in the cursory reference required to relate Thomas Berry's letters to the Civil War.

After losing over one third of his army in casualties of killed, wounded, and missing, Lee retreated with his remaining army toward Maryland. By July 7, he had reached the Potomac River near Williamsport where he found destroyed, the bridge by which he entered Maryland two weeks earlier with his supply train. The river which had been easily crossed by much of his army on entering Maryland was now rain swollen and impossible to ford. Lee was trapped with his back to the Potomac, facing a pursuing army which he fully expected would attack him.

Accordingly, Lincoln urged Meade to capture Lee's army of Northern Virginia while it apparently is within grasp of the Federals; however, harassing raids by Confederate cavalry, skirmishes with Lee's rear guard, and inclement weather impede the Army of the Potomac.

When General Willich spoke to the "boys" on July 5th, he was not aware of the surrender of Vicksburg to General Grant, which took place on the 4th of July, a day purposely selected by Grant. The Confederates surrendered Port Hudson four days later giving the Union control of forts along the entire Mississippi River, dividing the Confederacy, and severing the rebel's Trans—Mississippi communication lines.

General John A. Dix on July 5, was at Fortress Monroe where he had been in command since June 2, 1862. He was not "marching on Richmond", nor at that date was any other commander. Richmond will not be surrendered to the Union until April 3, 1865.

Tullahoma, Tenn.
July 13, 1863

Dear Estelle,

I have postponed writing to you for a few days as I have been anxiously looking for a letter from you so that I might know how Louella was. I received your fifth letter on the seventh inst. stating that Louella was attacked with the croup, but I am inhopes ere this, she is well as ever. I cannot help thinking and worring about her, for that is a very dangerous disease. I am inhopes I will receive a letter from you before many days. There has not much of anything new transpired since last writing to you. Our division is still here, and I rather think we will remain here quite a spell. Our regiment have moved to a new camping ground, a few rods and fixed up very comfortable quarters and we have very good times now. We have to go out on picket every four days. We went out yesterday morning and came in this morning. The picket line is about three quarters of a mile from our camp. I am inhopes that the day is not far distant when I can spend the Sabbath day a little different. The cars arrived in this place from Murfreesboro

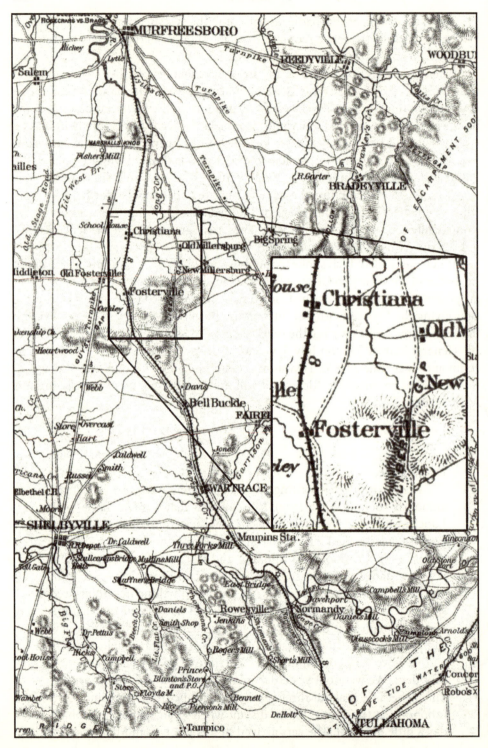

on the morning of the ninth about one Oclock. I was out on picket when I heard the whistle, it sounded good, it seemed as if I was in a civilized country once more. Prior to the arrival of the cars we was very short off for rations on account of the roads being almost impassable, but now we have full rations and are all right. When a soldier is put down to half rations it goes pretty rough. We are pretty well supplied with green fruit. George and me has stewed or fried apples about every meal. They detail ten out of every company most every day to go out to gather berrys. There is great many dewberrys, blackberrys and huckleberrys, the former and the latter berrys I never saw before I came here. The dewberrys looks very much like a blackberry, they grow on a vine or bush that runs along the ground. I was out Saturday, we went out about three miles most of citizens left here when Bragg skedaddled and good many left every thing in their houses, furniture and bed clothing. They was most all rebels in this vicinity. Quite a contrast from the people of Shelbyville, there was a general time of rejoicing amongst the men women and children of that place when our forces entered that town. We have had cheering news since the fourth, the surrender of Vicksburg to General Grant on the fourth, that day will be dearer then ever before to every loyal person and after that came the news that General Mead and Lee had a terrible battle and Mead came off victorious and Lee soundly thrashed. I hope and pray that Lee's army will be annihilated and forced to surrender. If we are successful there I shall look very soon for the glad tidings of peace proclaimed. I think it is a good thing that Lee invaded Pennsylvania which I think will prove his destruction and inhopes Morgan's raid into Indiana will place him in the same predicament. It seems that Mr Cramer obtained his furlough under false pretenses and the boys are all down on him. The Colonel is going to put him through, he said his wife was very sick and one of his children had broke his leg and they was in a bad fix generally. The Captain has found out that it is all a lie. I think it will go pretty hard with him, the Colonel says he would not give his grandfather a furlough after this. By his acting the rascal the rest of the boys will not get furloughs, that is the way it is in the army, when one does wrong the balance have to suffer for it. I do not know how far out the advance is but it must be quite apiece for the cars runs out twelve miles.

    I am very sorry to learn that your health is not good, you must take care of yourself as well as you can. I hope it will not be many months before this rebellion will soon be crushed out and I have the privlieges of returning to you again. I do not think the prospect ever looked brighter for a speedy termination of the war as it does at the present time. Let us hope and pray for the best. I have written a letter to Emeline and one to Arthur. I will have to close for want of more room. I close by sending my love to all enquiring friends and good share to yourself, hope this will find you and the children well.

From your absent husband and one that never forgets you,

T. Berry

Write often

(enclosed note)

My dear Birdie

I thought that I must express to you my feelings of love. You can only imagine how I long for the time to arrive when I can arrive at home, when we can embrace each other affectionately and share each others joy and sorrow. I want you to remember that when you have cares and discouragements before you that you have one that is continually thinking about you and one that you can depend on at all times and under all circumstances and I pray that our heavenly father will overshadow us both with the wings of his compassion and give us grace according to our troubles and cares and may the time soon arrive when I can return to you my dearest friend on earth and nothing but death will seperate us again. Oh I have thought if Louella should be taken from us by death it would be almost more then I could bear, but I feel that the good Lord will spare our lives and we will all see each other again. I feel assured that he will do for us what is best and may we put our trust in him from day to day and may we finally be one unbroken family in his kingdom. You say you guess we will need a hired girl so that we can be together most of the time when I get back. I think so too and I think so for it will take a long time to catch up. We have been absent so long a time. We will have good times when I return for I think it will make us both better and I know it will make me a better man. I did not know how well I did love you until I was seperated from you. I must close hoping this will find you and the children well. My health is firstrate, so good bye for the present. O for a good sweet kiss, from your kind and affectionate husband

Thomas Berry

Morgan, mentioned by Thomas, is Brigadier General John H. Morgan. Without General Bragg's consent, Morgan set out to raid north of the Ohio River early in July of 1863 with his brigade of 2,400 men. Pillaging and burning property useful to the Union as he traveled northward, he crossed the Ohio River at Bradenburg, some forty miles downstream from Louisville, Kentucky. Morgan captured steamers to ferry his cavalry across the Ohio, then set the boats on fire to prevent their use by the pursuing Union troops.

He continued his plundering on an eastward flight through Indiana to Ohio, and swept around Cincinnati toward the new state of West Virginia. Throughout the raid, Morgan had been eluding the Union army and local militia but was frustrated in his search for means to cross the Ohio River into West Virginia.

On July 19, at the town of Chester, Ohio, after an hour long battle with Union forces, Morgan lost in killed, wounded, and missing, 700 of his men. Morgan escaped with his remaining cavalry, losing 1,000 more of his men at Belleville, Ohio, the same day. He was finally captured with his remaining men at New Lisbon, Ohio, on July 27.

Morgan was sent to a penitentiary at Columbus, Ohio, from which he escaped on November 6, by tunneling. He made his way south and once again saw service in the Confederate army. Morgan was killed in action at Greenville, Tennessee, on September 4, 1864.

One of Morgan's men captured at Chester on July 19, 1863, was Louella's future husband, Private George A. Yocum. Yocum was arrested the next day and sent to Camp Douglas on August 23 that year where he was imprisoned until the end of the war.

The delayed pursuit of Lee's Army of Northern Virginia in the Eastern Theater by General Meade, allowed time for Lee to rebuild the bridge across the Potomac River, and by July 13, that river receded sufficiently to permit fording. On that night Lee's army built large camp fires at Williamsport to give the impression of an army encamped for the evening. Meade assumed the enemy would still be encamped the following morning at which time he planned to attack Lee's army.

In the dark of the night on the 13th, Lee's army crossed by ford and by the repaired bridge, escaping his trap and the Union army. When Meade finally made his charge on Williamsport on the 14th, Lee was safely in Virginia making his way down the Shenandoah Valley, much to Lincoln's chagrin and to Meade's embarrassment.

Tullahoma
July 17th, 1863

Dear Wife,

Its with the greatest pleasure that I improve the present time, in commencing a letter to you so that you may know how I am getting along. I am blessed with good health and enjoying myself, as well as can be expected under the circumstances, its not presumed that a man could enjoy himself very well, down here in dixie when he has loved ones at home. I received a letter from you day before yesterday and was glad to hear that Luella was as well as she was, if you or the children get sick dont delay sending for a physician if you think you need one, on account of saving a few Dollars. You say that you spent the fourth at home, I was inhopes that you was enjoying the fourth, if I was not. I have written before how I celebrated that day, I think by next fourth if our lives are spared we will have the privilege of celebrating that day together. My anticipations are pretty high now that the rebellion will soon be crushed out, and I think my expectations is based on a pretty good foundation which is the surrender of Vicksburg and Port Hudson and the scattering of Bragg's Army to the four winds of the earth and the driving back of Lees Army and the report has come to day that Charleston is captured. Our arms is crowned with success at all points. I think the rebels will soon be drove in the last ditch. It looks to me as if the fighting was about finished in the western department, Sherman and Grant will soon clean out Johnson. Bragg is reported to be at Atlanta with what force he has left. They have deserted him by the thousands, they are comeing in here every day, there was two regiments came in here yesterday officers and all and gave themselves up, and there is still great many in the mountains between here and Chattanooga, our regiment has been mustered to day for pay. I expect to get ten months pay, I presume we will get pay this week, as the paymaster is here. There was an order come last week to the effect that there should be five commissioned officers and ten enlisted men from each regiment sent home to recruit to fill up the regiments to their proper standiard. The talk is now that Lieut. Howell is going from our company. If he does, and I get my pay, I will send it home by him. I presume you have got the corn money before this time. When you loan any out, there must be a stamp a ten cent stamp I believe fastened on the note, or it will be of no account, which helps to pay the war debt. Be sure and keep enough money to keep yourself comfortable and if you loan Chambers the money you had better have it so that you can draw some when ever you need it.

It is still rumored that our brigade will be mounted, but there is nothing definite known about it by us. I am inhopes that we will not be mounted now. If I thought I should stay in the service until the three years was up I should prefer to be mounted, but as the prospect is now I should prefer it afoot, for I think the mounted men will have to remain in the service the longest for the purpose of hunting guerrillas.

We all have lost our knapsacks and contense, the roads was so bad that they was thrown away, but I think we will get pay for most of the things. My portfolio that mother gave me was in the knapsack. I would not taken a great deal for it. I believe that I never wrote what narrow escapes some of our company had at Liberty Gap. A ball passed through the crown of Livingstons hat while he was out on the picket line, and a ball struck a rail that Homer was sitting on, which he thought was about near enough for good health. Quite a number of the boys had the missles of death pass along close to them, there was one passed over in about two feet of Georges head, as it happened there was none that came any nearer then three or four feet of me. I gave them a few rounds wether it done any execution I cannot tell and I dont know as I wish to know, but I took deliberate aim on one reb. I must close by hoping that this will find you and the children well.

I remain yours as ever

Thomas Berry

No. 7

Continue to send postage stamps for they cannot be had here for love or money. I have received one on every letter and have received six letters. This makes seven that I have sent to you since my arrival at Murfreesboro. I wrote two there, and five since. I hope you will get them all.

Saturday after dinner, 18th

I was Corporal of the guard last night at Brigade headquarters for the purpose of guarding the paymaster and the greenbacks. There was one corporal besides myself and six privates. We went on guard at five Oclock I was up until twelve, when I was relieved by the other corporal, so I had a chance to sleep the balance of the night. Our regiment will be paid this afternoon or Monday. I will get ten months pay, and I will send you one hundred and fifteen Dollars. Our Chaplain Mr. Spencer is going home as soon as the regiment gets paid, and I am going to send it by him. All the boy's are going to send their money by him. We are going to get checks from the paymaster, and the chaplain is going to take them to Louisville and draw the money on them, and he will send the money home for us there by express which will be a safe way, for there is good deal of risk in sending money from here to Louisville for there is danger of it being captured by the Guerrillas, which will leave me fifteen Dollars. Lieut. Howell may not start home for a week, and he may not go the order may be countermanded. I dout there is much chance to get Volunteers around Altona.

As soon as you receive the money write and let me know.

We are having very pleasant weather here now, it has finally cleared off and stopped raining, I don't suppose its any warmer here then it is in Illinois.

All the boys in the Company that is with us is well except Mr. Haywood, he has been quite sick for quite a spell, but is on the gain now. Newtons health is tolerable good he looks better now then he has for a long time. Peter Tait is still at Murfreesboro and quite feeble.

Write often and all the news that you can think of.

From Thomas Berry to his birdie,
Estelle.

P.S. Since writing the above I have received a letter from you dated the 19th and was very glad to hear that you and Sylvester was well and Luella was on the gain. You say that I am in debt to you in the letter line. I hardly think not. I should have thought you would have received some of my letters that I wrote when we was on the march before you wrote the last one. The first letter that I wrote on the march was on the 30th of June, the next was the 2nd of July the next on the sixth...... and this one makes the seventh. I think Altona done nobly in raising money for the sick and wounded soldiers.

Thomas refers to the city of Charleston, South Carolina, headquarters of General Pierre P. T. Beauregard, commander of the Department of South Carolina and Georgia. Toward the end of 1862 and early 1863, Beauregard reinforced the defense of Charleston and the island forts and batteries in and around Charleston harbor. The Federal Government has been attempting a naval blockade of that harbor following, the surrender of Fort Sumpter, a blockade through which contraband continues to flow.

An attack was made upon Fort Sumpter April 7, 1863 in a futile attempt to silence the rebel guns and gain access to the harbor. The Federal fleet consisting of turreted ironclads of the Monitor class was soundly defeated. Employing a different strategy on July 10, 1863, the Union was successful in gaining an island foothold near the harbor entrance. The July 10th action, blown out of proportion, is that referred by Thomas. With an inferior number, Beauregard defended the Harbor and the city. The Confederates did not evacuate the city of Charleston until February 12, 1865.

"Johnson" is Confederate General Joseph E. Johnston, commander of mid-Mississippi and superior of General John C. Pemberton. Before the siege of Vicksburg, Pemberton did not follow Johnston's order to meet at a staging area and combine their armies in order to encounter the Federals with a formidable force. Grant took advantage of the divided Army of Mississippi, engaging Pemberton at Vicksburg while General William Tecumseh Sherman held Johnston to the west of that city.

The near six-month engagement of the Confederates in the Vicksburg Campaign was that same period Rosecrans spent at Murfreesboro skirmishing with Bragg's harassing forces. Neither Johnston nor Bragg could send sufficient troops to aid Pemberton, the former through the strategy of Sherman, the latter for fear of losing Tennessee to the Union.

Following the surrender of Pemberton of his army and the City of Vicksburg,

Johnston retreated with his five divisions to the east, pursued until July 17 by Sherman as far as Brandon, Mississippi, about 55 miles east of Vicksburg.

General Grant paroled the entire army of Pemberton from the Vicksburg surrender, sending it honor bound to the Confederacy for confinement until the soldiers would be exchanged under the terms of the cartel. Grant will later regret that action.

Bragg at this time is at Chattanooga, Tennessee.

The letters of June 30 and July 2 are missing. Ink was spilled on the line in which Thomas was accounting for his letters, making that line unreadable.

No. 8

Tullahoma
July 23rd, 1863

Dear Estelle,

I again drop you a few lines to inform you that I am well and for the purpose of keeping you posted as well as I can in our military and especially my own individual affairs. Our regiment was paid today up to the 20th of June. I was paid $139.95cts which is nine dols and cts more then I expected to get when I last wrote. I shall send you one hundred and fifteen dollars. I was going to send five more but the Captain had the above amount down on a paper for the Chaplain and he did not wish to change the amount specified, but I guess I can manage the balance for there is quite a number of sutlers and bakerys here. The Chaplain is going to start tomorrow morning and it will come from Chicago the same way that it was sent last spring. One of the bills that was paid to me was the round sum of one hundred dollars. Write as soon as you receive it for I will be anxious to hear if it gets there all right. If you have a chance to sell Fanny you had better do it. If you can't get any more than eighty dollars let her go and as much more as you can. Perhaps you had better wait until I come home before you go down to see Emeline and then we will go together and have a good time as the prospect is good at the present time for a speedy termination of the war. Our company was sent out yesterday to guard a foraging train of twenty wagons. Forage is tolerable scarce around here. We went out beyond Lynchburg about one mile, twelve miles to Lynchburg and they loaded the wagons with sheath oats, which was along tramp for a few oats and the roads was very rough and hilly. Lynchburg is a small place and the buildings looks as if they was built in the year one and they are very much dilapidated. There is very little enterprise in the mass of the southern people. There is very little improvements, they live and work the same as they did I should judge fifty years ago. The best thing I saw was a school in operation close to Lynchburg. Quite a large school house and I should Judge there was about fifty scholars. The first time I have seen children at school in the south. We did not arrive back to our camp before two hours after dark and we was quite tired and did not see a nairy armed rebel. We saw some rebels but they was citizens, the rebels are very scarce near here, they are afraid of Rosy's army. We have not had to drill any since our arrival here. We have good deal guarding and picketing to do which is the cause. We have had very good times since comeing here and live tolerable well as we have about all the blackberrys and apples that we can use, which goes pretty good with our hard tack and very healthy for the soldiers. The south is a great place for blackberrys and in fact all kinds of fruit. Their apples here is mostly natural fruit there is very little grafted. The boys are most all well and able for duty. Our company has an addition of three since I last wrote. Rosenleaf, Jasper Codding, they have been at Nashville since last fall. Theodore Whitney arrived here day before yesterday, he has been at Louisville for the past six weeks in the hospital, his health is tolerable good now. Peter Tait and Esq Allen is still at Murfreesboro, I understand that they are getting better.

You need not send any more stamps or paper, as the sutler keeps them now. I have bought eight stamps and some letter paper today.

I heard the other day that Arthur Taber and Mr. House was taken up as deserters but I do not hardly believe it or at least hope it is not so, write and let me know about it. I got the news from Captain, his wife wrote it to him. Write often, you cannot displease me by writing too often. I will close by wishing that this will find you and the children in the enjoyment of the best health. Yours as ever

Thomas Berry

I send my love to enquiring friends.

"Esq Allen" is Corporal Squire D. Allen. Neither Arthur Taber or Mr. House were from the 89th Illinois regiment. The captain is Captain Thomas Whiting.

Tullahoma
July 26th, 1863

Dear Wife,

Lieutenant Howell and John Tait is going to start for home today for the purpose of getting Volunteers. So I thought that I would drop you a few lines to let you know that I am well. I received your No. 8 letter day before yesterday and was glad to hear that the children was so well and that Sylvester was so mischievous for I think he feels well when he is mischievous. I am sorry to hear that you are not well. I hope the time is not far distant when I can come to you. I have sent one hundred and fifteen Dollars. The Chaplain started with it yesterday. I understand that Lieut. Howell will get the money at Louisville or Chicago and take it home for us. Write as soon as you get at. I think our brigade will be mounted as soon as they get the regiment filled up. I dont believe they will get many Volunteers. I will close by sending you my love,

Thomas Berry

No. 9

P.S. You can send them notions that I wanted you to send by Cramer, by John Tait or Howell, scissors and thread. Send some papers by mail, I guess they will come through. Mother and Hor is playing particular smash, write all the news.

Lieutenant William H. Howell carried Thomas' letter of July 26 to Estelle.

Tullahoma
August 6th, 1863

Dear Wife,

As this day is sat apart by the President for the national thanksgiving and praise, to giver of all good who has crowned our arm with success, thereby giving us great victories, I thought that I would commence a letter to you so that you may know how the day is spent down here in the army. All military doings is suspended except what is actually necessary. I have thought since reading the proclimation of the President that our nation could not help comeing out all right when it had such a man as Lincoln at the helm, for he acknowledges a higher power and looks to him for help in this our nations trial, may the Lord give him and all in authority wisdom and knowledge and may they look to him at all times for help, and may the time soon arrive when war and bloodshed shall cease and again be one united people, may the prayers that shall ascend to the throne of divine mercy for the speedy restoration of our Nation and the overthrow of the rebellion be answered is my prayer. Our Chaplain has not returned, I suppose we would have preaching if he was here. I believe I have never written anything to you yet about the morals of our regiment and company. The whole regiment has improved wonderfully. I believe I have not seen one of the boys playing cards since I returned which is quite a contrast what it was last fall. Some of the boys then was playing most of the times when they was in camp. Some of the boys got up a resolution last winter they they would not call upon Gods name in vain and good many has signed it. So we do not have a good deal of swearing. Our Chaplain keeps a regimental class book, all those that wish to have their names down can do so without any regard to what church they belong which I think is a very good thing. There is nine names down out of our company, I put down mine. George and I went to hear the Chaplain of the 49th Ohio preach two weeks ago, he is a Methodist and a good preacher. It was sacrament day with them and we had a good meeting. God can meet with his children in the army as well as he can those at home, all he asks is for the heart to be right and then he will bless them.

Afternoon

I have just received your letter dated the 30th of July and perused well its contents and was glad to hear from my birdie. I think you have taken a very sensible view about renting the farm for next year for I do not think it would hurt me any to act the gentleman one year if the war should close between now and spring. I think George Shears would be a good hand, I like the plan for the house being left vacant so we can move in anytime if we wish. Have a written contract and have the house left in your possession, for if you dont they can rent the house to who they please. Let him find grain, tools, team, and all expenses, and give one third of all small grain delivered in the half bushel, and one third of the corn husked and cribbed and one half of the hay put up in the stack. Also let him put in twenty acres of wheat and five acres of oats, or if he wishes let him put the five acres into wheat and the balance of the land into corn and do the farming in a workmanlike manner. If he accedes to the above terms rent him the place, let your father write the contract, and I will be satisfied.

My health is good, there is nothing new transpired since I last wrote only there has been rumors that we will have marching orders before long. It may be so and it may be only a camp rumor. The boys of our company are all well now. Mr. Newtons health is very good, he and four others have been detailed for three days as guards on the train between here and McMinville.

I will close by sending you my love, does Louella and Sylvester talk about their par. So good bye for the present.

Thomas Berry

P.S. Friday morning, last night just after we retired an order came for us to get ready to march at any time and have two days rations in our haversacks. So we had to get up and get ready, but all is quiet this morning. I dont hardly believe we will go at this time, but we are liable to go at any time. T.B.

Tullahoma
August 9th, 1863

Dear Estelle,

    As I wrote in my last letter that we had marching orders I thought that I would drop you a few lines to day, so that you may know that we are still remaining here, and all is quiet at the present time. Its no telling how long we will remain, for I presume that Rosy calculates to clean out Tennessee of rebels before long, I hear that the Generals are going to make a general movement on the rebs, at the same time. If they do and are successful, the rebellion will be apt to receive its death blow, if we are ordered from this place, I should not be surprised if I should get a chance to see Atlanta again for I do not think they will make a stand this side of that place. Our regiment went out on picket yesterday morning and was relieved this morning, about an hour before light this morning, two colored Gemmins came up to the picket line where I was on duty, which was on a road, on the roads they have two men, and one noncommissioned officer. We heard them comeing, but it was so dark we would not tell if they was white or black. When they got up in proper distance one of the sentinels halted them, and enquired who comes there, they said very promptly black men. They was ordered to advance, I enquired of them what they wanted they said that they had runaway from their masters and wished to get inside of our lines. They said that they had traveled most all night. I told them to wait until morning and I would take them to camp. They are coming in most every day. The 29th Ohio was out foraging last week and they brought in forty blacks, freedom sounds good to them. I bought some verses of poetry composed by a soldier that belongs to Davis Division and I thought that I would send it to you. Afternoon I guess I had something for dinner that you did not have, I had some good stewed peaches, and they went sumptuously. Peaches are just beginning to get ripe. Our cavalry caught about 40 rebs near here yesterday a part of them are bushwhackers. Our company are going to keep the above negroes for cooks, they are quite intelligent.

    I must close so good bye

                                                  Thomas Berry

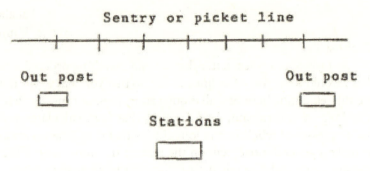

(Note enclosed with August 9th 1863 letter)

The above represents how we have to do picket duty. The station is where the company stays, and they keep four men and one sergeant or corporal at each out post and each out post supports four men more on the sentry line. Stations out post and sentry beats are all numbered and they are relieved every two hours, some times we have three reliefs and then it goes very easy. Our regiment has five stations. I guess you can understand it.

The Army of the Cumberland remained at Tullahoma until August 16, repairing the railway, roads, and bridges which were to be used on the march to Chattanooga. Rosecrans' six-week delay in pursuit of Bragg had its critics in Washington much the same as did his six month stay at Murfreesboro. General Meade also was subject to criticism for his delay in pursuing the Army of Northern Virginia following his victory over Lee at Gettysburg. That delay was in part due to counsel given by his generals.

Meade marched his army southward through the Shenandoah Valley in Virginia but was unable to stop the rebel retreat. Lee's army took refuge along the Rappahannock River north of Richmond.

The term 'bushwhacker' is used by the Federal forces in identifying a member of a guerilla band firing upon a Union soldier from undercover. Guerillas are a group of independent soldiers who attempt to harass and impede troop movement, generally working behind the lines, unlike 'raiders' who act openly as a band of riotous soldiers.

Part 8

Battle of Chickamauga

Bellefonte, Alabama
August 23, 1863

Dear Estelle,

You see by the commencement of this letter that I am down in Old Alabama. We left Tullahoma last Sunday afternoon at five Oclock. The orders came at two Oclock to get ready to march at five with three days rations in our haversacks. When the time arrived the 2nd division was on the march. We continued to march until the next morning at two Oclock, when we went in camp for a short rest. It took us all the above time to go about seven miles. It was a very dark night and the roads was very rough as usual the teams kept a getting stalled and some broke down, which made it slow getting along. We stopped close by Elk river. We took a short sleep and at five we was on our way. We went through Winchester quite a pretty place and very pretty scenery around it. We marched about twelve miles and went in camp about five Oclock. It was a very warm day and the soldiers fell out of the ranks by the hundreds. The 32nd Indiania most all give out. Willick had orders to go to such a place but he sent word on to General Johnson that he could not march his men as fast as they had done while it was so warm. After that we took it more moderate. There is any quantity of peaches along the road. I have never seen so many peaches before, most every house along the road there is a peach orcherd and the boys helps themselves. Tuesday morning we started about four Oclock our brigade was in the advance of the division, we passed through Salem, about ten Oclock we came to the Alabama line. In the afternoon we came to the mountains. The road was between two ranges of mountains, a very rich valley, splendid corn, Illinois cannot beat the corn that grows here in the valleys. I have seen that I could not reach the ears. We marched twenty miles, our company was out on picket that night. 19th marched ten miles, 20th we did not march any to day, our advance is passing over the mountains and the mountain is very steep and rough about two miles to the top. 21st our brigade commenced climbing the mountain as soon as light. We had to help the train up every company helped up two wagons, ten mules to the wagon. We went up without any trouble, marched about ten miles. Most all union folks that lives amongst the mountains. There is one hundred union men here hunting up the rebel bushwhackers, a great many men and women has come out and hurrahed for the Union as we passed by their log huts. 22nd marched about seventeen miles which brought us to Bellefonte which is on the Chatanooga R.R. We have had a pretty hard march on the account of it being so warm, I do not know as it is much warmer here then it is in Illinois but the load that we have to carry is what makes it go so hard. If I did not have anything to carry I could march all over Dixie and never mind but I am well rested out this morning and feel about as well as I did when I left Tullahoma. I presume we will remain here a few days to get recruited up and then start for Rome or Atlanta. I hear that the rebs are fortifying at Rome.

I got two letters from you soon after getting into camp last night dated 11th and 16th and was glad to hear from you after our march which keeps my spirits up to hear from home often. The cars runs within a short distance of this place. Excuse this scribbling as I have had a poor place to write. I am glad that Mr.Barnes wants the place for he will be an honest hand, you might as well sell the black sow if her bag is injured.

I remain your affectionate husband

Thomas Berry

Each opposing commander knew the defending of Chattanooga was not as important to the Confederacy as was the saving of Bragg's army, a lesson sadly learned by the Confederates at Vicksburg. Rosecrans, anticipating Bragg's next move, sent his armies on diverse routes from Tullahoma to encounter the rebel army which he knew would evacuate Chattanooga.

McCook's corps took the most southerly direction to the right and is now in Bellefonte, Alabama. The 21st Corps under Crittenden is moving on the left toward Chattanooga as General Thomas' corps is taking a middle route toward Bridgeport, Alabama.

Bellefonte, Alabama
August 25th, 1863

Dear Wife,

Our regiment is out on picket to day and I am one of the outposts which is a very good place to write as I am away from the noise and bustle of camp, so I concluded that I could not pass away the time any more pleasantly then writing to my birdie. My health is good and hope this will find you and the children the same. This is the second letter that I have written since our arrival at this place. Its called very sickly here, ague and fevers. I heard that most all the citizens that are left in the town have the fever and ague. We are camped in low bottom land and its very swampy. I suppose the Iasma that arises from the swamps

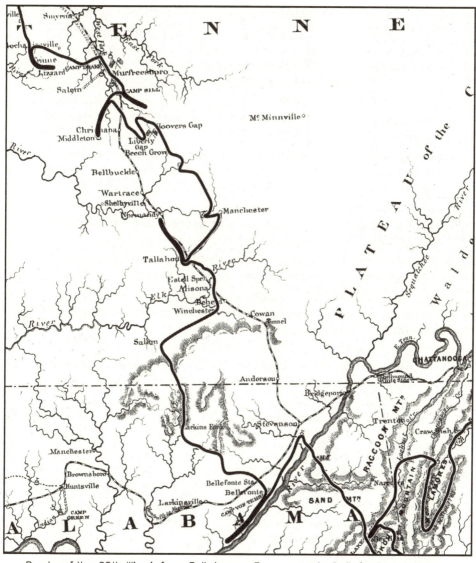

Route of the 89th Illinois from Tullahoma, Tennessee to Bellefonte, Alabama.

is the cause of its being so unhealthy. General Johnson has issued an order that no soldier should sleep on the ground in camp but must raise their bunks up from the ground and must build fires in front of their tents every night. He says if the above precaution is not heeded the hospitals will soon be filled with the sick. George and me have built us a good bunk about two feet from the ground. I believe I have never described how we built out bunks. Well, we drive down four crotches in the ground and cover with flat rails or poles and then cover with leaves or cedar limbs, which makes a very comfortable bed for a soldier, we are quite comfortable fixed again. Its no telling how long we will remain here, for we have no abiding place. I think I will get pretty well used to moving from one place to another. Some of Braggs army is close to the river on the other side. We are in about two miles of the river, when Rosy gets ready to move again they will have to fight or run. I guess they will be apt to run for it seems to come second nature with the rebs in Braggs army. I hear that our troops have commenced crossing the Tennessee river at Bridgeport. Rosencrans has pontoon bridges along that he brought from Murfreesboro, so that he can cross any time or place. I hardly think the rebs will make a stand this side of Rome or Atlanta, a few more weeks will tell. Mr. Camprumor says that our brigade will stay here until we are mounted, but Mr. Rumor is not noted for the truth and veracity in the army. I wish we would get our horses before long as I am about tired of marching afoot. I have done about enough of it to satisfy me that there is not much fun in it. The citizens have commenced coming in for the purpose of taking the oath of allegiance. There has three come in since I have commenced writing, they think the rebel cause has about exploded. We passed good many union men hunting up rebel bushwhackers. If any of the citizens holds out their union sentiments here under such embarrassing circumstances that they have had to pass through here by the rebels they ought to be well compensated by the Government for all losses that they have sustained, for they have had to pass through a firey ordeal, great many have saved their lives by hiding in the mountains. The rebels have had troops ascouring the mountains hunting up union men and deserters. We camped close by a house the night before we came here where the whole family was union, the strongest kind. One of the men belongs to our army to Negle's division. He was at home on a five days furlough he has been in the army fifteen months and it was the first time that he has seen or heard from his folks. He had an uncle shot in the field while he was ploughing by the rebels because he was a union man, he was an old man. They had a large peach orcherd and the trees was full of peaches. Gen Willick was going to put a guard around to keep the boys from touching the peaches but the owner went to Willick and told him the soldiers could have all the peaches they wanted and he did not wish any guard. They was quite poor people, our brigade gave them about forty dollars in provision and money which well paid them for the peaches that the soldiers took. I have received two letters from you since I have been here and I will endeavour to answer your questions. Our Chaplain is a Methodist, he was a circuit preacher before he came to the army, he was captain of a company until the death of our first Chaplain. He is a good preacher, he has good deal of influence and is doing great deal of good in the regiment. Those Gnewmans I believe, belong to Grants army, I have thought about their preaching great many times. Those names that are down on the regimental class book are the three Tait boy's, Joseph Mitchell, Wm. Stogan, John Hall, Jacob Craig, George Berry, and your man. I received pay for ten months and twenty days, which accounts for the nine dollars. Our place must be in pretty good demand I should judge by the number of applications for it. I guess you will be glad when you get it rented so that you will not be bothered so much. I do not think you could get a better hand than Mr. Barnes (except me) to carry on the place. You stated that Louella was going to send her par a piece of calico like her dress, you must have forgotten to put it in as it was not in the letter. It has been one year to day since our company started from Altona for the war. There has been a great change since then. The rebellion was in its full strength at that time and they had all hopes that they would gain their independence, but at this time gloom and despair overshadows the whole south. They see that their cause is lost. Those that lives to see the close of another year will see a greater change yet for I think the rebellion will be used up by that time root and branch to never spring up again. Peter Tait arrived here from Murfreesboro yesterday, his health is getting pretty good. We have thirty five men out on picket, all the boys in the company are in good health. I guess I have written about enough this time. I will close by sending my best respects to all enquiring friends. Yours as ever,

Thomas Berry

P.S. I visited the graveyard near this place, i will send you some of the inscriptions that are on the tombstones. You may commence again sending me postage stamps as the sutlers do not keep them now, and they say that they cannot get any.

"Negle's division" is the 2nd Division under General Thomas commanded by General James S. Negley.
Chaplain James H. Dill, "our first chaplain", died January 14, 1863.

In the woods and amongst the mountains of Alabama
Sept. 6th, 1863

Dear Estelle,
    Its been one week since I wrote last in that time we have marched

about twenty five miles. Last Monday our Division crossed the Tennessee River on the pontoon bridge. The river was about 80 rods wide where we crossed. The Tennessee is a very pretty river and went in camp about half of a mile from the river, and laid there until Wednesday morning, we was mustered for pay while we was there, there is three Divisions on this road besides about twelve thousand Cavalry, we are in about seven miles of Georgia line and the course that we are taken will lead us direct to Rome. On Wednesday we had to go up the Sandy mountain, over a mile to the top and very steep, but we arrived at the top with weary limbs, and marched about three miles and went in camp which ended that days march. Thursday we marched about fifteen miles, and received two papers from you and one letter dated the 25th Aug. containing a piece of Louellas dress, which is very pretty. Friday we went three miles and arrived at the foot of the Mountain and have not moved since then. The roads are so awful rough and mountainous that the army cannot make very fast progress. I do not think we will move from here today. I hope not for we have marched the last two Sabbaths. We are in a few miles of the lookout mountains and we will have to cross them, they say. There is conflicting reports about Chatanooga being evacuated. Some say it is and again some say it is not. A few more days will reveal the facts, we are in about 35 miles of Chatanooga. I have just heard which is considered reliable, that Bragg and Buckner is at Chatanooga. Burnside made Buckner fall back to Chatanooga. I presume that the rebs will try and make a big fight there, which will be their last fight in this part of the country, for I am satisfied that Rosy will be enough for them, with the help of Burnside. We are having very good weather for marching, only its very dusty. I stand it firstrate, we have very cool nights and heavy dews. Our regiment goes on picket this afternoon. I hope this will find you and the children well. Send postage stamps I have not but one more, I will close by sending my best respects to all enquiring friends.

Yours as ever,

Thomas Berry

Early in September a corps of Bragg's army under the command of Simon B. Buckner was ordered from Knoxville to reinforce Bragg, shortly thereafter General Burnside entered Knoxville to the exultation of the city's loyal citizens who had been under Confederate rule since March 1862.

Lookout Valley, Alabama

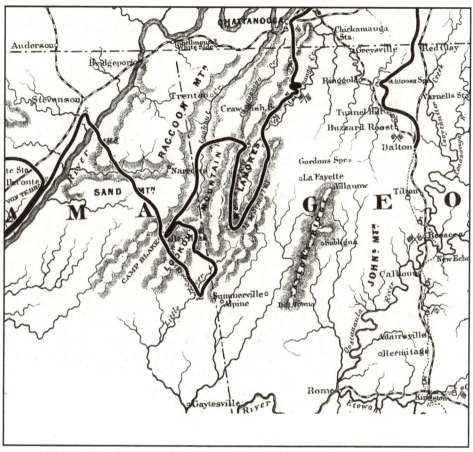

Route of the 89th Illinois between August 31 and September 4, 1863.

Sept. 9th, 1863

Dear Wife,

I again write you a few lines to inform you of our whereabouts and how I am getting along, my health is good. I have not been sick a minute since leaving Tullahoma. All of the boy's of the company never had better health then they have since we have commenced marching. There is great deal less sickness in the army when they are on the march then there is when they are in camp. The last letter that I wrote was the third of Sept. we was camped on Sandy ridge. Since then we have marched only about six or seven miles. We came to our present camp yesterday in a valley called the Lookout valley. The Lookout mountains are in sight. The prospect is that we will stay here a few days for we had orders to police our camping grounds and build our bunks, which we have done and it begins to look very much like a soldiers home. We are in about twenty one miles of Lebanon, the same distance from Trenton and eleven miles from Raulinsville and seven or eight miles from the Georgia line. You can tell about where we are by looking on the map by the above description. I should judge that we are in a very healthy location, we have good spring water. Bragg's army is at Chattanooga and I suppose he calculates to give Rosecrans battle, but I rather think that Rosy will get him surrounded and his communications cut off so that he will have to surrender without a great deal of fighting. A deserter from Braggs army came into our lines a few days ago, he stated that Bragg could not make his men fight again and they was deserting him every day. The last part I know to be true for there is not a day but some comes in our lines and great many are joining our army. They see that their cause is lost and there is no inducements for them to remain in the rebel army any longer. There is quite a force of rebels amongst the Lookout mountains. Our cavalry was sent out yesterday to rout them. I received a letter from you last night dated August 30th and was glad to hear that you and the children was well and that you had a chance to go down to Victoria to the quarterly meeting. I should have thought Mother could have spared you more apples. Has she many apples this year, how are they getting along.

We are camped on a rebel plantation. A very nice house the only good house I have seen since leaving Bellefonte, the owner is a captain in the Rebel army, it is now General Stanley's headquarters. If he ever gets back to the place again he will not find many rails on the place. The army does not burn anything for fuel except rails, there is not many rails left after the army passes by. I will close by hoping that this will find you well and I hope the time is not far distant when this war will be brought to a close and I have the privilege of returning to my loved one's. I send my love to all enquiring friends and a good share to yourself

From your Husband

Thomas Berry

P.S. This camp is called Camp Blake, its named after Captain Blake of the 89th Regiment that fell at Liberty Gap. Sept. 11th. We received orders in the evening of the 9th to be ready to march the next morning at five Oclock and that Bragg had evacuated Chattanooga and was in full retreat for Atlanta and General McCook was ordered to follow him with his corps. So yesterday we marched about seventeen miles. We had to cross another range of mountains called the Lookout mountains. We are camped in a valley. Our division and Davis is here. Gen. Stanleys cavalry had a blockade here to hinder our men from

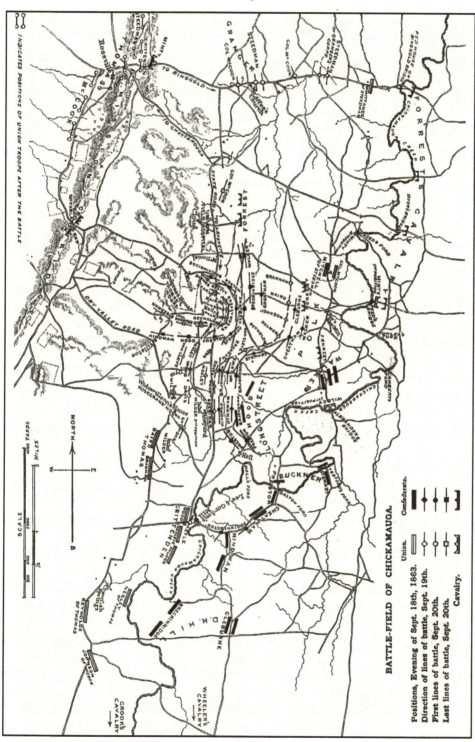

crossing the valley. The rebs had to fall back with some loss, they had all the advantage, our loss was about thirty killed and wounded. We are going to remain here today. I presume we will go to Rome or Atlanta, the rebs may make a stand at one of those places. We are close to the Georgia line and I heard that we are in thirty miles of Rome.

Sept. 12th afternoon. The mail will go out this evening so I will have a chance to send this. We have not moved since comeing here. Our rations have just come up. I think you will hear before long stirring news. We hear all kinds of reports about Braggs forces. One report is, which is credited, that Chattanooga is Rosy headquarters and Bragg is skedaddling and General Thomas is pressing him on the center, McCook is on the right and ready to receive him. I think we will have a big fight or a big surrender on Braggs part. I will close, if I am called in battle and should fall may we meet where war is not known. T. Berry

The "last letter" Thomas wrote was on the sixth of September. In that letter Thomas covered his activities of September 3.

In the Eastern Theater, General Lee had outwitted General Meade as the Army of Northern Virginia retreated following the Battle of Gettysburg. Meade's lagging pursuit afforded time for the swollen Potomac River to recede sufficiently for the passage of Lee's army on the night of July 13. Lee entered Virginia and marched his army south with Meade in futile pursuit of his capture. Lincoln was much distressed over the escape of the Army of Northern Virginia and over the lost opportunity to put an early end to the war.

On September 9, Confederate General James Longstreet left the Eastern Theater by rail with his division of Lee's Army of Northern Virginia for the purpose of assisting Bragg. The detachment of Longstreet's division from the Army of Northern Virginia left Lee in a weakened condition, whereupon Lincoln once again urged General Meade to attack Lee. To bolster his army, Lee offered amnesty to all his Confederate soldiers on unauthorized leave.

When Thomas started this letter on the 9th, he did not know of Bragg's evacuation of Chattanooga which was completed on that day. Bragg feared the Union army approaching Chattanooga would be reinforced by General Burnside from the north and was unaware of his forthcoming support from Longstreet, which would have given him the potential for holding Chattanooga. Longstreet arrived in the area with his division, joining Bragg on the 19th of September.

The Federals later learned that Bragg sent those "deserters" to misinform the Union army.

"Davis" is General Jefferson C. Davis, Union commander of the 2nd Division under McCook. Davis was mentioned earlier regarding the murder of General Nelson.

Rosecrans, acting on the assumption the evacuating rebels would not halt before reaching Rome or Atlanta, planned to intercept Bragg's army in its retreat. Leaving a token force at Chattanooga, he sent General Crittenden to trail Bragg south from Chattanooga, with two divisions marching toward Ringold, Georgia, and one division to Lee and Gordon's Mill on the West Chickamauga Creek. Rosecrans then directed General Thomas to Lafayette, Georgia, with the 14th Army Corps preceding the cavalry, and ordered General McCook to Alpine, Georgia. At their assigned locations, General Thomas was about 20 miles from either Crittenden or McCook and the latter two separated nearly 40 miles.

The 89th Illinois regiment with McCook's 20th Army Corps left Lookout Valley on the 10th, crossed the Lookout Mountain range which rises over 1,000 feet above the valley floor, and arrived at Alpine on the same day. "Gen. Stanley's cavalry had a fight here" on the 9th, skirmishing with rebel cavalry which retreated to the north, a tip off regarding the direction in which the main force of the Confederate army would be found. Lack of rebel foot soldiers at Alpine caused McCook to suspect Bragg had plans other than the full retreat assumed by Rosecrans. McCook immediately returned his army to the Lookout Mountain range, a precautionary move until the main force of Bragg's army could be determined by the Union cavalry.

When Crittenden entered Chattanooga on the 10th of September, it appeared to Rosecrans the town was securely under Federal control and that his separated corps would intercept a retreating Confederate army. He was wrong on both counts. Bragg had no intention of retreating from an engagement with the Army of the Cumberland nor was Chattanooga secured to the Federals. Bragg marched the front of his army south only as far as Lafayette and on the east side of Pigeon Mountain. On the west side of Pigeon Mountain is the West Chickamauga Creek.

Bragg had large troop concentrations near Steven's Gap through which General Thomas must pass to intercept his "retreating army". In that area on September 10, the advance of General Thomas' corps under General James S. Negley, came upon the Confederates, further revealing Bragg's strategy.

Bragg had set a trap which would have devastated piece-meal, Rosecrans' army if Bragg's subordinates had carried out his orders. The result of dilatory response to orders by rebel officers, whether or not justified, foiled Bragg's plan to engage the separated Federal army, or in military terms, to subdue the enemy in detail.

Rosecrans divided his army by miscalculation, not having full knowledge of the whereabouts of Bragg, a military error which caused him much embarrassment and caused the Union a tremendous loss in men and material. The corps of Crittenden, Thomas, and McCook were not within easy supporting distance when skirmishing began.

By September 13, Rosencrans was fully informed through information from his corps commanders of the location of Bragg's army. He then moved Crittenden to protect the roads back to Chattanooga, the only means of retreat for the Union army, and ordered McCook north to reinforce General Thomas who was facing the front of the Confederate army.

Confederate commanders, slow in following Bragg's orders, and on the verge of insubordination, caused delay in attacking the Union army in detail and allowed the time from September 13th to the 18th for the Federal armies to move closer together and prevent annihilation of Rosecrans' army. The Union army was also allowed time to prevent the rebels from cutting off Rosecrans avenue of retreat on the road back to Chattanooga.

From Thomas' diary:

Sat 12th

We are camped within a few rods of the Georgia line. We go on picket at four. The picket line is in Georgia.

Sun 13th

The Major came out to the picket line about sunrise and told us to come in and go up the mountain and join our Brigade upon the mountain as they had moved up before light. We marched five miles and camped, a retrograde movement.

Mon 14th

Marched eighteen miles. We are now near the place that we was on the 5th and 6th. The roads are awful dusty.

Tues 15th

We march tommorrow morning at six Oclock.

Wen 16th

Marched twelve miles. We are camped in Georgia one mile and a half from the line.

Chatanooga, Tennessee
Sept. 30th, 1863

My Dear loving Wife,

Its with pleasure that I take this opportunity to communicate to you this morning a brief sketch of our march here and of the great battle that came off on the 19th and 20th inst. I have written you two short letters since the fight but for fear that you have not received them both this will be a repetition of those two and some addition that you will like to hear as I suppose that you are anxious to hear all of the particulars. I will commence back to the 16th that day we marched about twelve miles and camped one mile and a half inside of the Georgia line. 17th we marched twenty five miles on the Lookout mountains in the direction of Chatanooga,(and enclosed you will find some flowers that I plucked on the Lookout mountains in Georgia) and arrived near the place where the great conflict was to come off about ten Oclock in the evening. It was a very hard days march and I was pretty well tired out, the dust was awful. You have never seen the depth of dust in old Illinois that we have here, after the army passes by. We partook of our repast of coffee and hard tack and then wrapped ourselves up in our blankets and laid our weary and jaded limbs down to rest. We had orders to sleep close to our guns, so that we could spring to them in a minutes warning. I slep soundly until four o'clock when we was ordered up. Then they gave each one of us 20 rounds of extra cartridges, which made sixty in all. We concluded by this time that we had something before us to do. About ten Oclock the 18th our brigade went out on picket. In the afternoon there was considerable cannonading on our left. At six Oclock at night we was relieved by the 2nd Brigade and we went in camp for the night and had a very good nights rest.

Now I come to the 19th and 20th, the days that never will be forgotten, it makes me feel sad. When I think of the many precious lives that fell victims to this unholy and cruel rebellion. Many a mother, wife, and sister at home have been bereft of some that was dear to them by the ties of nature. About sunrise our division was ordered to a new position about six miles from where we camped, in the direction of Chatanooga, which brought us within about thirteen miles of Chatanooga. The battle was raging all the time that we was a marching. About eleven Oclock we arrived to the scene of conflict, the missiles of death was doing its work, our brigade was brought right in the fight. The 32nd was thrown ahead and the 89th supported them, the bullets came as thick as hail, the supporting regiment lays close to the ground and the bullets and shells passes over. Its a pretty hard place on a persons feelings to be in when we are on the reserve, for we hear and see all that is going on and the wounded and mangled are brought back from the front through our lines. Its a heart sickening sight to see men mangled and agroaning. When we are in action we do not have time to think much about such things. After awhile the 89th was thrown ahead and the 32nd fell back to support us. We made a charge with a yell and the rebels skedaddled in a hurry. We drove them about eighty rods when we was ordered to halt and fall back as the rebs was trying to flank us. We fell back about thirty rods. We would have captured two pieces of artillery if we had not had orders to stop, as we had got in a few rods of it. Captain Whiting felt quite provoked because we could not have the privliege of capturing those pieces. Capt performed his part nobly. This was the time that Mr. Newton, Stoddard, Segreth, and two of the new recruits was wounded, J. Smith and Coy. Newton was wounded in the side and the ball lodged in his back. It is thought by those that carried him from field that he is mortall wounded, he fell in the hands of the rebels and I cannot tell his fate. Stoddard had his thigh broken. He also fell in the hands of the rebels. Segreth, Smith and Coys was able to get here and I learn are doing well, they was wounded in their arms. After we fell back there was quite a calm which proved to be a forerunner of a great storm. The rebs massed their forces and just at dark they came on us like an avolanche. We was compelled to give back and we was thrown in confusion. The bullets came like torrents of rain but they was finally checked, they also had a cross fire on us. They took good many prisoners that we know of. This was the time that we lost our missing Captain Whiting, Brother George, Theodore Whitney, R. Wilson, Nelson Burnerson, Rosy Rosenleaf are those that came up missing that night and we have not heard a word from them since but I feel pretty confident that most of them are prisoners. Some of the boys say that Captain Whiting was wounded in the leg. After we succeeded in checking the rebels the fireing ceased for that day. It did not seem that either army had gained anything that day. In the night our forces was building breastworks out of logs and the next morning the battle opened with renewed fury. It seemed as if neither party was going to yield. There was one continuation of volly without any cessation. I do not believe it has its equal in the history of the world and it was mostly an infantry fight. Artillery could not be used to a good advantage. Our brigade was held in reserve most of the forenoon and then we was brought in the fight. We was ordered over two lines of breastworks where our men was a laying and been a fighting and went about ten rods ahead and we gave them the best we had. Stryan, Hall, and Charles Bainbridge was wounded here, Stryan and Hall fell in the rebel hands. They could not get them off of the field. Swickerd, Star and myself carried Charley from the field. Our hospitals was close by but before we got him there the hospitals was all gone and commenced a retreat as the rebels was flanking us and we had all that we could do to get away with him and part of our forces commenced retreating. I thought they had our army pretty near surrounded at one time. We had to carry Charley on a stretcher about five miles and finally we succeeded in getting him in a wagon, Swickerd went with him to Chatanooga. We retreated about six miles and then formed another line of battle. We was overpowered by numbers, part of the Richmond army was here but after all they have not gained much. Their loss must have been great deal more then ours. On the 21st we was kept busy building breastworks and we was attacked on the left. I suppose they was finding out our position. Monday night we fell back to Chatanooga and went right to work a fortifying. We have a strong position here now and can withstand anything that they can bring against us. The rebels are in front in force and there has been some fighting every day with the exceptions of yesterday and today, but they have been repulsed every time. They have possession of Lookout mountain and they have a good view of our works. They have a signal flag on the mountain. I thought sure there would have been another big battle before this time but I think they feel pretty sore and do not feel over anxious to dip in. We have not had much rest for the last month but the worse is over with for the last two days we have had it more easy. Our regiment was out on picket yesterday in front. Their picket lines and our are in hailing distance. We could hear their drums and bugles very plain. They have a brass band and we had the privilege of hearing rebel music. I hope I shall hear before long that George is a prisoner and all right. You cannot imagine how I miss him. We have always slep and partook our meals together and for him to be gone it makes me feel lonely. I feel that I am under great obligations to our heavenly father for preserving my life through this battle. Let us give him thanks for the same and may the time soon arrive when I can have the privliege of returning to my loved ones, is my prayer. Mr Wales is with us now, he has been here three days, he looks quite healthy. I have received a letter from you since I have been writing dated the 24th with a postage stamp and was glad to hear from you. I hope Wessy will not get the mumps. I was glad to hear that Samuel was so good. Reynolds was not in the fight, he was taken sick and was sent back to Stevenson. I will close for this time, I send my best respects to all enquiring friends.

From Thomas Berry to his birdie
Estelle Berry

The "two short letters" are missing. Thomas apparently suspected they would become lost.

The Battle of Chickamauga began in earnest on the 19th of September, and fell heavily upon the center corps of the Union army. The battle raged on until sunset at which time it appeared the fighting was over for the day. Under darkening skies on that evening, a fresh Confederate division under General Pat Cleburne made a surprise attack against the mismanaged Federal army. General Thomas' corps, which at the time included General Johnson's division with Willich's brigade, carried the brunt of that attack. Thomas Berry told the story of that night encounter in which he lost many of his comrades including his brother George. The battle on the following day, September 20, saw the Union army retreating under fire.

"I thought they had our army pretty well surrounded at one time". Those words by Thomas are in reference to a military blunder which opened the Union line. General Wood pulled his division out of line by an order from Rosecrans who formulated that order from false information. As Wood pulled out, a huge gap occurred in the Union line through which poured the Confederates under General Longstreet, forcing most of the Army of the Cumberland to retreat, leaving on the battlefield only General Thomas' corps and those forces of other commands he was able to assemble. Among those other forces was that of McCook's 2nd division under General Johnson, including General Willich's 89th Illinois regiment.

Rosecrans, from his distant location at Rossville, thought General Thomas was defeated by the breakthrough of Longstreet. General James A. Garfield, Rosecrans' chief-of-staff, thought differently and insisted on further investigation. General Thomas was in dire straits. Without Garfield's assistance by bringing the reserve corps under General Granger to his aid, General Thomas would have certainly lost his assembled army to the rebels. Granger prevented the rebels from surrounding General Thomas' forces and allowed an avenue of retreat for the only Union army remaining on the Chickamauga battlefield late in the day of September 20, 1863.

General James A. Garfield [later to become the 20th president of the United States] saved the day for General Thomas' 14th Army Corps and associated units including the 89th Illinois regiment.

Rosecrans pulled his surviving army together at Chattanooga on September 22. Now begins that phase of the Chattanooga Campaign in which Bragg will attempt to regain the city he abandoned on the 9th of September.

Estimates of the forces engaged in the Battle of Chickamauga are given for the Union at 58,000 with 1,650 killed, 9,300 wounded, and 4,800 missing; for the Confederacy, 66,000 with 2,300 killed, 14,500 wounded, and 1,400 missing. These figures are strictly estimates and are given to portray as near as feasible the immensity of that battle, the bloodiest battle of the Western Theater.

Bragg settled his forces on Lookout Mountain and on Missionary Ridge, prominences which overlook the city of Chattanooga and the encamped army of Rosecrans, including the Union's line of communication. The term 'communication' is used broadly to include the army transportation line to a base of supplies and the line along which correspondence is carried to reach official authority.

PART 9

CHATTANOOGA

Rosecrans is now, on September 30, in a desperate condition with his communication line shut off and with food supply for men and fodder for animals running out.

The Confederate cavalry under General Wheeler is causing further destruction of the Union's communication line including the railroad line to Bridgeport. Bragg is intent upon beating Rosecrans into submission by slowly starving the men and animals of the Army of the Cumberland now in the rebel's net at Chattanooga.

"Mr. Newton", Private Winslow B. Newton, from Walnut Grove, was mortally wounded on the 19th, as was Private Elliot N. Stoddard, from Weller, Illinois.

No information is found regarding "Segreth". Thomas may have been referring to Private Michael Scragriff. Scragriff weathered the storm.

"J. Smith" is recruit Jasper A. Smith from Alton, Illinois who was later transferred to the 59th Illinois regiment. "Coy" is recruit William P. Coyce from Chicago who remained on active duty with the 89th.

Captain Thomas Whiting from Walnut Grove, was killed in the battle of the 19th, as was Private Hiram J. Rosenleaf of Copley, Illinois.

Thomas' brother George Berry with privates Theodore F. Whitney, William Stroyan, and John L. Hall, were captured and sent to Richmond, Virginia, ostensibly for transfer under parole to the Federal Government at City Point, as was Thomas Berry in January.

Private Robert Wilson, Corporal Nelson W. Burneson, and recruit Private Charles V. Bainbridge returned to active duty.

"Swickard" is Sergeant John W. Swickard, promoted to 2nd lieutenant on the second day of battle.

"Star" is Private George B. Starr from Walnut Grove.

Pressed flowers were found in the envelope with this letter.

"Mr. Wales", 5th Sergeant Harrison G. O. Wales, had been in the hospital since October 1862.

Chatanooga, Tennessee
Oct. 4th, 1863

Dear Estelle,

I thought that I must improve this pleasant Sabbath morning in writing to you. This is the first Sabbath that we have had the privliege of observing and resting since leaving Bellefonte, but I presume that it has all been necessary and for the good of the country at large, if it has not been in accordance with my own feelings and wishes. Two weeks ago to day we was in the midst of a great battle. Rosecrans was not to blame for fighting that day as the rebels opened the ball themselves. They thought they was going to crush Rosy and his brave army with their overwhelming numbers but they found themselves badly mistaken. Rosy could not hold the battlefield but he fell back in tolerable good order and he is in a position now that can hold all rebeldom to the contrary. I heard him say if the rebels get reinforcements he can and will be able to cope with them at any time. They continue working on the fortifications and have commenced building forts. The rebel houses have to suffer here that are in our way building fortifications. There has been great many torn down, the soldiers uses the lumber building soldiers houses. There was a splendid brick building torn down yesterday in a few rods of our camp. It was on an elevated position and they are going to erect a fort in its place so the house had to come down. The building must have cost six thousand dollars. McCook used it for his headquarters. The rebels continue to be in force in our front. We can see the rebel flag a waiving on the lookout mountain. They have a tolerable strong position. They have thrown some shells from the side of the mountain in our camp. I hardly think they will venture to attack us here but still they may if they do they will get mowed down by the thousands from our fortifications. I heard yesterday that Bragg and Longstreet said that they was going to be in Chatanooga to day but I can not vouch for the truthfulness of the report. Its all very quiet now. I dont think they will hardly come in. There will be good many tons of lead scattered broadcast before they get possession of this place. I do not pretend to know much about military matters but I think the only way they can rout this army from our present position is to get in our rear and cut off our supplies but I hope that danger will be seen to. We have been on half rations since our arrival here. Now I will tell you how much we get to eat per day. Two crackers and a half and about meat enough for one slice (and not very large) for each meal. We get all the coffee we want so you see we have not a very great variety. There is not much danger of getting sick on account of eating too much but I am willing to put up with considerable inconvenience if we can only clean the rebels out. Which will be done sooner or later for I am satisfied that this Government is bound to stand. I believe that the ruler of the universe is on our side and that he will bring about peace and harmony in his own good time. If the Lord is for us its more then all that can be against us.

  Our pickets and the rebels are getting quite friendly they exchange papers about every day and they traded for some of our coffee which is a great treat for them. It looks to me as if the death blow of the Rebellion will be struck in this section of the country. Its a great pity that Rosy did not have sufficient number of men to have anhilated Braggs army. If he had twenty five thousand more men the work would have been done. There will have to be another great battle. We kept a hearing during the battle that Burnside was coming with his army but no Burnside came and we lost the day. We have not heard anything more about our missing. I have learned that all the prisoners are sent to Richmond. If they are prisoners it will be quite a spell before we will hear from them. Same of our wounded has had a hard time of it. Some have lain on the battlefield one week without any care. Rosecrans got the privliege of going after our wounded. I believe they are all brought in now. We send our ambulances out to the picket lines and the rebels takes the same and go to the battle ground and bring back our wounded to their lines again. They will not allow any of our men to go to the battle field. Mr Rice of Chicago, father of Captain Rice of our Regiment that was killed has been here to get his sons body but could not accomplish his mission. He started back to day. I was in about six feet of Captain Rice when he was hit by a solid shot, he was struck close to his shoulder, it almost severed his arm from his body. The first thing he said was boy's I am killed, and looked around to his shoulder and said no I aint my arm is broke, boys carry me off. He was taken to the hospital and died that night.

We have tolerable easy times now and I am getting pretty well rested out. My health is good. We have quite cool weather now and the nights are very cold. We draw rations for forty five in our company. Some of the detailed men have been brought back. There is only twenty four that has guns. Some lost their guns in the fight. I am the only one that is left of my old mess that I had last fall, which was George W. Whitney, Theodore Whitney and Robert Wilson and they are all gone now. Old Dilworth is here he was brought here under guard, he does not do any duty for he will have to stand a court martial. All the wounded men of our regiment are going to be sent home.

Since I received the letter that you wrote when you was to Samuels I have received a letter from you dated the sixteenth. You spoke about moving back on the farm. I would not think of that for it would be too hard for you to go and manage things all alone and it would be hard getting anybody to go there and be interested in the work and I am afraid you would loose more then you could make by hireing the work all done. You had better sell Fanny. Let your father keep Nelly for the use of her, and if he does not wish to keep the colt you may sell it also. I was inhopes that Barnes would rent the place for next year. The way you wrote I have concluded he must have given up the notion of taking it. You state that the ladies of Altona have a dime sociable for the benefit of the sick and wounded soldiers of our country, and you wish to know which way I think would be the best to lay out the proceeds of the same, to the poor people at home or to the sick and wounded in our hospitals. I can very easily and quickly make up my mind on that subject. Send it to the Sanitary Commission by all means for they are doing a noble work. To be sure there is considerable rascality connected with it but never mind.

If the sick and wounded that are lying in our hospitals get one half that is sent them it will do an immense sight of good in the agregate, for such societys started all over the country would amount to great sum. If it is any body that deserves the gratitude, sympathy and benevolence of the folks at home it is the soldier, and especially the sick and wounded, for no one knows the privations and hardships that a soldier has to pass through except they have been soldiers themselves. Then I would say help the sick and wounded soldiers first and God will bless the giving. I must close.

From your affectionate husband,

Thomas Berry

I have written two letters to Harriet since the battle and one to Emeline to day. Kiss the children for par.

Under circumstance of contending armies at standstill, an agreement was often made to withhold firing between opposing pickets, such firing being of nuisance value only. The pickets would then converse and trade goods as Thomas mentioned. No such protection from bullets was enjoyed by officers.

Rebel pickets along the Tennessee River prevented the Federals from bringing supplies from Bridgeport to Chattanooga directly by boat. A survey of the river was necessary to locate docking facilities and thereby determine a means by which an alternate communication route would be established out of sight of Bragg's concentrated forces. On October 19, General William F. Smith, chief engineer for the Army of the Cumberland, dismounted his horse, and in the fashion of a picket, walked within sight of the enemy's pickets and studied the means by which the supply line would eventually be opened.

"We kept a hearing during the battle that Burnside was coming with his army..." Burnside, at Knoxville, had been ordered to reinforce Rosecrans. The general vacillated until after the Chickamauga battle and so remained at Knoxville.

Captain William A. Rice, Company A, 89th Illinois Regiment, was killed in action September 20.

Private James H. Dilworth remained in the regiment.

The Sanitary Commission was formed by a benevolent group of loyal civilians at the start of the Civil War. The group, consisting of ministers, doctors, nurses, professional, and lay men and women, urged a reluctant War Department to accept the services the Commission could offer to the military in terms of medical attention for the wounded, clothing, sanitation supervision, care of those dying and of the dead, and other aid not within the prerogative of the military to supply. The need for such a commission was soon recognized and was given administrative status within the area of its expertise. Members of the Sanitary Commission received no payment for their services. Compassionate Northerners contributed millions of dollars to aid the Commission in its work which was performed by member groups throughout all Union military areas of operation, including Federal prison camps which housed rebels. The South was not known to have such an organization.

Privates Robert Wilson and Wilford H. Whitney of "my old mess" will return to duty.

The two great Confederate armies in which the South made its largest investment of men, material, and money, and upon which it placed it highest hopes for victory in the rebellion are the Army of Northern Virginia under Lee, and the Army of Tennessee under Bragg. As Thomas is writing this letter, Lee is in Virginia maneuvering his army near the Rappahannock River in an attempt to subdue Meade or at least hold him at bay to prevent sending support to the Union army at Chattanooga. At the same time, Lee is preventing Meade from intercepting the Confederate communication line with Richmond. President Lincoln is becoming more exasperated with Meade for not attacking Lee in force, particularly since Lee is without the army of General Longstreet.

Bragg, with the Army of Tennessee, is preparing for the annihilation of Rosecrans at Chattanooga. The rebels are lobbing harassing cannon missiles from their positions on Lookout Mountain, but are hitting no vital Union military targets. Bragg is within siege opportunity but is content to starve the Army of the Cumberland into submission. The rebels control all rail lines, river routes, and Rosecrans' communication line to his base of supplies at Bridgeport. The only remaining route to the outside world for the Union army at Chattanooga is a long and tortuous horse trail through mountainous terrain north of the town. Mail is transported on that route but the trail is not adequate for supplying sufficient food, fodder, and military equipment needed by the army marooned at Chattanooga. Rosecrans' soldiers are on short rations and thousands of his horses and mules are dying of starvation.

At this time the Confederate armies of Lee and Bragg appear to be holding the Federal armies of Meade and Rosecrans at a standstill.

Chatanooga
Oct. 11th, 1863

Dear Estelle,

It has been one week to day since I last wrote to you and since that time our brigade has been on four days picket. We went out Tuesday morning and came in yesterday morning at four Oclock and did not loose a man. Although we have a fair view of the rebel pickets and they of us there is an understanding between the contending parties to the effect that there should be no picket fireing, which is a good thing as picket fighting amounts to nothing but is very annoying. Some of the officers thought that we was going to be attacked two or three times while we was out and they had the picket lines strengthened but nairy advance did they make, I guess it was their own imagaination. I shall be awfully mistaken if they attack us here but cannot tell for certainty what the imps will do but we are prepared for them if they wish to make the trial. The rebs are very bold in front and appear to be in force. They dug rifle pits within twenty rods of our picket lines whilst we was out, without any molestation. If I had my say about it they could not dig quite so close. They keep fires all along the picket lines but we are not allowed any and we have to pass the tedious hours of the night a shivering as it is very cold nights. They appear to have more confidence in us then we have in them. Last Monday afternoon they shelled us from the lookout mountain but it did not amount to much, wounded two and killed one negro is all the damage they done by shelling half of a day. Since that time they have removed the guns from the mountain as they found out that they could not accomplish anything from that position. It is rumored that the rebs are falling back and that there is four corps of our men getting in the rear of them, which I hope to be true. If Rosencrans is not properly reenforced it will be one of the worst blunders the Government ever made. We will not have to go out on picket again until the expiration of eight days. Yesterday the boys was all busy fixing their shanties. Mr. Wales, Starr, Higgins, Homer and myself have quite a comfortable mansion. About eight by ten, one story high and a fire place, how long we will have the privliege of enjoying the fruits of our labor we cannot tell. This Sabbath morning finds me in the enjoyment of good health and should like to have the privliege of going to church with you and the children, but cannot. I have not heard anything from our missing yet. Some more recruits came here yesterday, George Davis got back yesterday, he went back to Nashville, I asked him what he went there for, he said to get some things. It is a perfect shame enlisting him as he will never be of any profit, only in the way. Capt. Whiting did not like it because the Lient. got him to come. I will close hoping that this will find you and the children well. I received a letter from Elija Taber, and it was a firstrate one. We are beginning to get full rations I guess we will have a plenty in a short time.

From your Husband

Thomas Berry

This is the third letter that I have written to you since the battle and have received two.

Following his retreat from the Chickamauga battlefield, Rosecrans advised the War Department in Washington of his desperate situation. Conditions at Chattanooga were such as to warrant rousing President Lincoln from his bed late at night for a meeting with Secretary of War Edwin Stanton and other officials to determine a course of action to aid Rosecrans. Resulting from that meeting, among other decisions, was the movement of troops toward Chattanooga from the Army of the Tennessee and the Army of the Potomac.

Reinforcements are on the way, but the rumor, 'rebs are falling back and there is four corps of our men getting in the rear of them", is premature.

Fifth Sergeant Harrison G. O. Wales from Walnut Grove has been in the hospital most of the time since being mustered on August 27, 1862. He returned to the regiment briefly in October 1862, was returned to the hospital that same month staying there until September this year. His stay with the regiment will again be cut short. On the 27th of next month he will be returned to the hospital, reduced in rank to that of private, and will serve as a hospital nurse until November 1864 when he will once again return to Company G, from which he will be mustered out as a private on June 10, 1865, at age 53.

"Starr", Private George G. Starr is from Walnut Grove as is "Higgins", Private Washington L. Higgins.

"We are beginning to have full rations..." Those words would give Estelle less reason to worry, but food for the Army of the Cumberland still remains in short supply.

Chatanooga, Tennessee
October 14th, 1863

My loving Estelle

I have just received a letter from you dated the 4th and was very glad to hear from you and that our little family was well. I am well and we have tolerable easy times, but I presume it will not last very long. We hear nothing about our brave and noble brother soldier boys that are missing. O that we knew their fate if any of them fell on the battle field its not likely that we will ever hear anything about them. They might have lain on the cold battle field and died for the want of some kind and gentle hand to take care of them and administer to their wants, but we can only hope for the best. If our Captain has fallen our company has lost a noble man, a good officer and a patriot. He looked to the welfare of his company and was liked by all. Our company has suffered a great loss if he never returns. If any of our boys have fallen by the hand of death may their friends and loved ones at home live to see this wicked Rebellion crushed out and may they enjoy the land that those that have suffered and died to maintain.

The weather for the last two days has been very disagreeable, rainy and cold, hard time for those that are out on picket. I presume we will see pretty hard times this winter. There is quite a change going on in the army. The 2nd Division belongs now to Grangers Corps. It is now 1st Brigade 3rd Division and 4th army corps. The Division is commanded by General Wood. I understand that General McCook has been relieved of his command, for not doing his duty at the battle. General Granger's Corp's has been the reserved corps of the army but I presume it will take the front now. You had better keep on and direct your letters as you have until things get settled for they will come all right as you have directed them. We dont hear hardly any news, cant tell what is going on which makes camp life dull and monotonous but I hope everything is working right for our cause and inhopes that there will be a shaking amongst the dry bones of the rebellion before many days passes by. If this reaches you before the Lieut and John starts back I wish you would send me a couple pair of stockings if you can buy home made ones at the store. If you cant buy them let them go. The stockings that we draw are not of much account and do not last long. I wish that I could step in and see you and Louella, and Sylvester, I would call for a good warm meal. I hope the time will soon arrive when this war will come to a perpetual end. I believe I have nothing more to write so I will close by sending you my love and best wishes. Write often.

From him that never forgets you

Thomas Berry

General Grant is now assigned command of the armies converging on Chattanooga. Included in his command are the Army of the Ohio, the Army of the Tennessee, and the Army of the Cumberland. Grant's command also includes the two divisions sent from the Army of the Potomac which are under General Hooker. Grant is now planning strategy for the relief of the Union army at Chattanooga.

Chattanooga, Tenn.
Oct. 25th, 1863

Dear Estelle,

It has been quite a number of days since I last wrote to you but has not been the cause that I had forgotten my birdie in the least. For the past week we have been on duty most of the time. Last Sunday morning we went out on picket and remained there until Tuesday morning when we was relieved and returned to camp. Then the order came for us to move camp and take our position in General Woods Division which was about one mile and a half. So we had to pull down our houses as we had the privilege of keeping our lumber. There was a guard left to watch the lumber and the balance started for our new camp which is on a hill and a very good place. We have a good view of the rebel camps. Wednesday we had to work on the fortifications and it rained most of the time we concluded it was pretty rough to be obliged to work in the rain when we was tired and hungry. We are cut down to pretty short rations. The amount we draw now is, two thirds rations of crackers, half rations of meat, half of coffee not any sugar which is a very small allowance for men that are on duty most of the time. Thursday we had our lumber hauled and we erected our houses. We have made some improvements in ours, larger and higher. We have quite a comfortable mansion. If we only had plenty to eat we could get along very well. Friday morning at daylight we again went out on picket and was relieved Saturday morning. So you see that we are not idle much of the time. I received your letter dated Oct 11th Wednesday evening and was glad to hear that my little family remains well, my health continues very good. I do not think of anything more that would be interesting to write this time, so I will close by sending you my love, write often.

Thomas Berry

Sunday Afternoon

P.S. I have not heard anything about the missing of our company. Two of the new recruits are quite sick, Ross and Blair, balance of the company are well. We had inspection of arms this afternoon. We have inspection every Sunday. I calculate to go and hear the Chaplain of the 49th Ohio preach this evening. He preaches every Sunday evening when the regiment is in camp. I will close by wishing you Good bye for the present, hoping that I will have the privliege of seeing you before many months.

I remain your affectionate husband.

T. Berry

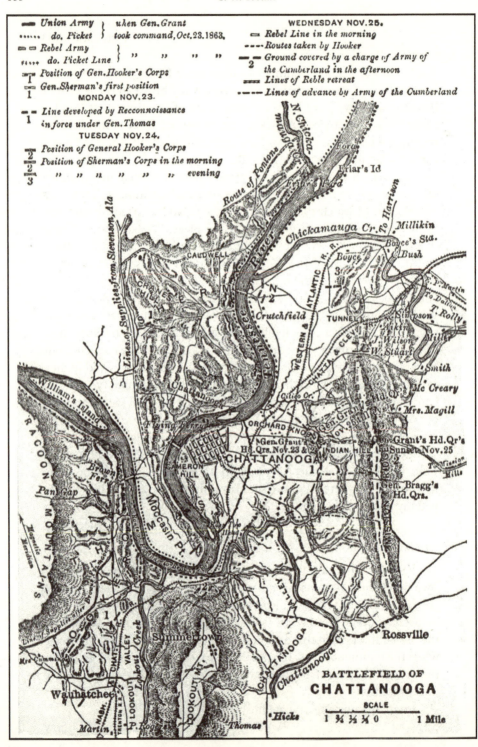

Grant replaced Rosecrans with General George H. Thomas as commander of the Army of the Cumberland on October 19. General Thomas reorganized his army causing Thomas Berry to "take our position in General Woods Division".

Rosecrans placed some of the responsibility for the Union loss at the Battle of Chickamauga on generals McCook and Crittenden, both of whom were immediately relieved of duty. [McCook and Crittenden were later acquitted in a court of inquiry, General Rosecrans was assigned commander of the Department of Missouri on January 28, 1864.]

The "fortifications" is a line of entrenchment, or breast works, roughly 2 miles in length forming an arc about one mile from the town toward Missionary Ridge.

"Ross" is Private William M. Ross from Altona, Illinois. He will recover and transfer to the 59th Illinois Regiment.

"Blair", Private John Blair from Walnut Grove, is terminally ill.

General Grant reached Chattanooga by way of Waldron's Ridge on October 22. He surveyed the area to formulate his plan for relieving the besieged town. Noting the condition of the underfed army, Grant issued orders on the 24th to open a "cracker line" to Bridgeport, but first the enemy pickets along the Tennessee River must be subdued.

Chattanooga, Tennessee
Oct. 28th, 1863

Dear Estelle,

    I have received the letter that you wrote at your fathers today and was glad to learn that you keep well. My health was never better then it is at the present time. Surely we have great reasons to be thankful to the giver of all things that our lifes and healths has been preserved until the present time. We have been in camp since I last wrote to you and have had nothing to do and not much to eat, which does not set very well on a persons stomach, especially when he has a good appetite. They cannot get provision here fast enough for the army. I am afraid it will be good while yet before we will be able to get full rations. I suppose they would soon get the cars running to this place if the rebels did not hold possession of Lookout mountain. Our forces are shelling the mountain to day and the rebs are replying. We have a plain view of the mountain and can see our shells burst very plain. The rebels have three pieces right on the peak of the mountain. I saw some of our shells burst very near them. It was thought night before last that we was going to be attacked as we had orders to have our equipments by us so we could get ready to fall in line at a minutes notice and take our position behind the breastworks which is about four hundred yards from here, but we was not disturbed. There was very heavy cannonading on the right of us yesterday. I understood it was General Hookers forces. General Grant has command of this department now. I look for a general engagement before long. I do not believe Grant will allow them quite as close as they be now. I do not care how soon it commences, if we have the men to make the victory certain. There will have to be some hard fighting in this section of the country, sooner it comes off the better. There is ten regiments in our Brigade now, which will make our picket duty pretty light as one regiment is on picket a day. No's of the regiments is as follows, 15th Wis, 87 Ind, 32nd and 8th Kansas, 25, 35, and 89th Ills, 15th and 49th Ohio.

I was sorry to hear that Mother was sick, I presume Louella is having fine times with Sarah. You are looking for a big price for the corn next spring. Did the frost injure our corn any and is it pretty good. How have the bee's done this summer, have they filled the box up with honey. Write all the news. W. Higgins of my mess is quite sick and two or three others of the company are complaining. What is the general opinion about the war closing very soon. I have not received any papers for quite a spell. I will close for the present by promising to write again in a few days.

From your affectionate husband

Thomas Berry

Direct as follows,
Company G 89th Ills, Vol.
1st Brigade 3rd Division
4th Army Corps
Army of the Cumberland by the way of
Nashville, Tenn.

General Grant ordered an abundant supply of food, clothing, and ammunition delivered to the base at Bridgeport. For the purpose of opening the 'cracker line', Grant ordered General Joe Hooker to clear the way from Bridgeport to Brawn's Ferry on the Tennessee River. General Hooker commanded the 11th and 12th corps from the Army of the Potomac. Hooker began his work on October 26, working his way from Bridgeport, on the south side of the river, clearing rebels from that stretch of the river, then marched into Lookout Valley and onward to Brown's Ferry.

Simultaneous with Hooker's work, troops from the Army of the Cumberland at Chattanooga silently floated sixty pontoons carrying 1,800 men down the river in the dark of early morning on October 27, past rebel pickets stationed along the Tennessee River, to Brown's Ferry. At Brown's Ferry they met with 2,000 of their comrades who had marched earlier that morning from Chattanooga through the hills north of the river and out of sight of the enemy, bringing materials to complete a pontoon bridge. Rebel pickets on the left bank at Brown's Ferry were overcome in the surprise attack by the Federals who then constructed a pontoon bridge across the river at Brown's Ferry.

Supplies were then transported from Bridgeport by steamer to Kelly's Ferry, then by wagon train to Brown's Ferry, across the pontoon bridge, and on the road north of the river to Chattanooga. The 'cracker line' was then complete, providing a supply route for the besieged Union army at Chattanooga.

The "heavy cannonading on the right" which Thomas heard on October 27, was the securing of Brown's Ferry by the Federals in which several rebel prisoners were taken.

Chattanooga, Tenn.
November 1st, 1863

Dear Wife,

I thought that I must drop you a few lines this morning to inform you that I am well and inhopes that this will find my dear wife and children in the enjoyment of the same blessing. I hold my own pretty well since I left home. I was weighed day before yesterday and weighed one hundred and eighty pounds. So you see that I have stood marching, fighting, short rations, and the exposure that a soldier has to pass through without loosing great amount of flesh. I believe I have not missed duty once since leaving Murfreesboro. No one could have made me believe before I enlisted that I could have endured the hardships and privations that I have passed through without a broken down constitution, but I find that a person knows not what he can stand until he has the trial. There has been some pretty hard fighting on the right of us since I last wrote. I have not heard the result yet only that our side repulsed them. There was quite a fight at midnight the past week between Hookers forces and Longstreets. We could hear musketry and cannonading very plain. We was aroused and ordered to have our things ready to fall in at a minutes notice. I presume that our officers thought that there might be an attack all along the lines. It's reported that boats come within a few miles of this place and that we will soon get full rations which I hope to be the case as this army has been very short off for provision, since the battle and very destitute for clothing, blankets and etc. Before we went into the fight we was ordered to pile up our blankets and extra clothing and the rebels got them they captured thousands of blankets knapsacks and clothing. If the rebels could cut off our supplies here they could soon make us surrender. One weeks time would be long enough, but I do not apprehend there is any danger of them being able to do it. The rebels continue to throw shells from lookout mountain most every day. I hear that our forces calculate to get possession of the mountain before long. I presume you can learn from the papers more about what is going on here then I know myself, for we can not depend much on what we hear in camp. I guess we have a dozen different stories about the fight on the right of us. All the boys in our company that are here are pretty well, only one reported to the surgeon this morning that was Higgins of our mess he is getting a little better. The new recruits of our company is not of much benefit to us especially as far as morality is concerned. Most of them are the offscourings of the earth, two or three are pretty good and will make good soldiers, if Howell cant find better recruits than he has the sooner he comes back the better it will be for the company.

We have had great deal of rain for the past few weeks and been cold and disagreeable. The Tennessee river is very high which is to our advantage. We have two brass bands in our company, the 25th Ills. and 8th Kansas has bands there is good many in this army, but its got to be to me like soldiering an old story.

I will close by wishing you goodbye and inhopes that I can return to you again.

Give my love to all of our folks and a good share to yourself. Write often

Thomas Berry

If you hear anything about the missing write as soon as you can.

The "fight at midnight" took place at Wauhatchie in Lookout Valley on the night of October 28 and into the early morning of the 29th. According to a report by Grant, which has been disputed, Longstreet's corps attacked a division of Hooker's army in an attempt to prevent operation of the cracker line. Hooker's losses in driving off the rebels are placed near 400 in killed and wounded, the Confederate loss is estimated to be about the same.

Supplies from Bridgeport are now being moved by steamer to Kelley's Ferry then portaged to Brown's Ferry and across the newly constructed pontoon bridge. The Tennessee River contains rapids between Kelley's Ferry and Brown's Ferry, impeding steamer traffic. From Brown's Ferry, supplies are transported seven miles to Chattanooga by way of a cleared road north of the Tennessee out of sight of enemy sharp shooters who are posted along the south side of the river.

Chattanooga
Nov. 8th, 1863

Dear Estelle,

I improve the present opportunity this morning to inform you how I am getting along. I am well and hope these few lines will find you and the children the same. It has been one week to day since I last wrote to you. Soon after I got my letter written and sealed I received a letter from you and also one from Emeline. Since that time there has nothing transpired of much interest to write so you will not hear a great amount of news this time. Emeline is quite anxious for you to come down and see her. But I guess you had better put it off until spring. We can tell pretty well by that time if the war is going to close during the term of my enlistment. General Willich told us when we was out on picket the past week that General Sherman was comeing up in the rear of the rebel army that is in front of us with thirty thousand men. If that is the case they will have to leave here as we will have a very large army here in supporting distance. I think everything is working well in this department. There must be about one hundred thousand men near this place which I think is more then the rebels have and we can whip them if they have not two men to us one. We begin to get more rations, we will soon have plenty. The worse time is over while we remain here. It makes the boys feel good deal better since we have commenced drawing more rations. Boats comes within seven miles of this place so they do not have very far to haul the provision. Its all quiet along the lines. Each army attends to their own business only they watch each others movements pretty close. The rebels throw some shells from the Lookout mountain most every day but I hear that it does no injury. They had better save their powder for I think they will need all they have after awhile. The rebels sent down a raft in the river a few days ago and it tore our pontoon bridge away and it took about two days to repair the damages and it stopped our men from hauling provision to us. Which made us go hungry a few meals. I believe the rebs would just soon have us starve as not. Captain of Company B received a letter from Lient Adams, he is in Libby at Richmond. He was reported killed. He states that there was forty seven taken the same time that he was but did not say how many belonged to this regiment only mentioned those that was taken that belonged to his company. It may be that some of our boys was taken the same time and did not say anything about Capt Whiting. If Capt was taken prisoner I should have thought he would have known it, as the officers are kept together and he would been apt to have mentioned him in his letter. I will close by wishing you good by for the present. I look for another letter from you to day.

    From your affectionate husband.

Thomas Berry

    I will send you Emelines letter

P.S. We have been mustered for pay again, I presume we will get pay before a great while, we will get four months pay. I do not know how I will send it home this time without I send it in letters. I presume it would go all right as I guess you get all the letters that I have written since comeing to this place. If we get four months pay, I will send you forty two dollars and keep ten, I have seven dollars left yet. Well I have made out more of a letter then I expected to when I commenced. How I wish I could see you and the children. Kiss them for me.

From him that never forgets you,

T. Berry
(Enclosed is letter from Emeline)

At Grant's request, Sherman was made commander of the Army of the Tennessee on October 23. That army is now on its way to Chattanooga. Grant's plan is to place Sherman northeast of the town, Hooker to the southwest, and General Thomas in the center facing Missionary Ridge. In that configuration the Union armies would converge, climbing the mountainous country against Bragg's army.

The Army of the Ohio under command of General Burnside is in a tenuous state at Knoxville, Tennessee, defending the town from encroaching rebels. Confederate General Longstreet left the area of Chattanooga on the 4th of November to engage Burnside causing Lincoln much concern for the loyal citizens of East Tennessee. The president prevailed upon Grant to go to the aid of Burnside. Grant communicated with Burnside who assured Grant he would wage a delaying skirmish with Longstreet to protect Knoxville until Grant lifted the siege of Chattanooga by disbursing Bragg from Lookout Mountain and Missionary Ridge.

Rations for the men and fodder for the few remaining animals are starting to flow into Chattanooga. Thousands of horses and mules have died of starvation with one report placing the number at 10,000. Those animals were replaced by those brought by Hooker.

The officers and men of Bragg's army must have been disenchanted upon seeing the revitalization of the Army of the Cumberland. Particularly should Confederate president Jeff Davis be disenchanted after visiting the scene earlier and being told by Bragg that capitulation by the Union army at Chattanooga was only "a matter of time".

Chattanooga, Tenn.
Nov. 19th, 1863

Dear Wife,

This is to inform you that I have received two letters from you this week dated the 7th and 10th and was very glad to hear from you for it does me good to hear from you, if I cannot have the privliege of seeing you and the children, so the oftener you write the better. I received two papers that you sent last week.

You got disappointed in your visit to the burg. I have written a letter to Eliza Taber if you had went down when you calculated I guess it would have come while you was there. I have written one to Uncle Clint. I will have quite a number of correspondents if they all write. I do not get any letters from your folks which seems as if they did not think much of their son—in-law, but I hope its otherwise. Our regiment was paid last night. I received $46.45cts. My years clothing bill was settled it amounted to $47.52cts, which was $5.52cts more then we are allowed, which is $42.00. Some of the boy's clothing bill overran the amount that is allowed as high as forty dols which left them a small sum. I think my years clothing bill was quite reasonable. We are paid up to the first of November. My next yrs clothing bill will not be near as much for I am not going to draw any overcoats or dress coats. I am going to send you forty dollars and I will have twelve left which will be as much as I will need, I think there is not much use of thinking of buying anything to eat here for they ask about ten prices for everything. I do not know yet how I will send the money. I am going to try and get a draft. I would rather not send it by mail for there is considerable risk, there may be considerable mail robbing as all the scoundrels knows that the army is being paid off.

Enclosed you will find the likeness of General Willick, our Brigadier General. I have written about him quite a number of times, so I thought I would buy his likeness and send home so that you may know what kind of looking man he is. I gave fifty cts for it. I want you to take good care of it for I will want to see it after I get home.

I saw General Grant the other day and was considerable disappointed in the looks of the man. He is a very common ordinary looking man, does not put on any style, and I should judge he does not feel half as big in the position that he holds as the majority of our captains and Lieutenants.

I received a letter from Harriet last week stating that George was a prisoner in Richmond which makes three of our company that we have heard from George, Codding and Hall.

Our Regiment worked two hours and a half this fore noon on the fortifications and have to work the same length of time this afternoon. We work one day out of a week on the fortifications and twenty four hours out on picket every week. We have quite easy times now and the weather is quite pleasant. You must cloth yourself and the children warm this winter for if my life is spared to return home I want to see my little family looking well and healthy.

I will close for Uncle Sam will soon want me to use the shovel.

I will close by sending you my constant love, give my best respects to all enquiring friends,

From your Husband

Thomas Berry

Do with the money as you think best and it will be all right.

When Thomas "saw Gen. Grant the other day", it was on November 16, when Grant made an inspection of the area with Generals Thomas, Sherman, and others to review his strategy for attacking Bragg. From Thomas Berry's diary for that day:

Mon 16th

89th worked on fortifications by Fort Wood. General Grant, Thomas, Reynolds, Brannon, and General Smith. They have been viewing the rebels on Missionary Ridge through their glasses. General Grant is a very common looking man.

The main body of Sherman's Army of the Tennessee is being delayed by heavy rains and is still enroute to Brown's Ferry.

Thomas' brother George, Private Jasper C. Codding from Victoria, Illinois, and Private John L. Hall from Lynn, Illinois, will not be sent to a Federal camp as parolees according to the cartel to which the Confederacy is honor bound. All Union privates captured in the Battle of Chickamauga are instead being sent to the Confederate's infamous Andersonville Prison in Georgia from which no prisoner exchange will be made.

On the day Thomas wrote his letter of November 19, 1863, President Lincoln dedicated a cemetery at Gettysburg, Pennsylvania, to the soldiers who fought and died at the Battle of Gettysburg on July 1, 2, and 3, 1863. It is not out of place with Thomas' letters to include here, Lincoln's Gettysburg Address:

Four score and seven years ago, our fathers brought forth on this continent a new nation, conceived in liberty and dedicated to the proposition that all men are created equal.

Now we are engaged in a great civil war, testing whether that nation- or any nation, so conceived and so dedicated-can long endure.

We are met on a great battle—field of that war. We are met to dedicate a portion of it as the final resting place of those who have given their lives that that nation might live.

It is altogether fitting and proper that we should do this.

But, in a larger sense, we cannot dedicate, we cannot consecrate, we cannot hallow, this ground. The brave men, living and dead, who struggled here, have consecrated it, far above our power to add or to detract.

The world will very little note nor long remember what we say here; but it can never forget what they did here.

It is for us, the living, rather, to be dedicated, here, to the unfinished work that they have thus far so nobly carried on. It is rather for us to be here dedicated to the great task remaining before us; that from these honored dead we take increased devotion to that cause for which they here gave the last full measure of devotion; that we here highly resolve that these dead shall not have died in vain; that the nation shall, under God, have a new birth of freedom, and that government of the people, by the people, for the people, shall not perish from the earth.

Chattanooga, Tenn.
Nov. 22nd, 1863

Dear Estelle,

I thought that I must write my loving wife a few lines this afternoon so that you may know that we are still at Chattanooga, but I dont think we will remain here many day's. We had marching orders last Friday afternoon to march Saturday morning at four Oclock. The order was countermanded Friday evening about eight Oclock, I understand the reason why we did not move was that General Sherman had not got up in the position that was assigned him. I presume we will have warm times near here before many days. They gave one hundred rounds of cartridges to the man. I dont hardly think we will attack them here in front if we do we will have rifle pits and breastworks to contend with. I rather think we will make a flank movement and force them to fall back. We can shell them from our forts here. There is a very strong fort within a few rods of our camp called fort Wood named after our Division General. There is six 32 pounders and four or five smaller pieces in the fort there is a ditch around the fort ten feet deep and about twelve wide and a rifle pit around that, which makes a very strong fort and a hard place to take. The fort was visited last Friday by General Hooker, Howard, Granger, Thomas, Sheridan and Johnson. So you see that I have had a chance to see quite a number of our Generals. Fighting Joe Hooker is a very fine looking man, tall and well built, face quite red, and very quick motioned and looks as if he would not be afraid to hurt the rebels when he has a chance. If the rebel army is strong enough here to contend against our force I look for another great battle.

The church call is sounded and I will close and go to meeting promising to write again soon if we do not march. I have not sent the money yet.

Yours affectionably

Thomas Berry

Fort Wood is on a promontory in the fortification line to the east of Chattanooga, between the town and Mission Ridge.

Grant is now on the verge of attack and is only waiting the arrival of the Army of the Tennessee which is still delayed by storm swollen rivers and creeks.

Bragg sent a letter to Grant advising Grant to evacuate the citizens of Chattanooga, a pretext to delay Grant, pretending a rebel assault upon the town was imminent. Bragg had hoped to hold Grant until rebel forces attacking at Knoxville would be victorious and return to reinforce him. The ruse did not work on Grant.

> On Missionary ridge three miles from Chattanooga
> Nov. 26, 1863
>
> Dearest Wife
>
> We have had another great battle and it has resulted so far in a great victory and complete rout of the enemy. We have captured about twenty thousand prisoners, and any quantity of artillery and small arms. The battle commenced Monday afternoon. Our division was in the advance, drove the rebels one mile and a half and gained a strong position without a great loss on our side. Tuesday there was not any fighting in front of us, tremendous fighting on the right, General Hooker took possession of lookout mountain. Wednesday the battle opened on the left and in front of us. In the afternoon our whole core was in the fight and we stormed and took possession of Missionary ridge, their strong hold, drove them from their breast works. In the afternoon it is stated we took 15,000 prisoners. Our corps captured 64 pieces. Our brigade captured about thirty pieces. Our regiment was in the advance, we marched up the ridge under a heavy fire of artillery and musketry. The lead and shells was poured in our ranks, but we gained the top of the ridge and drove them without a very heavy loss, only one killed in our company, that was one of the new recruits, Jacoby Wayman, he was a good fellow. Six wounded, Dick Bernerson, slightly wounded, Homer Wagner, slightly wounded, Wash Berkhart, hit by a shell, not much hurt, the balance are the new recruits. There was thirty seven killed and wounded in our regiment. Lieutenant Young of Company A was killed. Captain Rowel was wounded. We have drove them and defeated them at every point, it is a great and decisive victory. I have passed through it without a scratch, surely we have great reasons to thank our heavenly father for preserving my life through another great conflict. This is Thanksgiving day and we as a nation have great reasons to thank the ruler of the universe for his signal favor in giving us this great victory, three cheers for the Stars and Strips, they are following the rebs, good bye to the confederacy.
>
> Yours in love
>
> Thomas Berry

Thomas is writing about the Battle of Missionary Ridge. That battle took place on November 23, 24, and 25, and was the last major battle in the Chattanooga Campaign. The Federal victory on Missionary Ridge secures Chattanooga for the Union and is causing Bragg to retreat toward Dalton, Georgia. Large Union forces cannot remain long on the heels of the retreating Army of Tennessee since it is now necessary to concentrate on the relief of Knoxville where Confederate General Longstreet with his corps from the Army of Northern Virginia is pressing hard against fortifications of that city.

General Burnside is defending Knoxville with his Army of the Ohio but is penned within his lines of defense. His under fed army is being sustained by loyal citizens from in and around the city. At risk in the dark of night, loyalists float barges containing food and fodder down the Holston River to a pontoon bridge where supplies are rescued by the hungry army at Knoxville.

Sergeant Richard J. Burnerson, corporal George Homer Wagoner, and private Washington Borkhart are recovering from their wounds and will continue to serve in Company G. The corrected spelling of their names was furnished by the Illinois Adjutant General's Report and the National Archives Trust Fund, Washington, D.C.

General Thomas' corps was the first to enter the three day battle which started on the 23rd. That was not according to Grant's original plan. He wanted the three armies to start the battle on the same day but the Army of the Tennessee was not yet in position and would not be until the 24th. Grant's concern for Burnside, due to the rebel forces converging on Knoxville, caused him to start the battle early. The effect could have been the return of Bragg's detached army to the relief of Burnside, and of course, to the relief of President Lincoln.

Sherman's army was finally in position on the 24th. That army stormed Missionary Ridge from the north as Hooker came over Lookout Mountain. The advance of the two armies was intended to distribute Bragg's army on Missionary Ridge and minimize concentrated enemy forces against the Army of the Cumberland in the center. On Tuesday the 24th, General Thomas' corps waited that advance, and as Thomas wrote, "Tuesday there was not any fighting in front of us...".

On the 24th, Private William Stroyan, taken prisoner in the Battle of Chickamauga, died of his wounds at Atlanta, Georgia, in rebel hands.

The third day of the battle saw the Union armies converging to chase Bragg from the area, lifting for good the siege of Chattanooga.

"Jacoby Wayman" is Private Jacob Wagmen, a recruit from Altona, Illinois. Lieutenant Erastus O. Young, Company A, was from LaSalle, Illinois. Both were killed on the 25th.

Union losses in the three-day battle are estimated at 5,800 in killed, wounded and missing; the south suffered over 6,600 casualties.

Bragg escaped with his remaining army into Georgia with Sherman in pursuit. Now Grant will turn his attention to the situation at Knoxville.

Chattanooga
Nov. 27th, 1863

Dear Wife,

I wrote you a letter yesterday in a hurry so that you might know that I have passed through another great battle without receiving a scratch from the enemy. The battle commenced Monday afternoon by a general movement all along the lines. Our division was in the advance in front of us. We drove the rebels back about one mile before dark and gained a strong position without much loss on our side, did not loose a man in our regiment as our regiment was in the reserved line. We captured good many prisoners. As soon as we had gained the intended position we commenced throwing up breastworks and before morning we was pretty well fortified against an attack. Tuesday the ball opened in earnest on our right all quiet on our left. Hooker attacked them on Lookout mountain and there was tremendous hard fighting but before night he drove them at every point and took possession of the mountain which was a grand thing and captured a nice batch of prisoners. Wednesday the fight commenced on the left, the rebels massed their forces on the left for the purpose of crushing Sherman, but they was foiled in their attemps. In the afternoon our Corps was brought in the fight in front of us and we stormed and took possession of Missionary ridge. We drove the rebels from their rifle pits at the bottom of the ridge and took most of them prisoners and then pushed on the top of the ridge and the rebs poured volleys of musketry and artillery, the leaden hail, bursted shells and cannon balls passed through our ranks but did not impede our advance, only helped to press us on the faster. When we arrived at the top they took to their heels and I presume some of them are running yet. Some places I noticed our men and the rebs was about nigh enough together to shake hands but they shook hands with the cold lead. At one point I noticed the stars and stripes and the rebel flag floating close together but soon the rebel rag had to come down and the stars and stripes went up and still floats over Missionary ridge. Our company lost only one killed that was Jacob Wayman and the balance slightly hurt by shells and bullets. I gave you the names in the other letter. They are all doing well, we come off remarkably well for considering the fire that we was under. As soon as we drove them from the ridge the battle was closed here. We have gained one of the greatest victory of the war. They have been drove at every point and are still being drove by our forces. Yesterday afternoon we had marching orders to go to Knoxville as Burnside was hard pressed and we was to take four days rations. In the evening the news came that Burnside had given them an awful thrashing and the order was countermanded and we was ordered back to our old camp, and it seems good to get back once more to our little shanties. We are again under marching orders. General Hooker and Sherman are after the rebs and pressing them hard. Sherman captured three thousand prisoners today. We may not leave here and still we maybe ordered away at any moment. We appear to be held here in reserve for the purpose of going to any place that is hard pressed. I hear that we have taken thirty thousand prisoners. This army has accomplished and is still accomplishing a great thing, which must be one of the greatest death blows to the rebellion. If our armies are as successful at other points as we are here I expect to come home to my dear wife and children before many months passes by, if my life is spared. I feel that the Lord has done great things for us here and we have great reasons to bless his great and holy name for the great victory that we have won here. You must excuse this bad writing as I am writing by a poor light and cannot see the lines on the paper on account of the light being so dim. I have received your welcome letter this evening that you wrote on the nineteenth. Also received one on Tuesday while we was in the breastworks close to the enemy. I will close for the night by wishing you good night

From your affectionate husband

Thomas Berry

Saturday morning 5 Oclock the 28th

We are going to march this morning as soon as light for Knoxville Tennessee. I will not have a chance to write again until we get there, I dont suppose. I hope this will find you and the children well. I have not sent any money home yet, I was going to send twenty dollars in this if we stayed here to day, as it is I do not like to risk it as our whole Division is going and it would be more risk, so I concluded I would keep it with me. I am pretty well fixed for the march as I have bought me a good woolen blanket and a pair of good boots. They both cost me $6.50 and I have a rubber blanket and half of a shelter tent, so I can keep comfortable. I picked up a good rebel knapsack and haversack on the battle field on Missionary ridge. Also a piece of calico which I send to you in this. I will have to close and commence getting my breakfast and be ready to march

From your husband

T.B.

After 3 P.M. on the 25th, Grant ordered the Army of the Cumberland to advance on Missionary Ridge from the position it gained on the 23rd. Thomas says of that advance, "We drove the rebels from their rifle pits at the bottom of the ridge and took most of them prisoners and then pushed on the top of the ridge...". At that lower entrenchment of the enemy, the Federals were expected to regroup after taking the rebels, and await further orders.

General Grant was watching that operation from the promontory of Orchard Knob. Turning to General Thomas he asked who gave the order to proceed up the ridge. The general told Grant he did not give the order. The same question was asked down the rank of commanders with the same negative response. When General Granger was asked, Granger gave the same answer and added "When those men get started all hell can't stop them." Thomas Berry said the "leaden hail, bursted shells, and cannon balls" passing "through our ranks...only helped to press us on the faster."

The inquiry pressed by Grant interestingly reveals priority in the minds of many in high military rank. The question could be paraphrased to 'Who lessened my authority and told those men to subdue the enemy without orders from me?' Of further interest is the spontaneous action of men and officers who had seen their comrades killed, maimed, and taken prisoner while following 'orders' in the recent battle of Chickamauga, and were themselves starved for two months by that enemy before them. The elements were present to brave mortal combat beyond military orders.

Because of the urgency to relieve Burnside at Knoxville, Grant gave orders to General Thomas regarding the movement of Granger's corps toward Knoxville once the rebels were cleared from the Chattanooga area. Grant gave those orders prior to the Battle of Chattanooga, or as it is often referred to, the Battle of Missionary Ridge. The order included transporting supplies by steamer up the Tennessee River to the mouth of the Holston River, and up that river to Knoxville. The men were to carry 40 rounds of ammunition and four days' rations.

Part 10

Knoxville

One mile and half from Knoxville Tennessee
Dec. 9th, 1863

My Dear Wife,

You see by the commencement of this letter, that I am good ways from Chattanooga. We left that place the 28th of Nov. two Oclock in the afternoon. Most of the army left the same time with the exceptions of Hookers, he was after Bragg. Grangers and Shermans forces was sent here to reenforce Burnside and give Longstreet a thrashing. Burnside had him whipped and on the retreat before we arrived and Burnside, Sherman and all of Grangers men except our Division are pushing on after Longstreet. Our division was left behind and its reported that we are going to garrison this place. I wish the report would turn out to be true for I have done as much marching as I care about doing. We marched four miles the first day, we had three days rations in our haversacks. We came through on the south side of the Tennessee river. The 29th, we crossed the Chickamauga river on pontoons marched about twelve miles and camped for the night close to Harrison Station. The 30th, we marched twenty five miles passed through Georgetown a small village. I believe there was eight Union flags brought out by the citizens along the road that day as we passed by their houses. One oldish man brought out the stars and stripes and waved it to the breeze and the tears trickled down his cheeks, he appeared to be overjoyed to see the union army a coming amongst them. I wonder what the copperheads of the north would think of that. We stopped for the night one mile and a half from the Hiwassee river. Dec 1st, we crossed the Hiwassee river on a steamboat, our boats run up the river. We drawed two days rations of hard tack there and marched four miles as it took good while to cross over all the troops. 2nd, marched twenty miles. 3rd marched about twenty miles, camped close to Sweetwater station, on the railroad that runs from Dalton to Knoxville. A very nice and neat looking place three churches and some very nice buildings and it looked as if the inhabitants enjoyed themselves in times of peace. 4th marched twelve miles through a rich farming country, good many foraging parties was sent out and brought in beef, pork, potatoes, flour and meal. We have lived on the country with the exceptions of five days and still we are living on the inhabitants. Foraging parties are sent out every day and they take anything that will eat, so we live pretty well. We have had a good deal better fare since we have been on the march than we did at Chattanooga. 5th marched 18 miles, crossed the little Tennessee at Morgantown. 6th marched twelve miles passed through Mary'svile, quite a good sized town. 7th marched ten miles which brought us within one mile and a half of Knoxville. How long we will remain here I cannot tell, but I hope the report about us staying here will prove true. Its also reported that we are going back to Chattanooga, time will tell. I should like to stay here firstrate, if we stay here I calculate to take parson Brownlows paper. I believe Grant is pushing things pretty well. The army was in a poor condition to leave Chatanooga on account of clothing. I was very lucky before we started I bought me a pair of boots and a good blanket. I would have suffered if I did not have them. Great many are about barefooted and without blankets and it goes pretty rough for them. We have had very pleasant weather since leaving Chatanooga.

T. Berry

General Granger did not move his troops toward Knoxville until the 28th despite the early orders, to march immediately following the defeat of Bragg in the Battle of Missionary Ridge. Even on that date, as Thomas tells us, "The army was in a poor condition to leave Chatanooga on account of clothing." General Sherman with his command was also on the march that day toward Knoxville.

The siege of Knoxville by the Confederates was repulsed by General Burnside in the final major battle on November 29. On receiving word of Bragg's defeat, Longstreet realized it would only be a matter of days before he would be confronted by a major Federal force marching on Knoxville. He continued hammering at the door of Knoxville with "minor" skirmishing until December 4, at which time he withdrew his forces to the northeast, two days before arrival of the Federals from Chattanooga.

During Thomas' march on the 4th of November, Private John L. Hall of Lynn, Illinois, taken prisoner at the Battle of Chickamauga, died at Andersonville Prison.

Camp near Knoxville Tenn
Dec. 11th, 1863

Dear Wife

I thought that I must drop you a few lines this morning so that you may know that we are still near this place, but dont expect to remain long. We had orders to march this morning. I presume we will leave sometime to day or tomorrow. We are going back to Chattanooga. I

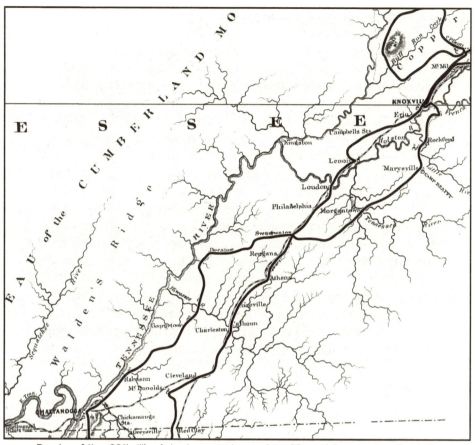

Route of the 89th Illinois between November 28 and December 7, 1863.

will not have a chance to write again until we arrive at that place. I wrote a letter to you day before yesterday about our march here. The last letter I received from you was at Chattanooga, we have not got any mail since we left. I took a tramp down in the city of Knoxville yesterday for the purpose of seeing the sights. Its about the size of Galesburg and quite a pleasant looking place. There is some very nice buildings. I took a good look at Parson Brownlows office its a very inferior looking building. Built of brick and wood, the front is a small frame and the back part where his office is is built of brick. He is not publishing his paper now as he was advised by the military authorities to leave when Longstreet was beseiging the place. I guess Longstreet is about played out now as I understand he is completely surrounded. And we know that he was badly defeated when he tried to take this place. I also went to the fort that Longstreet tried to take. It was one of the greatest slaughters that has transpired. In this same length of time

our men in the fort killed and wounded five hundred of the rebels so I was told by a soldier that was there at the time. He said the ground was covered with rebels. I noticed places the ground was covered with blood. He showed me where there was thirty of the rebs piled on top of each other in the ditch by the fort. He said only one got on top of the fort and he was the color bearer. Just as he reached the top he hurrahed for Jeff Davis and was completely riddled with bullets. Longstreets men are good fighting men. Our side only lost twelve men, the fort dont begin to be as formidable as fort Wood is at Chattanooga. East Tennessee never will be under rebel rule again. I dont think Burnside has done a good work here and I think General Grant will complete the job. It looks to me as if the rebellion was playing out pretty fast. We live pretty well, we draw flour, meal, pork, beef, potatoes and molasses. We do our own cooking. You know I can make pancakes. We drawed three days rations last night. I was glad to hear that brother Charles was comeing all right again. He must be about right if he could drive a team to Altona. It will be a good thing for him and for Mother, it was very unexpected news. I hope this will find you and the children well. I will close by wishing you good bye until I have a chance to write again. Write often. I am sorry to hear that your Mothers health is so poor. My love to all enquiring friends
Yours

Thomas Berry

As Thomas was writing this letter, Longstreet was retreating toward Rogersville, about 60 miles northeast of Knoxville, from which point on December 14 he marched back to Bean's Station to counterattack the Union force in pursuit of his retreating army. In that attempt he suffered further loss of over 450 casualties. Union forces curtailed further pursuit and Longstreet marched again in retreat to winter quarters in eastern Tennessee.

The fort referred to by Thomas is Fort Sanders, recently named for the Federal cavalry commander, General William P. Sanders, who was killed while buying time for Union soldiers to strengthen defensive positions around the fort. For two days General Sanders with his brigade of near 700 men, held ground between the fort and the enemy against the infantry and artillery fire of Longstreet's army. General Sanders was killed in that action on November 18. The fort stands about 1/2 mile to the west of the town and is fronted by a "ditch" with steep 7 foot sides. Rebels who worked their way into the pit had no way of scaling the walls except over their comrades' shoulders.

Confederate battle flags of the 13th and 17th Mississippi regiments were reported to gain the parapet as did the flag of the 16th Georgia, but only to the disaster of those who attempted to rally to the colors. Most of the rebels in the pit were easy targets with no escape except surrender.

Thomas refers to casualties suffered November 29, in the time period of Longstreet's concerted attack on Fort Sanders. For the larger time period of the siege of Knoxville between November 17 and the evening of December 4, Union casualties are placed near 700 in killed, wounded, and missing, and near 1,300 for the Confederates.

To the relief of loyal citizens of Tennessee, they are now no longer subject to control by the Confederacy although rebels continue with spurious raids into their state.

With Federal control of the Mississippi River dividing the Confederacy geographically, this latest Union victory at Knoxville, along with the major Federal successes of the past six months including those at Gettysburg, Vicksburg, Murfreesboro, and Chattanooga, signals the demise of the rebellion. The North is becoming stronger in all areas of military significance where the South is weakening militarily, politically, and economically. Furthermore, hope for foreign military intervention on behalf of the Confederacy has diminished. Yet, warmongers in Richmond refuse to heed the warning signals and will invite the further ravishing of Confederate states by recklessly prolonging the war in a desperate and futile effort to save the Confederacy.

President Lincoln entertained no doubts regarding the suppression of rebellion as he prepared for the day of capitulation by the Confederate military. On December 8, 1863 he addressed the first session of the 38th Congress, then in its second day, to reveal his Proclamation of Amnesty and Reconstruction for the states and citizens of the rebelling South. Buoyed by the show of confidence in his administration as evidenced at the polls during the 1863 state and national elections, the president set parameters within which the congress would establish laws for restoring a republican form of government to the rebelling states. The 38th Congress would also set terms providing for amnesty, restoration of civil rights, and the return of confiscated property (except slaves) to qualifying citizens; but the president maintained for his office the constitutional power to withhold or grant pardon to individuals guilty of crimes against the U.S. That power would be used in judgement of those who held high office in the Confederate government and its military forces.

The task set before the 38th Congress was not to be easily dispatched since the northern congressmen as well as the loyal citizens were torn asunder by their sympathies toward the rebels. Those sympathies ranged from unrestricted amnesty with complete restoration of civil rights and property, to total suppression with vindictiveness. Furthermore, there persisted in the north, prejudice of the slave and freedman to a greater degree than existed in the south. A political tightrope would be walked by Republicans and Democrats alike who were grooming their respective parties for the upcoming 1864 national elections. Fortunately for the Republicans, the Union armies were victorious in major battles of the current year. As a result of those victories the voters provided their party with a majority in Congress, unlike the elections of the previous year when on September 3, 1863, Thomas wrote Estelle, "The Union army appears to be losing ground".

The Republicans had in their favor the policy of the present administration regarding emancipation, a moral issue and a fact urgently desired by the North. The onus would be placed on the citizens in the 1864 national elections to balance prejudice against morality.

> Three miles from Strawberry plains
> and about sixteen miles from Knoxville
> Dec. 22nd, 1863

My Dear Wife,

    I feel in pretty good spirits this morning on account of receiving a good supply of news last evening, which was the first mail that we have had since leaving Chattanooga. I received three papers from Emeline and a letter written by Aunt Sylvia and Eliza Tabor, which furnished me with good deal of reading. I hope Louella and Sylvester have got along well with the mumps. I presume its best time for them to have it while they are small. My health is good, all of the boys of the company are well. We have now heard from all the boys that are missing with the exceptions of Capt Whiting, Newton, and Rosenleaf. I have given up all hopes of seeing Capt and Newton. We have heard that Stoddard died in the hospital near the battlefield.

    This is the third letter that I have written since our march from Chattanooga. In the last I wrote that we had orders to go back to Chattanooga, that order was countermanded and on the sixteenth we marched here for the purpose to help whip Longstreet. We learn that the old rascal is retreating into Virginia so we will not get a chance to fight him. We have very good times here camped in a good place, pleasant weather, plenty to eat and there is a nice running spring within six feet of my tent. George Davis is going to be discharged and sent home. They are making out his discharge papers now on account of mental disability. All of the officers in the regiment is down on Howell for enlisting him, and surely it was perfect insult to the company. It will be apt to go pretty hard with Avad Stowell, there was two or three deserters shot at Chattanooga, I never wanted to see him back with the company again as he is an unprincipled wretch. Captain Rowell of our regiment has died of his wound that he received at the battle of Chattanooga. He was acting Major at the time and was a good officer.

We have not many commissioned officers left.

Our Chaplain got back yesterday and I am very glad of it as he is a fine man and a good preacher. I have not had a chance to go to a meeting in a long time and it almost seems as if there was not any Sundays in the army as it is not respected any, which I consider to be very wrong. Emeline wrote that Charles voted this fall, if that is the case he must be pretty well restored to reason.

I have no idea where or when we will be sent from here but we are always ready to go. Write often and all the news and all about Charly. As soon as I learn that you get my letters from here I will commence and send you some money as I have not sent any yet. You and Mrs Leet are taking good deal of interest in the welfare of the poor and needy, there is nothing lost in helping the poor. (Do you wear white bonnets, the Sisters of Charity wore white bonnets at St. Louis)

Sally Palmers son, the one that lived in Texas came to see me Sunday. He has been a Lieutenant in the 14th Ills Cavalry, but has resigned on account of poor health. He appears to be a very fine man. I also saw Wm Spaulding he is going home. From your affectionate husband,

Thomas Berry

Thomas has not yet learned of the deaths of Captain Whiting and privates Newton and Rosenleaf, all of whom were killed on the battlefield of Chickamauga.

Strawberry Plains is on the Holston River, approximately 30 miles west of Longstreet's command which at this time is between Russellville and Greeneville, Tennessee.

Avid Stowell remained with the regiment.

Captain Henry L. Rowell from Chicago, 89th Regiment, Company C, died December 3, of wounds received in battle on Missionary Ridge.

With the beginning of winter several minor engagements continue throughout the land and on inland and coastal waters. Raids are conducted by detached units from armies both North and South and guerrilla warfare, by rebel and loyal citizens alike, pester the respective enemy.

Sadly, most minor clashes are vendettas of no consequence in deciding the outcome of the rebellion and serve only to breed enduring animosity. General John Hunt Morgan is ruthless at times, but his raids serve a military purpose for the Confederates, unlike others which are using the war as an excuse to serve only their personal lust and aggrandizement such as W.C. Quantrill and his murdering guerrillas.

Major armies on both sides are content to seek comfort in winter quarters, during which time they will be reorganized, replenished with supplies and men, and enjoy rest as best they can in the abnormally cold winter. During this rest period strategy will be planned for the coming spring campaigns. Cavalry of both North and South remain active for reconnaissance and harassment. One of the exceptions to the program of comfort in winter quarters is that of the Army of the Cumberland, and particularly the 89th Illinois regiment of that army.

With exception of his detached corps under Longstreet, Lee's army is in winter quarters in the Shenandoah Valley and near Richmond, Virginia. Bragg's army is at Dalton, Georgia, where Bragg halted his retreat from Missionary Ridge.

The Union Army of the Potomac under General Mead is in winter quarters along the Potomac facing Lee's army of Northern Virginia. Grant's armies are in the Knoxville and Chattanooga area of Tennessee, and spread to the Mississippi River between Vicksburg and New Orleans. His armies at Knoxville and Chattanooga are facing Bragg's Army of Tennessee.

The two great Southern armies of the rebellion are confined to the heartland of the Confederacy, with the Union armies of Mead mainly to the north and east of them and the armies of Grant and Sherman to their west. On the southern and eastern borders of the Confederate states, an effective blockade is preventing free flow of shipping, and the Confederacy is hemmed by the Union armies of General Nathaniel P. Banks at the Gulf of Mexico, and that of General Benjamin F. Butler with the Army of the James, at Fort Monroe.

Excursion of the 89th Illinois regiment to Strawberry Plains, a locale between Knoxville and the rebel army to the east, serves the purpose of extending the forage

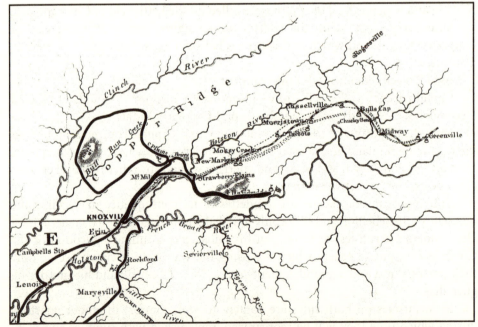

Route of the 89th Illinois between December 12, 1863 and April 19, 1864.

area of the Union army. The advanced position also limits the area of Longstreet's forage and provides ready combat of rebel forces attempting to disturb the Union army in winter quarters around Knoxville.

General John G. Foster became commander of the Army of the Ohio on December 11, replacing Burnside who was then assigned to command the Ninth Corps. General Burnside and his Army of the Ohio were later commended by President Lincoln and the U. S. Congress for their meritorious action at Knoxville.

Strawberry plains, Tenn.
Dec. 28, 1863

Dear Wife

Its with the greatest pleasure that I improve the present opportunity in writing to you so that you may know how I am getting along down here far from home and in the land of dixie. We returned last night on a four days forage expedition. The 25th Ill.regt. and the left wing of the 89th guarded the train. We traveled about thirty five miles before we got to where there was forage. We marched about twenty five miles Christmas. I spent Christmas last year a foraging, I hope I will spend the next Christmas with my dear family at home. On the 26th we got our wagons loaded with corn and started back. I stopped to a citizens house and got a square meal, which I called Christmas dinner, if it was on the 26th. It seemed good to set down to a table and partake of a good dinner. Its the first time I have eat a meal of victuals in a house since leaving you at Galesbury. About all union folks through this part of the country. The man where I got my dinner had two sons in the federal army. Well we arrived back to our old camp last night and found the balance of our Brigade gone to Strawberry plains and we started this morning and rejoined the same. We are camped close to the place, the cars comes here. I rather think we will remain here quite a spell. I received a letter from you last night dated Dec 13th and was glad to hear that the children had got over the mumps and that you was comfortable. It does me good to hear that you and the children have enough to eat and to wear, if I am deprived of the many comforts of life. I am sorry that you are troubled with catarrh, you must try and cure it if you can. I am glad to hear that your mothers health is improving. Colbourn that you enquired about was detailed teamster a few days before the battle of Chattanooga, I have not seen him since but suppose he is all right. Lamphere is with us and is well, he is a very nice young man. The boys of the company are well only pretty tired after the forage expedition as it is very muddy on account of recent rains, from your affectionate husband

Thomas Berry

This is the sheet of paper that you sent me. Excuse bad writing and with a pencil as I have a poor place to write. Yours in love T.B.

"Colburn" is Private Henry E. Colburne, a recruit mustered into the 89th Illinois regiment September 1, 1863, from Altona, Illinois.

Private William B. Lamphere from Waren County, Illinois, was mustered into the 89th as a recruit on October 10, 1863.

The "cars" referred to are on the Tennessee and Georgia Railroad. Generally, the use of the word "car" is in reference to the railroad, and the word "train" in reference to animal drawn wagons.

General Braxton Bragg resigned his command of the Army of Tennessee at Dalton on December 2. That post was temporarily assumed by General William J. Hardee until assigned by December 27 to General Joseph E. Johnston. Bragg then became military advisor to Confederate president Jefferson Davis, determining strategy for the Confederate armies, a move which dissatisfied many rebel commanders including generals Johnston and Longstreet.

Thomas closed out the year with these brief entries to his diary:

> Tues 29th
> Our Company was detailed this afternoon to
> work on the bridge about 3/4 of a mile from our camp.
>
> Dec 30th
> We are busy today making ourselves as comfortable as the circumstances will admit.
>
> Thurs 31st
> This ends the year 1863.

1863 was the pivotal year of the Civil War. The year began with the Battle of Fredericksburg in progress, a battle in which the Confederates could claim victory. The rebels were also victorious in the first week of May at the Battle of Chancellorsville despite the loss of General "Stonewall" Jackson, mortally wounded by his own men in a case of mistaken identity. Southern elation generated by those two battles soon was lost to depression as Confederate General Braxton Bragg was being chased from Tennessee in June by the Army of the Cumberland in the Tullahoma Campaign.

At Gettysburg on July 1, 2, and 3, where General Lee's Army of Northern Virginia was defeated by the Army of the Potomac under General Burnside in that pivotal battle, the tide began to change in favor of the Union. The fourth of July saw the surrender of Vicksburg, followed by Federal victories at Chattanooga,

Missionary Ridge, and Knoxville.

Even the least objective observer of the Civil War should have seen the inexorable result of a continuing rebellion. There was certainly no doubt in President Lincoln's mind regarding the outcome of the war as he outlined his plan for restoring the rebelling states to the Union in his address to the 38th Congress on December 8th with a Proclamation of Amnesty and Reconstruction. Yet, the Confederate administration pressed even harder on its distressed citizens to provide men, material, food, and fodder to carry the lost cause into the following year.

Close to Strawberry plains Tenn
January 1st, 1864

Dear Wife,

I will commence this morning by wishing you a happy new year. Our lives have been spared to see the commencement of another year. May we give thanks to our heavenly father for the protecting care that has been over us the past year and may we try to live nearer, and put more trust and confidence in our Saviour the coming year, that we may have his smiles and approbation continually. May we realize more fully that we derive all our blessings from him both temporal and spiritual and may we feel that it is not only our duty but a privilege to bless his great and holy name, that we may have his holy spirit to guide us in the path of duty and holiness.

It turned very cold last night and its very cold this morning, coldest weather I have seen in the south, which makes the boys hug the fire pretty close as we are not fixed very well for such cold weather. But I am inhopes that it will not remain so long. Our brigade has been detailed to work on the railroad since Christmas. They are building a bridge across the river close to this place. A man from Chicago is boss of the job. It will take about one week more to complete the bridge. One regiment a day works on the bridge our company has worked one day.

I must close as the mail is going out.

Thomas Berry

"Very cold" indeed. The temperature was found to be "below zero" throughout the entire operations area of the war on New Year's Eve and on the following morning.

The "bridge" is a railroad bridge crossing the Holston River. The rail line from Knoxville to Holston River is the Tennessee and Georgia R.R., from the river heading east the line becomes the East Tennessee and Virginia Railroad. The entire line is referred to as the Virginia and Tennessee R.R., a military line alternately used and destroyed by Union and Confederate armies throughout the war.

Strawberry Plains Tenn
Jan 11th, 1864

Dear Wife

I thought that I must drop you a few lines this morning so that you may know that we still remain here and give you the news in general. Since I last wrote our regiment has been offered a chance by our Brigadier General, to reenlist in the Veteran Corps and most of the regiment quickly responded by putting their names down, and we have got the recommend of our Division and Corps Commander, also General Grants, all we want now is the acquiescence of the war department and then the 89th will be a veteran regiment and we will have the four hundred Dollars bounty. I put my name down. I have about nineteen months more to serve any how on the first enlistment, and I am satisfied the war will be closed before that time, and so I thought the bounty would come very handy. We will be mustered in for three years or during the war and have thirty days furlough. Our Brigadier told the Colonel that if we are accepted we will be thought be furloughed the first of March. The whole regiment will go together, or at least all those that have reenlisted. Those that have not reenlisted will be put in other regiments and companies to serve out their term of enlistment. All of our Company that is here have reenlisted with the exceptions of two Sprouses, and James Livingston. We may not be accepted as the order from the war department reads that they must be in the service two years before regiments can reenlist. Well if we are accepted you may look for me home. The balance of the Brigade have reenlisted as they all have been in the service two years. The 49th Ohio have started home, and I hear that the 15th leaves today. I do not know what you think about it but I thought you would endorse my proceedings, let me know what you think of it.

I received your letter dated the 27th day before yesterday and was very glad to hear that you and the children was well. Santa Clause must be quite liberal to Louella and Sylvester, tell them that they must keep those things nice as par wants to see them when he comes home. We are quite comfortably fixed here now. George Starr, W. Higgins and myself messes together and we have quite a comfortable abode with a fireplace. We keep fire most all night, as it has been very cold since New Years. Our Brigade is still working on the R.R. bridge. We do not have any picket duty to do. I have not seen an armed rebel since the fight at Chattanooga.

I have not sent any money yet, I think I will wait and see if we are accepted, if we are and get our furloughs I can bring it home and save the risk of sending it by mail. I believe I have written all the news so I will close by sending my best respects to all enquiring friends and my warmest love to you.

Thomas Berry

P.S. You say that you hope I will return just as good as I left you, I do not think I have changed any yet, and I am sure that my love to you has not diminished in the least.

Yours as ever, T.B.

12th

The mail leaves camp at 10 Oclock this morning, we receive mail about once a week and I get one regular from my birdie every week since they have commenced comeing here, and it is a welcomed visitor, for it does me good to hear from you and the children.

John Lamphere has been sick quite a number of days and has been sent to the hospital. His lungs are very much affected, he cannot speak out aloud, the balance of the company is well. Those that we left at Chattanooga have not come up yet and we have not heard from them since leaving that place. If our regiment happens to be accepted and get furloughs home, we must go down and make Emeline a short visit. It aint best to build a very great castle in the air about comeing home, for fear it will explode and we get disappointed for there is nothing certain about being accepted. There is some more room so I concluded I would tell you what we had for supper last night. We had some good baked beans and pork and they was good you had better believe, the first I have had since I have been in the service, also hardtack and coffee which made a No. 1 supper for a soldier. We are very well fed and clothed now. I will close by hoping that this will find you and the children well.

From Thomas Berry to his birdie
Estelle Berry

Desertions are reported by both North and South as armies are stagnated in cold and uncomfortable winter quarters. No doubt some of those desertions are a result of concern for the comfort of families left behind. Later, a proffer of amnesty brought many back into the fold.

At this time Florida, Louisiana, and Tennessee are working to eliminate slavery from within their borders, and the Federal government is ready to provide provisional governors in those states as a preliminary step for restoration to the United States.

The standing of Confederate President Jefferson Davis is lowered in the minds of Southerners as Davis demands more support for the Confederate cause. Southerners are now protesting the expansion of conscription which includes men to the age of forty-five.

>In Camp Close to Knoxville, Tenn.
>Jan. 22d, 1864

Dear Wife

You see by the above that we are again back to Knoxville, and very near the place where we was camped when we first come to this place. We arrived here last night after a long march out to the front and back again. We left Strawberry plains the 14th of Jan. We went to Danridege which was 18 miles from the plains. We arrived there the 14th. Our Colonel told us to make ourselves as comfortable as we could, as he thought we would stay there quite a spell. The boy's went to work in earnest building themselves huts and we was very soon well fixed. But there was very soon a change in the programme, the next day there was a cavalry fight close to the place. Some of Sheridans troops was sent out and when they saw our Infantry a comeing, they retired. We also had orders to fall in at a minutes notice. Sunday afternoon the 17th, the rebels again attacked our cavalry close to town. Our brigade was ordered out, we was kept in line of battle about one hour and a half when the fighting eased and we was marched back to our camp. Our forces drove them back. In the course of the evening, orders came for us to fall back to Strawberry plains that night, as the enemy was in too great a force in front of us. They had to get the train started first and they had to go very slow as the roads was very bad. We commenced marching back three Oclock the next morning. Our regiment and about one company of cavalry was the rear guard. We marched about ten miles when we was attacked by a force of rebel cavalry. But our cavalry held them at bay, we was deployed out in line of battle. After quite as squirmish with our cavalry, they thought they had better keep off at proper distance. They followed us a few miles and dispersed. Well, we arrived back here last night and we have learned since we have been here that we was scarred before we was hurt as the rebels commenced retreating from Danridge the same night that we did. I hear that some of our forces have gone out there again and its reported that we are going back in that section of the country again, but cannot tell anything certain about it, but I dont think we will remain here long for they will keep us going as it is not our luck to remain at one place very long at a time. Lamphere was sent to the hospital at Knoxville, and we have learned since our arrival hear that he has died, but have not heard the particulars yet. Our Doctor is going over to town to day and he said that he would go to the hospital where he died and learn the particulars about his death. When I hear I will write it to you as Mrs. Scott would be anxious to hear the particulars about him I suppose.

There is one thing that I have never answered that you wanted to know, whenever I commenced writing I did not think any thing about it. It is the amount of pay that Berkhart gets per month. He only gets thirteen Dollars per month. I have not received a letter from you for quite a spell, we do not get mail very often but I presume you have some on the way for me. The weather is quite pleasent now, but the roads are bad my health continues good and hope this will find you and the children the same. I will close by sending my best respects to all enquiring friends, and my love to you

From your husband

Thomas Berry

Uncounted skirmishes throughout the Civil War, such as those mentioned by Thomas near Dandridge on the 16th and 17th, and that of the 18th nearing Strawberry Plains, were not deemed of sufficient consequence to find space in recorded history.

In camp at Mary'sville Tenn.
Jan 25, 1864

Dear Estelle,

The mail is going to leave here today, so I concluded that I must drop you a few lines so that you may know where we are at the present time. We arrived here yesterday. This place is about seventeen miles southeast from Knoxville. We passed through this place on our march from Chattanooga to Knoxville. I think we will remain here sometime. Its a very pleasant place to camp and the weather has been delightful for the past few day's. I wrote you a letter the 22nd. I have heard nothing further about Lampheres death. The boys of the company are all well, only some had bad colds and they are policeing the company grounds and I must close and help as I have not much news to write this time. I presume we will get a mail tomorrow or at least I hope so for I want to hear from you. I have not received a letter for quite a while. Write often.

From your affectionate husband

Thomas Berry

There are three regiments gone home on furlough out of our brigade. I dont think our regiment will be accepted in the veteran service. Good bye birdie, I hope the time will soon arrive when I can see you. Kiss the children for par.

Marysville, Tenn.
Jan. 31st, 1864

Dear Wife,

    I thought that I must drop you a few lines this Sabbath morning so that you may know that we still remain here, we arrived here one week ago today, as you have been informed if you have received my last letter. I am well with the exceptions of a bad cold. Most all of the boys of the company have had colds. We have had delightful weather for the last two weeks, which I suppose is quite a contrast from the weather up north. I received a letter from you dated Jan. 10th day before yesterday also one from William which I must answer before long. I am very sorry to learn that you and the children do not enjoy better health. You wish to know where I would want my loved one's buried if either of them should be taken away by the hand of death, and also who to preach the funeral serman. If in the providence of God death should enter my household and take away any of its inmates (which I do hope and pray may not be the case) I should want their remains to be buried in the Victoria burying ground, as to who should preach the funeral serman, I do not know as I have any choice, only I should prefer a Methodist preacher. My prayer is if it is consistent with God's holy will may our lives be spared to see each other again and live many happy years together and train up our dear children in the nurtur and admonition of the Lord, and finally when our day of probation is ended may we be one unbroken family in the kingdom of our Lord. I will close by hoping this will find you and the children well,
    Yours in the bond of Love,

Thomas Berry

Marysville Tenn
Feb 4th, 1864

My dear Wife

    I again improve the present opportunity for the purpose of conversing with you for a short time by the method of the silent pen. I received your welcomed letter dated the 17th yesterday and was very glad to hear that my loved family at home was blessed with tolerable good health and inhopes that this will find you as it leaves me in the enjoyment of good health. I will have to give up that you have beaten me on the weight of hogs. Surely that was a good sized pig to weigh 520 lbs. Its a great inducement for farmers to raise things now as every thing brings such good prices. If I had not come to the war I could have made farming pay pretty well but so it is and I think it will all come out right yet. There has nothing of much interest transpired since I last wrote. We still remain here in camp. I have heard two sermons since we have been to this place. The meeting was held in one of the churches of this place. The first sermon was preached by the chaplain of the 24th Ills, and the other by a chaplain that belongs to Woolfords cavalry. Our chaplain has resigned and gone home. We are very comfortably fixed and have enough to eat such as it is. Our rations consist of cornmeal and beef, coffee and some sugar. I have a corndodger for breakfast, corndodger for dinner, and a corndodger for supper which makes a very steady diet. We get flour sometimes, the citizens brings in things every day to sell to the soldiers, pies and cakes eggs and some butter. It dont take them long to sell out and the boys are so hungry for a change that a person dont stand much chance to get anything. I have bought one dozen of eggs for 25cts and a dols worth of biscuits and cakes. The southern women dont know how to cook. They cant cook a good corn cake, I wish you could see some of their pies that they bring in to sell.

You say that you get all of my letters so I concluded that I would send you twenty dollars in this and run the risk. Write as soon as you receive this and give me all the news. I should like to step in this morning unexpected. I have not received any papers from you for quite a spell. I wish you would send me some linen thread in your next letter. The clothes that we drawed are poorly put together, which makes thread an indispensible article. I will close by sending you my love

Thomas Berry

The 24th Illinois regiment is in the 2nd brigade, 1st division of the 14th army corps.

"Wolford" is Colonel Frank Wolford, a veteran of battles in East Tennessee early in the war and at Mill Springs in January, 1862. Wolford gave pursuit of John Hunt Morgan in the latter's raid through Kentucky, Indiana, and Ohio in July of 1863. He presently is in the cavalry corps of the Army of the Ohio under General John M. Shackelford. Shackelford's cavalry, after the siege of Knoxville, gave chase to Longstreet as far as Bean's Station, Tennessee. After a battle at that place on December 14, 1863, in which Longstreet was frustrated in his attempt to entrap his pursuers, the chase ended and Shackelford returned to Knoxville. Longstreet then sought his winter quarters where he remains at this time.

Marysville Tenn.
Feb 7th, 1864

Dear Estelle,

This is to inform you that I have received your letter dated the 24th stating that Emeline was with you and was very glad that she took the pains to come up and see you and the balance of the folks. I hope you have had a good and pleasant time agoing around with her. She complimented Sylvester pretty highly in her letter, but I was not ignorant of the fact. I presume she has started back before this time. I should have liked exceedingly well to have been with you. I presume you have went down to Victoria with her to see Harriet and Mother. You must write all the news how George's folks and Mother is getting along all about Charles and everything in general for I like to hear what is going on up there in civilization. I think we will remain here sometime. Its a very pleasant camping place and we have comfortable quarters. I wish you could take a peep in our little cozy edifice. If you could look in at the present time you would see your man a writing with quite a number of letters by his side that he has received from his loved one that he has been perusing before he commenced this letter. And I guess you could tell by his looks that he is thinking about home and its associations. And a little to his left you would see George Starr sitting leisurely a reading from a paper that he has received from home and is trying to pass away the time as pleasantly as he can. And to the left of him W. Higgins is a writing a letter it may be to his sweetheart for what I know. By our pleasant fire place you could see our cooking utensils which consist of two frying pans, a small tin pail that we do our mixing in, one plate apiece, knives spoons and tin cups for our coffee. And a little back you could see on a shelf, our meal sacks and pretty good supply of pork, which we have bought. Our bed is raised up from the ground about one foot, made of poles pine boughs and hay. Our house is about eight by nine and is built of pine logs and covered with our shelter tents. Our chimney is built of the same material and lined with stone and mud. We can burn wood about three feet long. We put in a good backlog and we can have a good fire all night if we wish. If you could take a look through our company grounds, you could see the boy's almost all busy doing something. Some are washing their clothes, some chopping and others are cleaning their guns to have them in good shooting order so that they will bare inspection. And if you could look in a tent close to mine you would see a small boy and he is not very well. I believe you would say that Lieut. Howell robbed the cradle when he enlisted him. I do not know but you will think that I have written enough nonsense so I will change the subject. General Willich starts for home to day for Cincinnati, as he has leave of absence for a few days. He called our regiment out to wish them good bye. I hear that we are accepted in the veteran service and the General said he would get us furloughed home as soon as he could. He did not say that we was accepted, I heard a few days ago that he said we should go home on a furlough if we was not accepted.

There is preaching in the Churches in this place every Sabbath. There is two citizen ministers living in this place. One an aged man and the other a young man. I heard the latter preach yesterday he preached a very good sermon. The text was Remember now thy creator in the days of thy youth.

I reckoned up yesterday how many miles we have marched since leaving Murfreesboro last June, according to my calculation we have marched five hundred and fourteen miles. It would have been much easier to have traveled a thousand miles in Illinois. I have passed through three battles Liberty gap, Chickamauga, and Missionary ridge. Chickamauga was the most terrible and destructive battle. I hope we will not have as much hard marching and fighting in the same time to come.

It looks to me that we must have another battle in east Tennessee. Our force have fallen back from Strawberry plains and have burned the bridge that our brigade help build. I do not think our men have got paid for working Sundays building the bridge. Our company was detailed two Sabbaths to work on the bridge which I considered very wrong. Our nation is not sufficiently punished yet, for her national sins to have peace. We ought as a nation put more trust and reliance in God for help in this our nations distress and trial.

I will close by sending my best respects to all enquiring friends.

From your husband T. Berry

Enclosed is five Dols, I sent twenty in my last.

The 89th Illinois infantry regiment was not admitted to veteran corps status nor did the 89th receive the inferred furlough.

Knoxville Tennessee
Feb 22d, 1864

Dear Wife

It has been sometime since I have written to you, the reason is that I have not had a good chance to write since the sixteenth. On the evening of the sixteenth about nine Oclock orders came for us to get ready to march immediately. I had just got to bed and expected to get a good nights sleep but it proved otherwise. Well we roused up struck tents and soon got ready to obey uncle sams orders. There is no use for a soldier to grumble but I thought it was pretty rough to leave our houses after we was so comfortable fixed. We was soon on the march, we took the road that goes to Knoxville so we concluded that we was destined for that place. We marched all night and it was very muddy as it had rained all the preceding day which made marching very hard. Before morning it turned very cold and since that time it has been very cold until last evening, since then it has been moderateing down considerable. We arrived close to Knoxville the next day and went in camp about one mile and a half from the city. Since we have been here, we have received two months pay. First of March there will be two months more due us. I believe the reason why we was ordered here was that they expected that Longstreet was going to attack this place as it is reported that he has been heavily reinforced. They are getting ready to receive him as they are working on the fortifications night and day. Our company worked on a fort yesterday. You wish to know what has become of the boys that was left at Chattanooga. They all came up to the regiment while we was marching from Strawberry plains to Danridge with the exceptions of Homer Wagner, he was left back to guard company books. Schuyler Atherton is with us and well. Few days before we left Marysville our division train came up with the headquarters stuff, Homer came along with the train and he accidentally shot himself through the arm, near shoulder and I understand very bad which is a bad affair. I wrote to you that Lamphere had died in the hospital at Knoxville but I am happy to state that has proven to be a false report. I saw him as we passed through the place. He is getting along very well, he has not got his speech yet. He cannot speak above a whisper, otherwise he is tolerable well. You need not look for me home this spring for veteranism has played out with us. I have received two letters from you since we left Marysville. We get mail every day now. If you can sell my half of the corn planter for seventeen dols you had better sell. I wanted Samuel to buy it last spring but he would not. If he is not willing to pay the above price we can keep it. Tell him if he hires it out, to pay you half of the proceeds. I am glad to hear that your father has bought him a farm I think he has a good place.

 I guess Brinkerfoff will be a good man to carry on the farm the comeing year as he is an eastern man. I wish I could be home to commence spring work but I cant. The rebels are going to make another desperate effort this spring. I will close this by sending my best respects to all enquiring friends

From your affectionate husband

Thomas Berry

Enclosed ten Dols which makes thirty five I have sent to you. Write often.

Yours as ever.

Longstreet, with his army attempting rest in winter quarters 60 miles away, made no overt action threatening Knoxville. One might surmise from past absurd marching orders suffered by the 89th regiment, the reason for returning the troops to Knoxville was for payroll distribution only.

General John N. Schofield was placed in command of the Army of the Ohio on February 9. The interim commander of that army, General J.G. Foster, was assigned to the Department of the South.

Part of the Army of the Cumberland is at this time at Ringgold, Georgia, in a march toward General Johnston's Confederate army at Dalton. General Thomas is attempting to determine the location of the main body of the Army of Tennessee without engaging in a major battle. A second purpose of the march on Dalton is to feign an attack which will deter Johnston from sending segments of his army to augment Longstreet or to the west in aid of the rebel army in Mississippi.

Morristown, Tenn.
March 1st, 1864

Dear Estelle,

I hear that the mail is going out today so I thought that I would drop you a line to let you know where we are at the present time. We arrived here last night, about twenty six miles from Strawberry Plains. This place is where Longstreet had his headquarters all winter. I do not know where he is now. Rumor says good many things about him. We are to remain here today. I do not know how much further we will go. Its reported that we are going to Bristol. I have just received yours of the 17th, glad you received the 20 Dols. I think you might as well wait until the war is over before you buy a sewing machine. I have not time to write any more for the mail is going right out.

So Good bye

T. Berry

Morristown, Tennessee, was the repository for military supplies and confiscated personal property removed from Kentucky by Bragg's retreating army in late October 1862. A vestige of rebel military equipment discarded in Morristown by the rebels and discovered by the 89th regiment would give the impression

"Longstreet had his headquarters all winter" at that location. Longstreet's army marched in the vicinity of Morristown while seeking winter quarters following his retreat from Knoxville and the pursuing Federals last December. Longstreet moved his army to the Russellville—Greeneville area for the winter, about 30 miles east of Morristown, where his army is now foraging amid loyal citizens who occasionally harass the wintering army.

> New Market, Tenn.
> March 4th, 1864

Dear Wife,

This is to inform you for the first time since last spring that I am sick. I have the chills, I have had three shakes, they come on every other night. I have not felt well since we left Marysville, that night march was too much for me through the mud. I do not believe there was any use for us to march that night. They marched us very fast and we would get very warm, there was two streams to pass over and we had to stop about an hour for the troops to pass over and I would get very cold, which I think is the cause of me being sick at the present time. I reported to the surgeon this morning, he gave me some medicine to take at nine Oclock and some at three and some this morning. He has excused me from duty. I am inhopes I will get it broke up before many days. Its a hard place to be sick. If I was at home I should think I was sick enough to be to bed most of the time. When I last wrote to you we was at Morristown eighteen miles from here. I had a shake the night before, I did not mention it in that letter, the next day we came back to this place which was day before yesterday, and have remained here since that time. I do not know how long we will stay here. The order is to be ready to march at any time. There is quite a number of rumors about our next move, one is that we are going to have thirty days rations and march on towards Virginia. And another report is we are going back to our old department. I do not put much reliance in camp rumors, I suppose Longstreet is leaving as fast as he can. I dont suppose Mr. Mitchell knows of the death of his little child yet as he was left back to Knoxville so to guard headquarters stuff, as the letters all come to the regiment. West Swicherd is there. He was sick with a bad cold. Mr. Colbourn is driving a team, I saw him before we left Knoxville, he was well. I will send five dollars in this letter, which will make fifty that I have sent. I have ten dollars left. I hope when you hear from me again that I will be well and inhopes this will find you and the children well. I will close by sending you my love,

> Thomas Berry

When Grant was ordered to aid the Army of the Cumberland at Chattanooga in the fall of 1863, he placed that army under the command of General Thomas. Grant then united that army with the Army of the Tennessee under General Sherman. (The Union Army of the Tennessee is not to be confused with the Confederate Army of Tennessee, the former named after the Tennessee River, the latter after the State of Tennessee.) Additionally, two corps from the Army of the Potomac under General Hooker were sent to assist Grant in defeating Bragg.

In the reorganization of the Army of the Cumberland under General Thomas and in the melee of the ensuing battle and the chase of Longstreet at Knoxville, the commands of divisions and regiments were shifted to fit battle conditions. As a result, the 89th Illinois regiment is now separated from the main body of the Army of the Cumberland which is still in the Chattanooga area, giving credence to the camp rumor that the 89th is 'going back to our old department'.

New Market, Tenn.
March 10th, 1864

Dear Wife,

In my last letter I wrote that I was quite sick with ague. I am about well at the present time. For the last two days I have improved very fast. I think that I have got it broken up. If we should not march for a spell I may not be troubled with it again. I am afraid if we have any hard marching to do very soon it will bring it on again. I think by the appearance of things that we will remain here quite a spell. There was two regiments sent back to Strawberry plains out of our division to rebuild the bridge across the Holston river. I do not think we will go ahead very far until that is completed and another thing we have not men enough here to advance against a very large force of rebels. If the report is true about Longstreets forces going to Richmond and to Johnstons army there is not much need of a very great force to hold Tennessee. I believe there is a quite a force of rebels in front of us yet, we hear of Cavalry skirmishes every few days near Morristown. All the forces that we have here is the 23rd and 9th Corps and our Division. Part of the 23rd is mounted, and they are the poorest disciplined troops in the army. On the march they scatter all over the country, they appear to have very poor officers, I would not put much dependence in them in a fight. The ninth is good deal better. Hester of our company was sent to the hospital yesterday, he was taken down very sudden with the fever. Also one of the recruits by the name of Coys. He was wounded at the battle of Chickamauga he came to the regiment a few days ago. He says he was exposed to the small pox at Knoxville. He is broke out, the doctor says it is the measles. David Sprouse and Brown is not very well, the balance of the boys that is here are well. Dick Burnerson, Mitchell, Swisherd, George Davis, Atherton are at Knoxville. I presume most of them will be up in a few days or at least I do not know what should hinder them as I hear that they are well with the exception of Mitchell. His health is not very good, he had a fit when he was on the march from Marysville to Knoxville. Colbourn was here yesterday and is well and hearty. We have been on half rations since we left Knoxville. We draw hard tack, for a few days we get most full rations of meat coffee and sugar. We can buy some corn bread once and awhile so we get along pretty well but the citizens charges a round price for what they sell, provision is very scarce and there is good many families suffering for the staff of life. The Government has to feed great many families at Knoxville which is one reason that we cant get any more. If the war continues a year longer I do not know what the inhabitants will do to support themselves, there is not horses enough left in east Tennessee to cultivate the land. The rebels have made a clean sweep of most every thing that they could get away that would be of any service to them, cruel war.

I received your letter written the 28th yesterday and the paper that you sent the same time one day sooner. We have a daily mail now. We was at Morristown when I received your letter containing the thread which came just when I needed it. Was glad to learn that you received 25 Dols up to that time. I wish it was so that we could go on the farm this spring. I know that I could enjoy peaceful life better then I ever did before with my loving birdie and children. There is one thing if the war does not close very soon the three years will wear off after awhile. I shall never put my name down again. I have been pretty near disgusted with the army lately. The way we have been fooled around from one place to another and accomplishing nothing. The night we left Maryville our Lieut Colonel and quartermaster was drunk as they could be. He could not give an order and did not get over it for a week, he is a poor tool and I presume there was some drunk that held higher positions. There has been great change in our brigade since Gen Willick went home. I understand he is promoted to a Division Commander. I wish he had the command of our division. He never allowed any gambling, since he left gambling has been carried on a big scale. There can be seen squads of men all round a gambling away their money and its growing worse most every day. The army is a bad place for the youth of our land. I received a letter from Homer a few days ago. He is in the hospital at London and his wound is improving some he says that he is getting along as well as could be expected. Our regiment is not accepted and I am glad of it. I should like to help you set out the shrubbery first rate but I cant. I hope the time will soon arrive when I can come home to my loved ones that are dear to me. I believe I have written all the news so I will close by sending you my best love and wishes.

Thomas Berry

George Davis got me to send his folks forty Dols, he was paid over fifty Dols.

President Lincoln had been troubled by the idiosyncrasies of men in high places since the beginning of the Civil War. Upper echelon military officers in many instances used insubordination as a tool to subordinate Lincoln as a military leader, politicians pressured the president to gain popularity, and the press attempted to run the war by editorials inconsistent with Lincoln's long-term plans. From the beginning of the war until early in March 1864, Lincoln had two huge managerial jobs to perform, the administration of the United States government and the administration of the Civil War.

The 38th Congress relieved Lincoln of managing the war when it acceded to Lincoln's request to place U.S. Grant in charge of all Union armies. Following that act of Congress, the President happily conferred the rank of lieutenant general on Grant, appointing him general-in-chief of the Union armies on March 9, 1864.

Grant caught Lincoln's eye because the general accomplished victories, among which were those at Forts Henry and Donelson, Vicksburg, Chattanooga, and Knoxville. Lincoln selected Grant for that high position because "he fights". No matter the cost of victory in war, which is forgotten by the general public long before the victory, approbation and reward goes to the triumphant commander. Lieutenant General Ulysses S. Grant formally took command as general-in-chief of all United States Armies on March 17, 1864.

At this date the rebellion is a lost cause. The Confederacy no longer has the strength to win, only the strength to prolong the war. Most citizens of the South should by now be fully aware their rebel armies are surviving only by retreat, that the resources of the North are increasing where those of the South are diminishing, and that large Union armies stand ready to wreak havoc, if not vengeance, amongst them. Reasoning by those citizens should now prevail to the extent of suing for peace to stop further carnage and destruction on southern soil. But such reason prevails only in a democratic society, not under rule of an oligarchy, and the war goes on.

Thomas commented on the enlistment of George Davis and upon his fitness as a soldier in his letters of 10/11/63 and 12/22/62. Davis was subsequently listed as a deserter. One might speculate from those letters, on the possibility of maneuvering Davis to desertion to save the face of his recruiting officer.

"Swisherd" is Lieutenant John W. Swickard from Walnut Grove.

Grant is planning the Spring Campaign for 1864. The objective of the campaign is the capture of the two great Confederate armies assembled east of the Mississippi River, the Army of Northern Virginia under Lee, and the Army of Tennessee under Johnston.

Even though several Union and Confederate naval units and army corps are clashing elsewhere within and outside Confederate states, submission of Lee and Johnston would render folly further attempts to continue the rebellion. Renegade armies would soon realize all support of their efforts is withdrawn with the surrender of the two mightiest armies of the South, and with that loss, even the most obdurate of the Confederate hierarchy must concede defeat. The strategy of the Federal campaign is sound, but first the campaign objective must be met.

Grant is aware of the renewable resources available to him and of the restraint to be exercised by the Confederates in expenditure of Southern men and supplies. He accordingly is preparing an all-out offensive. As commander in chief of all Union armies he elects to have his headquarters in the field and will take personal command of the Army of the Potomac, an egoistic prerogative to be suffered by that army. Grant plans to enclose Lee's army, and in that endeavor will employ the several Union armies in the east including the Army of the James under General Benjamin F. Butler located near Fort Monroe. From the Valley of the Shenandoah Grant plans to use the army of General Franz Sigel, and the Army of the Potomac will come from the direction of the Federal capitol.

To Sherman he gave the armies of the Ohio under General Schofield, the Army of the Tennessee under command of General McPherson, and the Army of the Cumberland under the command of General Thomas. He will order Sherman to march those armies south against the Confederate armies of General Joseph E. Johnston, leaving nothing in his wake that would be of military value to the South.

Union armies are being readied for the Spring Campaign of 1864 which will commence on a date yet to be set by Grant.

> In camp at Strawberry plains, Tenn.
> Mar. 25th, 1864

Dear Wife,

You see by the above that we are back to Strawberry plains. Our Division left Morristown the 18th and arrived here the 20th and our brigade has remained here since that time. The 2nd and 3rd brigades have gone up the river. We are camped close to the bridge. I think we will remain here sometime for the purpose of guarding this point and bridge. There is a good R.R. bridge across the Holston river and also a pontoon bridge. Colonel Hotchkiss has command of the brigade and has command of this post so I think we will stand a good chance to remain here without something unlooked for takes place. We have a pretty strong position here, we have two forts built here and still making more, its a very pleasant place. The 23rd corps is between here and Morristown. We had quite a snow storm yesterday. It snowed the greater part of the day. The snow is about six inches on a level. The sun has come out warm and bright this morning which will soon make the snow disappear. Christopher Brown of our company died the 15th of this month. He was sick when we was at New Market and was sent to Knoxville. He was not sick very long, his limbs commenced swelling up. I think it must be the dropsy. The convalescents are coming up that belongs to our company. Russel Smith came up yesterday, Andrew Reynolds, Craig and Wooley are at Knoxville. They was sent back to Nashville the 16th of last Sept. Our brigade doctor has been sent back to send forwards all that is able to come to their regiments.

I received a letter from Mother a few days ago written by Charles. She wants all his brothers and sisters to throw in something for the purpose of getting Charles a suit of clothes. If you are a mind to you may send Mother couple Dollars for that purpose. I received a letter from you the 18th and the Northwestern the 20th. I wish you would send me by mail a diary one without dates, also a course pocket comb. You can most anything by mail. There has been shirts, hats, and great many things come by mail to the boys of the regiment.

I will close by sending you my best wishes and love,

Thomas Berry

In his letter of March 10, Thomas said Christopher Brown was not "very well", and in this letter, he tells us Christopher died the 15th of March. The Illinois Adjutant General Report sets the date of Christopher Brown's death at March 1, 1864.

There are many facets to the Civil War aside from the strictly military operations of the Blue and Gray. One such is domestic, revealing the perfidy of powerful men in the north who use their influence giving rise to rebellion against Lincoln's administration and to Federal conduct of the war. Another is international, involving the shameful conduct of France in attempting to invade and claim the State of Texas, taking advantage of the United States while it is heavily involved with internal affairs.

An offshoot of the former is the six-day draft riot in New York City in the past year resulting in the death of over 500 citizens and the loss of millions of dollars by fire and looting. That copperhead influence continues in its attempts to disrupt the Federal war effort. In the latter facet, Napoleon III is attempting to maintain a monarchy in Mexico in defiance of the Monroe Doctrine and against the will of loyal citizens of Mexico who want to be free of European domination. Mexican loyalist Juarez is carrying the brunt of battle with the French puppet Maximillian. The latter compels the United States to rebut, committing the Federal Government to military operation at the expense of its war effort. That military operation is known as the Red River Campaign.

"Wooley" is Private David Woosley from Walnut Grove.

Strawberry plains,
Tenn. March 26th, 1864

Dearest Wife,

I feel in pretty good spirits this afternoon. So I will inform you the cause of it. Lieut. Howell and John Tait arrived here to day about noon and I received a package that my dear birdie sent to me. As I took each article out one by one my mind wandered far away where my loved ones is, for I knew that only a few days ago they was put there by the hand of my loved one, who was the choice of my youth and hope of my future life. I hope the day is not far distant when we can show each others attachment around our own fireside. The package came in good order, the cakes came all right and they look more like civilization in the shape of cooking that I have seen since I crossed Mason and Dixies line. I will cook the dried corn to morrow, I know it will be good. A very nice pair of scissors something that I have wanted for a good while, thread, needles, pins come in good and the papers will help pass a good many tedious hours. I think great deal more of the things then I would the same articles if I could buy the same things here. I will close by hoping this will find you well as it leaves me.

From your affectionate husband

Thomas Berry

P.S. Tell Louella and Sylvester that par thanks them very much for those crackers that they sent. Enclosed is five cts a piece for them, tell them that par says they may go to the store some pleasant day and buy them some candy and tell them that they must not forget their par.

Thomas must have enclosed ten one cent pieces, two half dimes, or one dime in order for Louella and Sylvester to each receive "five cents apiece". The five cent nickel has not yet been coined by the U.S. mint.

Part 11

Sherman's March on Georgia

Strawberry plains
April 6, 1864

Dear Estelle,

    I thought that I must drop you a few lines this afternoon to inform you that we are under marching orders. We are going to start tomorrow morning at five Oclock. I understand we are going in the direction of Knoxville. I do not know where will be our destination but I think we will rejoin the army of the Cumberland in front of Chattanooga. We are relieved here by Tennessee troops. My health is firstrate again. I feel as well as I ever did and think I can stand it to march with any of the boys. I have not received a letter from you since a week ago last Sunday. I have been looking anxiously for the past two or three days but have looked in vain.

    Mr. Mitchell and myself build us a fireplace yesterday and we was very comfortably fixed but we will not have the privliege of enjoying it very long, such is the life of a soldier. I will close by hoping this will find you and the children well and may the Lord bless and protect us and may we have the privliege of again seeing and enjoying each others presence again is my prayer.

    From your affectionate husband,

Thomas Berry

Thursday evening the 7th

    We arrived at Knoxville in about two hours and marched about three miles on the road that leads to Loudon. I presume we will pretty near make that place tomorrow. We have marched nineteen miles today its 25 miles to Loudon from here. I presume I will have a chance to send this tonight as I have learned that we will get a mail this evening. I presume we will be pretty near Chattanooga when you hear from me again. Good bye my loving birdie.

T.B.

Friday evening the 8th

    We have not moved yet, its thought we will start this afternoon. The mail just came and I will have a chance to send this. I received a letter from Charles he thanks me very much for sending him that Dollar he wrote a good letter. I expected one from you but was disappointed. Write often.

Roster
Company G, 89th Ilinois Regiment
January 1864

NAME	ILLINOIS HOME TOWN
Captain William H. Powell	Walnut Grove
1st Lieut. Peter G. Tait	Copley
1st Lieut. John W. Swickard	Walnut Grove
1st Sgt. Richard J. Burneson	" "
Sgt. John B. Smith	Lynn
Sgt. Harrison G.O. Wells	Walnut Grove
Cpl. Squire D. Allen	" "
Cpl. Thomas Berry	" "
Cpl. Orange G. Haywood	" "
Cpl. John B. McLaughlin	" "
Cpl. George H. Wagoner	

PRIVATES

Schyler Atherton	Walnut Grove
Jacob Borkhart	" "
Washington Borkhart	" "
Christopher Brown	" "
John Campbell	
Nelson Chimberg	Weller
Charles Collinson	Walnut Grove
Henry G. Collingson	" "
Jeffrey Cragan	Lynn
Jacob F. Craig	"
Jacob B. Cramer	Weller
James H. Dillworth	"
Michael Doyle	Walnut Grove
Albert W. Elsworth	Lynn
William S. Fitch	"
William Ferman	Clover
Henry Goddard	Lynn
Levi Hager	"
Andrew J. Harris	Victoria
Isaac Hester	Walnut Grove
William B. Hicks	Lynn
Washington L. Higgens	Walnut Grove
David Kerr	Lynn
James Livingston	Walnut Grove
Richard H. Lyman	Lynn
James W. McLaughlin	Walnut Grove
Joseph B. Mitchell	" "
James W. McLaughlin	" "
William H. Nesbitt	" "
Jocob Preston	
Andrew M. Reynolds	Victoria
Benjamin F. Riner	Walnut Grove
Isaac Roosa	" "
Charles Rowe	Henderson
Michael Scagriff	Walnut Grove

Herman P. Smith	" "
Russell M. Smith	" "
Matern Spohr	Lynn
David E. Sprouse	Weller
Isaac Sprouse	"
Thomas Sprouse	"
George B. Starr	Walnut Grove
Edward W. Stephens	" "
Adad G. Stowell	" "
William D. Taggart	Weller
Horneston P. Tait	Copley
John Tait	"
William Tait	"
David Thompson	Walnut Grove
Andrew Topper	" "
Jacob Ulmbaugh	Lynn
William E. Ward	Walnut Grove
Wilford H. Whitney	Knoxville
Robert Wilson	Walnut Grove
David Woosley	" "

RECRUIT PRIVATES

Charles V. Bainbridge	Walnut Grove
James M. Bailey	Galesburg
Robert Bell	Abdingdon
Adelbert Boves	Peoria
John Brown	Oneida
Henry E. Colburn	Altona
William P. Coyce	Chicago
George W. Davis	Altona
John W. Davis	Galva
Theosore O. Depue	Knox County
Henry E. Dudley	Altona
William E. Ford	"
Lewis L. Goole	Knox County
Thomas C. Hubbell	Altona
George W. Huling	Chicago
Henry L. Lautz	Lynn
William B. Lamphere	Warren County
Charles W. Mitchell	Altona
William Morrison	Aurora
William H. Nelson	Altona
Chester P. Palmer	Young America
James H. Pemble	Knox County
Josiah Piatt	Altona
Andrew J. Rays	unknown
Needham Rogers	Altona
William M. Ross	"
George W. Shoop	Abingdon
Sylvester H. Smiley	Warren Co.
Jasper A. Smith	Altona
James T. Stormant	Warren County
Elias Umbaugh	Altona
George O. Wright	Abingdon

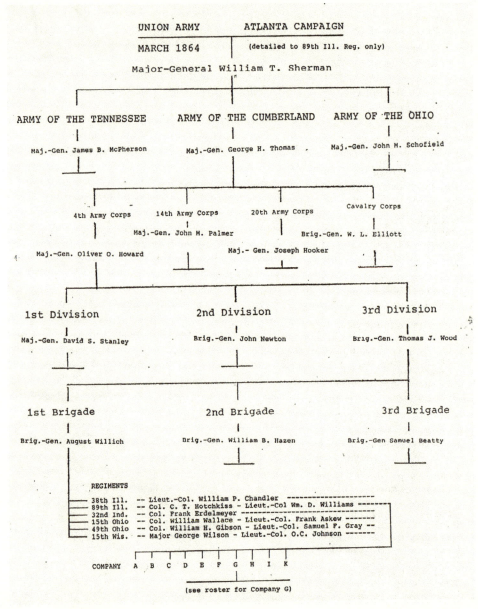

Organization chart of the Union Army before Atlanta, March 1864.

The 89th Illinois regiment was given "marching orders" for the purpose of joining Sherman's proposed march into Georgia against General Johnston. The Confederate Army of Tennessee is still at Dalton where Johnston took command of that army replacing Bragg. Although strategy has been outlined for the spring offensive, Grant has not yet given the order to move.

As Thomas writes this letter of April 6, the State of Louisiana, now partially under Federal protection, has adapted a constitution under the Union flag abolishing slavery.

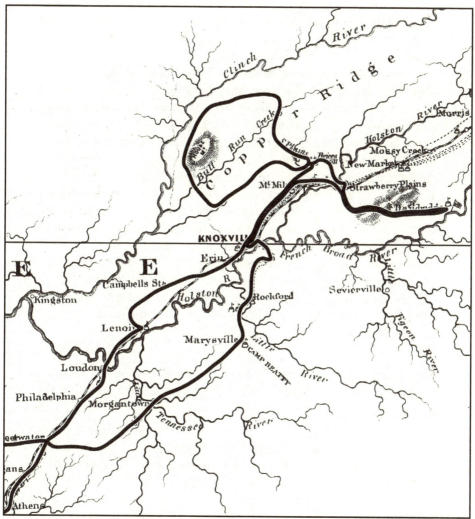

Route of the 89th Illinois between December 12, 1863 and April 16, 1864.

Loudon, Tenn.
April 11th, 1864

Dear Wife,

This is to inform you that we arrived here yesterday forenoon. We are camped close to the river. We are on the north side of the river, the town is on the opposite side. We are going to cross here. One brigade of our division crossed yesterday, one will cross to day and ours tomorrow. They have to cross on a ferry boat. The bridge that the government is building here is pretty well completed. I should judge by the looks that they will have it so that the cars will pass over it in a few days. Its a very long and high bridge. Our destination is Cleaveland about twenty five miles from Chattanooga on the R Road. Sheridans Division is camped here or rather Wagners, as he has the command of that division now. They have been here good while. I received your letter yesterday dated April 3rd, also the diary and comb and they was very thankfully received. I am going to copy off whats in my last years diary in the one that you sent me and send it to you by mail. Mr.Cramer came to the regiment yesterday. He planned his family matters pretty well to be at home when the young soldier came along (I am afraid I would not been as successful as that). I should have thought that Mrs. Newton had better have waited a spell longer before she had her husbands funeral sermon preached. Our doctor saw him the next evening after he was wounded. He say's that he thought he could not have lived twelve hours longer but we know nothing further about him. He may possibly be alive yet, that is how it stands.

The boys of the company are all well. My health is good and inhopes that this will find you in the enjoyment of the same blessing.

Yours as ever

Thomas Berry

You are a pretty good salesman. I hope it is so about Captain Whiting being alive. Tell Louella that her par thanks her for her letter that she sent me.

Evening of the eleventh

Our brigade crossed the river this afternoon and went about two miles and camped. We expect a mail to night if we do, I will have a chance to send this good bye my birdie dear.

"Sheridan's Division" was the 2nd Division, 4th Corps, in the Army of the Cumberland at the Battle of Missionary Ridge under the command of General Philip H. Sheridan. General George D. Wagner was then in command of Sheridan's Second Brigade. Sheridan is now with Grant as commander of the cavalry corps in the Army of the Potomac.

In the past week, Longstreet left his winter quarters in northeast Tennessee to join Lee who is anticipating Grant's next move.

On April 8, 1864, the 13th Amendment (abolition of slavery) passed the U.S. Senate by a vote of 38 to 6.

In camp eight miles from Cleveland, Tenn.
April 17th, 1864

Dear Estelle,

We arrived here yesterday afternoon, arrived at Cleaveland about one Oclock and marched eight miles towards Chattanooga. We are to remain here today. I do not know how much longer. I finished copying the diary this morning. I have stood the march very well up to last night. I have a shake of the ague in the night. I feel pretty well this morning. I hope this will find you all well. I received your letter last night dated the 10th. I think you have sold Fanny well. Write as soon as you receive this. I have copied the diary by odd spells on the march.

Yours as ever,

T. Berry

As Thomas writes this letter near Cleveland, fighting continues in other areas. Those encounters are characterized by the many small and detached Rebel armies escaping Federal forces and conducting raids on small towns and Union garrisons throughout the Confederacy and into loyal states. Much of the territory won by the Union and left unsecured or guarded only by small garrisons, is again overrun by

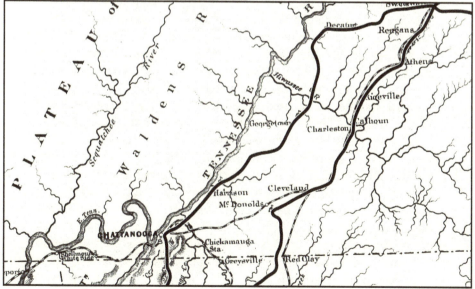

Route of the 89th Illinois between April 17 through May 5, 1864.

Rebels who garner support from the two large armies of Lee and Johnston. Typical of such action occurred on April 12, 1864, when a cavalry corps from Johnston's wintering army, under command of General Nathan Forrest, attacked and vanquished a small garrison at Fort Pillow on the Mississippi River in Tennessee. Fort Pillow had been evacuated by the Rebels and occupied by the Union early in June 1862. The garrison consisted of less than 600 men, about half of which were black.

The number of black soldiers in the Union army is increasing, to the discontent of the Confederates. Jefferson Davis will demand all escaped slaves captured while in the service of the Union army be returned to their owners, and no black soldier taken prisoner by the Rebels will be exchanged. As a result of the Confederate president's stand on that issue, Grant will not permit restart of the exchange program. At this time there are more Rebels in Federal prisons than there are soldiers in the combined armies of Lee and Johnston.

Letter from Estelle to Thomas:

Walnut Grove
Apr. 17, 1864

My Own Dear Loved One,

It is well perhaps that I cannot express my feelings tonight. Oh this lonely heart pining for that dear one far away. Can it be we must be seperated so long and perhaps never meet again in this world, Oh can it be. I ought not to write this evening I feel too sad, it is hard to live in this unfriendly world alone. I try to keep up courage and get along till you return but should it be otherwise we would not be long seperated for the blow would crush me it seems, for the thoughts of it is so terrible. The coming campaign is so much dreaded, but enough of this. I was over to the farm Friday I think Mr. Brinkerhoof is going to do very well. He seems to be taking care of the garden and orchard firstrate. He is trimming off the trees, they need a good deal of trimming too. He is going to plant potatoes, sorghum and corn, no small grain at all. New corn shelled No.1 brought 89 cents last week. I expect mine to go for No. 1, Mothers did. I still think it will be a dollar by the first of June. I am trying to clean house and goes pretty hard with me, everything has lived through the winter but the peach trees, I guess they are all dead. I have received two letters from you within the past week. I will try to send you some paper this week. We are all well at present and hope this finds you the same. Butter is 30 cents per lb here and 50 at the burg. Everything is high. I must close for it hurts my head very much to write my desire is that the lord will continue to bless you and keep you faithful and may your example have a good influence over your comrads and may they be constrained to follow you as you follow Christ this from your affectionate wife

Estelle Berry

Letter written by Thomas on unused part of Estelle's letter.

April 25, 1864

My dear Estelle,

I received this kind and affectionate letter yesterday and I am glad that I have one dear one that thinks of me. Still I can well assure you that your love for me is warmly returned. There is not hardly an hour in the day but what I think of you and the children. It does seem hard and cruel that we should be thus seperated from each other. If our lives are spared to see each other again, our seperation will no doubt be the means of making us think more of each other and we will live happier together. I dont mean by the above that we did not live happy together but rather our happiness will be more complete. I long for the time to arrive when we can have the privliege of embracing each other again and give you a good warm kiss.

I have had a bad toothache for about one week, our regimental doctor has not instruments for pulling teeth and he told me that I could not get it pulled any place nigher then Cleveland. So I got a pass today to go to that place to get it pulled. When I got there I found a regular dentist and he pulled it out root and branch and charged only one Dollar. I heard in Cleveland that our forces was moving out toward Dalton. We are not out in front. There is thousands of troops in front of us. I dont think of much more to write I have plenty of letter paper but I thought I could write this short letter on the same sheet.

I will close this letter by sending you my warmest love. Remember me at the throne of grace that I may be under the protecting care of our heavenly father continually and may the time soon arrive when we shall clasp each others hand again in love and friendship. May we both live in such a manner that when we are called from this world we can meet death with a smile and meet each other where seperation of friends is not known.

From your ever true husband,

Thomas Berry

Be sure and make that visit to Peoria for I want you to enjoy yourself as well as you can. I think you can spend two or three weeks very pleasantly down there.

Grant's spring offensive is well advertised. When Estelle wrote on April 17, she was well aware of the "coming campaign", and Thomas learned of the Union's proposed move to Dalton while he was in Cleveland on medical leave. The advance notice is giving Lee and Johnston time to prepare their respective defenses against the proposed Union offensive. The Confederate generals know an attack is imminent, only the date and time, which has been determined by Grant, remains unknown to them.

Grant ordered his army commanders to begin the spring offensive on May 5. By starting the Eastern and Western Theaters on their campaigns simultaneously, neither Lee nor Johnston will afford the practice of sending troops in aid of the other.

Despite the ominous threat of Union armies marching on Confederate soil, Southern spirits are lifted by news of Rebel victories in scattered areas. The Confederates repelled and inflicted heavy loss on the Union army and navy in the ill conceived Red River Campaign which began early in March and is still continuing with the Federal army and navy in full retreat. That campaign, ordered by the Federal Government and issued by Henry W. Halleck, who at that time as general in chief of the Union armies, was prompted more for diplomatic than military reason and is now miserably failing. That campaign was initiated against the better judgement of several generals including Grant, who at the time was not yet promoted to his present rank. European interests in the territories of Texas and Mexico in defiance of the Monroe Doctrine prompted the Federal government to initiate the Red River Campaign.

Federal losses in the Red River Campaign, the loss of Fort Pillow, and Rebel conquests of small Union garrisons including one this past week in North Carolina, give the South reason to hope for further success in the continuing struggle. Those "lesser" victories which give rise to Southern confidence are of little concern to Grant in his strategy for the grand Spring Campaign, of little concern except for the Red River fiasco. At Red River is the slowly retreating army of General Nathaniel P. Banks upon which Grant plans for augmenting Sherman's march through Georgia. Even without Banks' immediate help, Grant will begin his Spring Campaign.

Thomas would have been pleased to know the Federal government on April 22, 1864, began stamping the words "IN GOD WE TRUST" on United States coins.

May 5th, 1864

Dear Wife,

This is to inform you that we are under marching orders. We are to commence marching to day at twelve Oclock. I think there will be a great battle between here and Atlanta. Before this reaches you it is not impossible but I will have to be called in the deadly conflict again. I feel to put my trust and reliance in our heavenly father knowing that I will not fall by the missiles of death without it is not in accordance to his divine providence and will. If I should not have the privilege of meeting you again in this world may we prepare to meet each other in the haven of eternal rest where wars and wickedness and separation of friends is not known.

My health at the present time is good. I received you letter dated April 24th day before yesterday and was very glad to hear that you was well and that Sylvester is getting rugged again. I believe I have nothing more to write this time. Give my best respects to all enquiring friends.

From your husband

Thomas Berry
to his birdie Estelle

The day Thomas wrote his letter of May 5, is the day Grant set for the opening of the Spring Campaign. "We are under marching orders" to serve General Sherman's purpose of staging his armies for the offensive drive against Johnston's army which is still at Dalton. Johnston has posted troops at strategic defensive positions in the hills and ridges north and west of Dalton, and in the mountain gaps through which the Federals must pass on the shortest route to Dalton.

In the Eastern Theater on this day, the Army of the Potomac is engaging General Lee in the Battle of the Wilderness in the State of Virginia.

Sherman's first objective is the capture of Johnston's army, his second objective is the occupation of Atlanta, both are included in the operation known as the Atlanta Campaign which is now underway. Sherman's armies are marching south with the Army of the Cumberland in the center, the Army of the Ohio on the left and the Army of the Tennessee on the right. The right and center are both in Georgia at this time, the army on the left is at the Tennessee—Georgia border.

In camp four miles North East of
Ringgold Georgia
May 6th, 1864

Dear Wife,

In my last letter I wrote that we was going to march that day about twelve Oclock. We struck tents and marched about seven miles and the next day came here, and have remained here since that time. We are out in front. The rebs are said to be in force about four miles from here at buzzards roost. I suppose they have a pretty strong position but its generally thought that we outnumbered them greatly and that we will have an easy victory, but time will only tell the true facts. It is reported that we have over one hundred thousand men in supporting distance. There is about thirty thousand in the fourth Corps which is commanded now by General Howard, the one armed man. Gen Thomas old Corps the 14th is on our right also General Hooker. The 25 corps is on the left. There was another corps passed through

Chattanooga yesterday for the front. I feel confident of success and victory in the comeing campaign and think it will open before many days. I think that Atlanta and Richmond will be occupied by our forces by the Fourth of July. I dont care how soon the battle will commence if we have to fight them the sooner we get at it the better. This is a very rough and willy country.

I received that pepper you sent me about half of an hour before commenced marching. It came all right and am much obliged. I dont suppose we will get any more pay until this camapaign is over. We have to pay due us from the first of January. The boys of the company are all well. There is forty five in the company at the present time. General Willich is back and commands the brigade. The boys of the brigade gave him some hearty cheers when he arrived. He went around and saw the boy's first before he went and saw the Colonels. I will close for the present hoping this will find you well

From your affectionate husband

Thomas Berry

On Tunnel Hill
Saturday evening the 7th.

The whole army moved out this morning, and we are now on tunnel hill. We have met with but little resistance so far. There has been some cannonading and skirmishing, our loss is very light. There was a large force in advance of our division. I hear that they had three or four wounded and one or two killed. We are in about four miles of Dalton. We can see some rebels on a high eminence about two miles from here. I believe they call the hill Buzzards Nest. I presume we will get them off by a flank movement. Its generally thought that the rebs will not make much of a stand this side of Atlanta. I think everything is working well and that the rebellion will receive its death blow before many weeks. The mail is going out soon and I will close by wishing my birdie good bye. I will write as often as I have a chance, so you may know how I am getting along.

Yours as ever

Thomas Berry

Buzzard's Roost is a hill protruding from Rocky Face Ridge. The rebels are well entrenched on that hill overlooking the Union army as it approaches Dalton.

The "one hundred thousand men in supporting distance" are in Sherman's army calculated as follows:

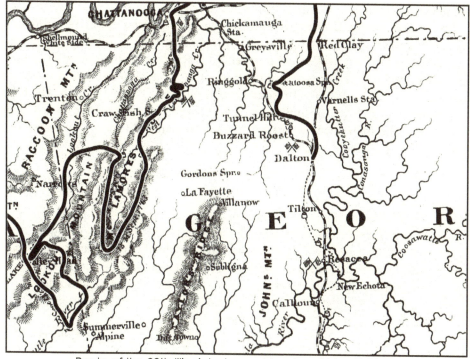

Route of the 89th Illinois between May 6 and May 7, 1864.

Sherman's Army

ARMY	COMMANDING GENERAL	NUMBER OF MEN
Army of the Ohio	John M. Schofield	13,559
Army of the Cumberland	George H. Thomas	60,773
Army of the Tennessee	James B. McPherson	24,465

The above total of 98,797 does not include armies near the Mississippi River under Sherman's command which might have been considered within supporting distance but were not included in Sherman's immediate drive through Georgia.

The "one armed" is General Oliver O. Howard, a veteran of several battles including that of Seven Pines or Fair Oaks, Virginia in which he lost his right arm in fight on June 1, 1862.

Characteristic of Sherman's pursuit of Johnston is the "flank movement" mentioned by Thomas. As the center of the Union army moves directly on the main body of the Confederates, Sherman's wing armies will attempt to cut off the rebel supply line and gain the rear of the Confederates. Johnston's strategy is to make brief stands, inflicting as much loss to Sherman as possible, then pull back to the next defensive position. Johnston cannot risk an all-out battle with an army twice the size of his. Johnston will attempt to stretch out Sherman's army, causing the

Federals to lengthen their supply line which not only becomes more vulnerable, but also requires leaving Union garrisons to protect the ground left in federal hands. The Union army will therefore have fewer men at the front the further it travels into Confederate territory, while the Confederates move closer to their base of supplies.

Both generals at this time are fighting a war of attrition, Sherman inflicting loss on an army with limited resources, and Johnston buying time in which he plans the army confronting him will be reduced by his strategy, and by those Union soldiers in Sherman's army who are not reenlisting and will soon have served out their enlistment period.

May 20, 1864

Dear Wife

I have not time to write much. We are at Kingston and pursuing the rebels very close. They are making a stand here so they can get away with their train, fighting every day. We fought them hard two days near Resaca and routed them. We lost in our company near tunnel hill, one killed and two wounded. Jacob Craig killed, E Ward and Smiley wounded. A bullet passed through the rim of my hat and just glazed my forehead, my health is good. Good bye

T. Berry

Near Kingston Georgia
May 20th, 1864

Dear Wife,

I dropped you a line this morning and I supposed then that we would be on the march or in a fight by this time. The rebels left last night and the 23rd corps is after them. We can hear considerable cannonading. We are going to remain here to day the first days rest we have had since the army commenced moving. I will commence back to the eighth. We was on tunnel hill at that time and the rebels was in front of us on a very high ridge called rocky ledge and a very strong position, back of that ridge is a high eminence called buzzards roost and a very strongly fortified position. It would have been almost impossible to have got them out of their works by square fighting, Sherman took a flank movement on them and they had to travel.

On the eighth our brigade was kept in line of battle all day and there was very heavy skirmishing in front of us on the side of rocky ledge. On the 9th our regiment was put on the skirmish line along said ridge which is very steep and almost perpendicular in places and we advanced and drove back the rebels lines under a heavy fire. They had the advantage of us greatly. They could look right down on us. We lost in our company one killed and two wounded. Jacob Craig was killed, he was shot in the head. Ed Ward had his right arm broken and Smiley, one of the new recruits was hit near the hip. It was about a tight a place that we was ever in. There was very heavy fighting on the right and left. We was relieved about sundown. The rebels also gave me a very near call a bullet passed through the rim of my hat and just glazed my forehead which is nigh enough to suit me. On the tenth it was very quiet along the lines except skirmishing in front of us. On the 11th we went on the skirmish or picket line about sundown, we remained the line all night. There was firing most all night. The yanks and the rebs would talk a spell to each other and then they would shoot a spell. Our boys would tell them to come down and get some coffee and they would tell our boys to come up and get your nigger. We was relieved the morning of the twelfth about the sunrise, and we went back on the tunnel hill. About noon the rebels made a demonstration to our left and our division was ordered out to stop them and we soon got in the position to give them a warm reception but it turned out to be only a feint to cover their retreat. We laid in line of Battle that night, the next morning the whole rebel force was gone. Our forces was soon in hot pursuit. We arrived at Dalton about noon, we marched until after dark and camped for the night. Most of the Corps is in front of our Division. On the 14th we came upon them again in another strong and fortified position near Resaca and our forces advanced right up to them and the ball soon opened in earnest. Our Corps and the 23rd Corps engaged them first and before night General Hooker got his men in position and opened on them. Our men took two lines of their works, our loss was quite heavy. On the 15th the battle commenced about sunrise. In the afternoon General Hooker charged the rebel lines took good many prisoners and quite a number pieces of artillery. General Willick was wounded in the shoulder. Its reported that he was going to make a charge with his Brigade if he had not got wounded. On the morning of the Sixteenth about one Oclock the rebs made a charge and a yell but was repulsed and then they skedaddled, I suppose it was done to deceive us. At daylight the rebs was all gone. If they had fought us one day more we would have about annihilated their army. We just got our men and artillery in position to make it count. Sunday afternoon our men commenced pouring in volleys of shells and balls in their ranks. A prisoner stated that one volley of twelve guns killed and wounded about three hundred of their men. Our artillery is superior to theirs. They was afraid to reply to our guns on Sunday. Our men was soon in pursuit of them again and have been close to their heels and have been skirmishing with them every day. Yesterday they was obliged to make a stand here or else loose their train. We could see their train very plain. There was pretty heavy fighting here yesterday afternoon, part of our division was in the fight. Our regiment has not been engaged since we left rocky ledge. This morning the rebs was all gone from here. Our corps has been in the advance since we started and I hear that another corps is going to take the lead. We are 58 miles from Atlanta. There is three columns on the march, we are in the center. We follow the R R tracks. There is seven corps here, Atlanta is bound to fall. I hear that Grant is going nobly, I will close by wishing you good bye

Thomas Berry

The cars run from Chattanooga to Kingston, the first train came up this morning. The army has full rations and every thing is working well. I think this campaign will close the rebellion. May the Lord crown our arms with great victory is my prayer.

With his penchant for writing Estelle, the interval between Thomas' last two letters of May 7 and May 20, indicates the extent to which the 89th Illinois regiment has been engaged. Thomas recalls events of that time starting with May 8. The Army of the Cumberland was threading its way through the precipitous ridges and hills between Ringgold and Dalton, drawing fire from advanced rebel troops on Rock Face Ridge (Thomas refers to it as 'rocky ledge') and the hills protruding from that ridge including Tunnel Hill and Buzzard's Roost.

To the right of the Army of the Cumberland on the west side of Rocky Face, was McPherson's army, and to the left and rear was that of General Schofield. The armies on the right and left are for Sherman's strategy of 'flank movement', attempting to divide and intercept the Confederate Army as it is pushed to the south by General Thomas' army.

The 89th regiment occupied Tunnel Hill on May 7, as Thomas told us. On the 8th, the rebels were "fortified" on Buzzard's Roost and retreated from that post only after "Sherman took a flank movement on them". That flank movement was made by cavalry and infantry of McPherson's army on May 9, as he passed around Rocky Face Ridge through Snake Creek Gap and approached Resaca, south of the main body of Johnston's army. His orders were to destroy the railroad at Resaca and thereby cut the Confederate's supply line to Dalton.

At Resaca was a small rebel garrison which was outnumbered by McPherson's troops, nonetheless the ensuing skirmish caused McPherson indecision, he delayed a major encounter, leaving the railroad intact, and giving Johnston time to reinforce the garrison with some of the troops which had been facing the Army of the Cumberland. The larger army now at his front forced McPherson to decide on returning that evening toward Snake Creek Gap and await further orders.

The rebels remaining along Rocky Face Ridge continued to skirmish with General Howard's army, gradually pulling back to the south. On the night of May 12, the Confederates evacuated Dalton. "Our forces was soon in hot pursuit" on

May 13. The rebels fell back to Resaca where a battle took place on the next two days, forcing further retreat of the Confederate army beyond Ringgold, the place from which Thomas wrote his letter of May 20, and the present headquarters of General Sherman. The Union armies plan to rest here for the next three days.

"Rocky Ledge" is Rocky Face Ridge, one of the many ridges in that area of Georgia.

"Ed Ward" is Private William E. Ward from Walnut Grove. As a result of his injuries he was hospitalized (until discharged on January 4, 1865).

Private Sylvester H. Smiley was sent to the hospital at Chattanooga (where he died of his wounds on July 14, 1864).

The three columns mentioned by Thomas are the 4th corps under General Howard in the center, and the flanking columns, the 14th and 20th corps under generals Palmer and Hooker respectively.

The "seven corps" he mentions are:

4th — Gen. O.O. Howard	20th — Gen. Hooker
14th — Gen. John H. Palmer	23rd — Gen. Schofield
15th — Gen. John A. Logan	Cavalry — Gen. Washington L. Elliott
16th — Gen. Grenville M. Dodge	

As we saw earlier, the above armies have an aggregate of near 99,000 men. Sherman's armies are opposing Johnston's Army of Tennessee now consisting of close to 70,000 men.

"Grant is doing nobly" only because of the superior size of his army as compared to Lee's Army of Northern Virginia. With over 100,000 men, Grant opened the Spring Campaign on May 5, at the Battle of the Wilderness. In that fight Grant lost an estimated 17,600 men in killed, wounded, and missing, twice the loss suffered by the Confederates. Lee outwitted Grant throughout that and the next battle at Spotsylvania where Grant lost another 18,000 men. In two weeks, Grant has lost the equivalent of one—half of Lee's army. Grant at this time is moving his army to the North Anna River and toward another battleground, unaware that Lee has anticipated his plan, and will once again outwit the general—in—chief of the Union armies. Generals Sherman and Grant are outweighed by superior military minds, those of Johnston and Lee, and only a majority of troops on the side of the Union will overcome the imbalance.

Near Kingston Georgia
May 22nd, 1864

Dear Wife,

I again drop you a few lines to inform you that we are still here and that my health is good. I believe the whole army is resting and I hear that they are getting ready for a twenty day's march and its rumored

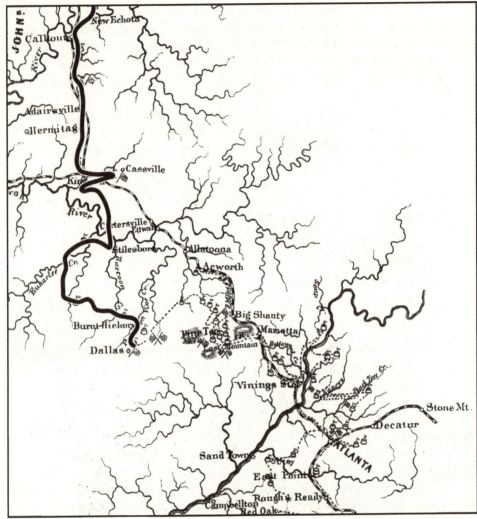

Route of the 89th Illinois, May 1864.

that Johnsons army is breaking up. Some going to join Lee and some to other places. They might as well for General Sherman has men enough here to very soon devour the rebel army under Johnson. If the report is true I presume it will change Shermans whole programme, and we may have some long marching to do. If you should not hear from me again for a good while you must not think it strange. There was fifteen hundred deserters came into our lines last night. They are deserting every day. The bugle is just blown in the 15th Ohio for preaching, I will stop and finish after. I have heard a very good sermon. The text was, war a good warfare, which is very appropriate both temporally and spiritually.

I have been to see the 102 Ills. they are camped about two miles from here. I saw George Cumming, he is well. Their regiment lost heavy about eighty killed and wounded.

The weather is getting pretty warm. We are 58 miles from Atlanta, the boys of the company are all pretty well. You wish to know if Haywood is promoted, he is promoted to a sergeant, he was a corporal. Give my best respects to all enquiring friends. Write often.

From your husband

Thomas Berry

When Thomas wrote on May 22, General Johnston's army was still very much intact around Allatoona, about 17 miles southeast of Kingston.

Since leaving Tunnel Hill on the 13th, Thomas Berry has marched some 50 miles, yet, vouching for his physical condition, he was not too tired to walk the distance to and from the 102nd Illinois regiment to see George Cummings, George Berry's brother—in—law. That regiment is in the 1st Brigade, 3rd Division of the 20th Army Corps under General Hooker.

General Sherman, not knowing the exact location of Johnston's army plans to circumvent the area of Allatoona by a march through Dallas. That march will take his armies away from the railroad, his line of communications to his base of supplies, therefore Sherman orders 20 days supplies be carried in his wagon trains.

As before, General Johnston anticipates Sherman's move and leaves Allatoona to intercept the Federals by moving to the west into the areas of New Hope Church and Pickett's Mill.

"Haywood" is Sergeant Orange G. Haywood from Walnut Grove.

With Union garrisons left behind, including one at Kingston, Sherman marched his armies from Kingston toward Dallas on the 23rd. The Army of the Cumberland under General Thomas was in the center of the southern march, with General Schofield's Army of the Ohio on the left and the Army of the Tennessee under General McPherson on the right. Crossing the Etawah River on that day, the Army of the Cumberland passed through Stilesboro on a path toward Pickett's Mill. The march continued until the 25th when the Army of the Cumberland was in the area of Dallas, New Hope Church, and Pickett's Mill, all within a three mile radius. There General Thomas found the Confederates, preceding him by one day, were in force at his front.

On the evening of the 25th, the 20th Corps under General Hooker attacked, engaging the rebels for two hours at New Hope Church. Hooker was repulsed at a place dubbed "Hell Hole," where the Federals suffered heavy loss. That encounter was in the rebel's favor, since early arrival permitted time for construction of effective fortifications against the anticipated move by Sherman. The following day saw but little skirmishing since both armies were busy extending entrenchments for the inevitable battle to follow.

May 26, 1864

My Dear loving Wife,
    I wish I could see you and be with my little family again. If I live to return to you again I shall be a happy man and I think we will be a happy family when we can get around our own fireside again. There is not a day passes by but what I think of you and our dear little ones. I believe our heavenly father will preserve our lives and that I will have the privliege of seeing you again.
    Remember me in your prayers and may our prayers ascend to the throne of grace for each others protections and guidance. From your husband who loves you dearly.

Thomas Berry

T. Berry

E. Berry

Lou. Berry

S. Berry

(Names circled with words "One bond of love")

General Howard's 4th Corps encountered the rebels at Pickett's Mill on May 27. The 89th Illinois Regiment was foolishly ordered to rush the well-fortified breastworks of the enemy which was manned by the veteran troops of Confederate General Patrick R. Cleburne's Division of Hardee's Corps. The gallant Federals were repulsed with heavy loss.

The rebels gave a lesson to the Union generals at the Battle of New Hope Church on May 25, when Hooker tried in vain to assail well-constructed breastworks of the Confederates under General Johnston. That lesson was wasted on generals Sherman and Howard. Two days later, under command of Sherman, General Howard gave orders which resulted in the repeat of that slaughter of May 25.

In an attempt to turn the enemy's right flank, not knowing where that right flank was, Howard, at five thirty in the evening, sent wave after wave of loyal and courageous veterans against well-established breastworks of the enemy. The attack was made in narrow formation providing easy target of Union soldiers for the wide front of rebels who were entrenched behind barricades supported by heavy artillery. When darkness put an end to the carnage, 700 Yankees lay dead before the rebel breastworks.

With the rebels in control of the field before them, they took 200 wounded Union soldiers from the battlefield as prisoners. No momentary truce was requested by General Howard to retrieve his dead and wounded, emulating the stubbornness of Grant who saw such practice, however honorable, to be an admission of defeat. (At the Battle of the Cold Harbor, Grant let his wounded lie for three days on the battlefield rather than call for a momentary cease fire to remove them. Of 7,000

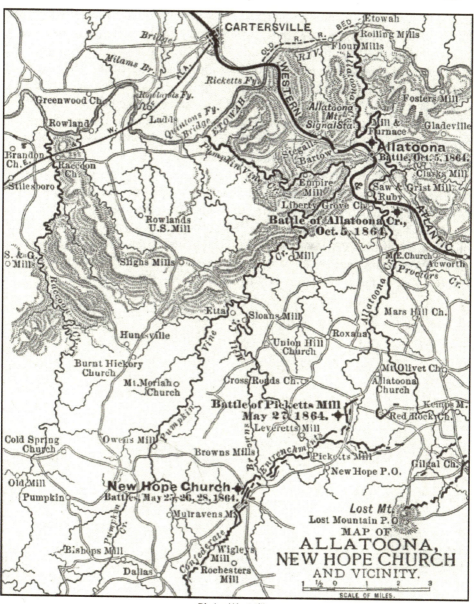

Pickett's Mill.

men left dead and groaning in agony on that battlefield, all suffered within one half hour of fighting on June 3, 1864, two only survived Grant's pride when finally removed from the field on June 7.)

General Howard explained his order to advance at Pickett's Mill, with his decision that regardless of the limited chance of success, it is sometimes necessary to assault a well-fortified position. General Sherman explained the carnage of his loyal soldiers by saying it was necessary to prove to Johnston that he, Sherman, whose proven strategy was the use of flank movement, was not above making a direct assault upon breastworks of the enemy.

It appears the explanations of blunders by commanding generals, regardless of how weak or non sequitur, are sufficient to excuse and forgive the terrible waste of human life, particularly so while sitting in counsel with their peers.

Among the many dead and dying left on the field of battle at Pickett's Mill on the night of May 27, 1864, were five mortally wounded men of Company G, 89th Illinois regiment: Private Isaac Hester, Private Andrew M. Reynolds, Private Andrew Topper, Corporal Squire D. Allen and Corporal Thomas Berry.

Epilogue

U.S.A. General Hospital No. 1
Chattanooga, Tennessee
July 15, 1864

Mrs. Estelle Berry,

Mr. Wales of our Co., (G., 89 Ills) who is here in Hospital with me called my attention to an advertisement in day before yesterdays "Chattanooga Gazzette", asking for information in regard to two men of our Co. who were missing after the battle of Dallas, Ga. on the 27th of June, and one of those inquired after was your husband; presuming, of course, that you had sent here for information, being in doubt as to the fate of Thomas, and as I have seen and talked with brother Peter since that time, he has given me all the particulars of the battle, with the names of those who fell, I will use the privelige of an old friend and give you the substance of my conversation with him so far as it relates to Thomas.

Peter told me that they were advancing up to the enemy's breastworks when Thomas fell very severly wounded; he instantly turned very pale and Peter thought that the ball struck him just below the breastbone and passed out at his back injuring the spinal column, and that he could not live; our men were eventually driven back and the rebels occupied this ground on which our wounded men lay before they could be gotten off; after dark a party from our Regt. commanded by Lieut. Swickard of our Co. was out back to try and get off our wounded as the Rebels had fallen back inside their fortifications ere nightfall, and the boys got up very near the place where Thomas lay when the rebs charged on them again and came very near capturing the whole party; so our men were obliged to retreat without getting a single man; when the boys got up so near Thomas after dark that night; they said that they did not think he was dead, but that he made no movement or noise of any kind.

Estelle we have been friends in our younger days, and it sadly grieves me now to say that I can give you no hope that Thomas lives; the prevailing opinion in the Co. is, that he did not live more than through that night at least; I know that this is terrible news to communicate to you, but if you have hitherto been in doubt and this will set your mind at rest and alleviate any of your sorrow I shall have been amply remunerated for writing this letter; furthermore, if there are any questions you wish to ask or information you wish to obtain that I can furnish you with, write without any hesitation and I will be only too glad to find out and let you know; unless you are already possessed of all the particulars; as soon as my attention was called to the article in the paper it occurred to me that you had not been able to obtain any definite knowledge of your husband's fate and had taken that method of satisfying yourself, or rather telegraphed to Sanitary Commission and they had advertised, and hence the reason that I have written this letter.

Permit me to add here, that in these terrible afflictions our religion is the only thing that will sustain us and enable us to feel that "God does all things well"; I fully believe that Thomas was a true Christian and was ready for the great change; no nobler man or braver soldier ever performed his duty in Co. G., than was Thos. Berry; let it be a part of your consolation to know that he fell doing his duty as a true man; that for his country his life was demanded and that the sacrifice was not withheld; but let your chief consolation come from the knowledge that he has gone to rest with God, our Saviour and all the friends who have passed on before; that his work here was done and well done.

And yet Estelle we may all be mistaken; Thomas may be yet alive, I would not say hope not, at all; but in what I have written I have endeavored to impress upon your mind the idea that it is almost impossible that he could have lived after the wound he received. I deeply sympathize with you in this sad bereavment; the burden of my prayer daily is "Oh! Lord comfort those who are called upon to mourn;" I have been tried in the furnace of affliction too; brother John was mortally wounded in the same battle where Thomas fell.

This has been a very hard campaign and has brought sorrow to many hearthstones; may God be a father to the orphans and a husband to the widows.. All things are working well for the cause; every man that falls only makes that cause dearer to us than ever before; may God hasten forward the end is my daily prayer.

If you wish to write for any information to me, as I have already said "do so without any hesitation" I will gladly furnish you with any that I can possibly obtain. Direct to the Regt. the same as when you were writing to Thomas

Accept with this my heartfelt sympathy and believe me ever truly your friend.

Wm. Tait

Private John Tait was moved to Chattanooga where he died of his wounds on July 19, 1864.

College Hill
Nashville, Tenn.
July 18th, 1864

Mrs. Estelle Berry,

    As an old friend I feel in duty bound to write a few lines to you and give you all the information in my possession of Thomas's fate. I was close to him when he fell and his wound was a very dangerous one to say the least. I fear that the ball struck his spinal column. If so he must have died on the field that night for he was perfectly helpless. He was wounded within one hundred feet of the enemy's works, about half an hour before sunset 27th of May.

    I sent four men back after dark to bring off the dead and wounded but the enemy charged on the line and drove them from the field. One of the men got within twenty feet of Thomas but it was so dark that he could not see whether he was alive or not and he had to run from the spot to save himself, so he did not get any nearer to him.

    Poor Thomas if he has sacrificed his life it was in a glorious cause and to you and your children "his little family" I offer my sincere heartfelt sympathy in your great loss. He was a noble man and one of the best of soldiers facing danger without fear.

    Thomas lived a good christian life which is a very rare thing in the army and was respected and loved by all his comrades in arms who sincerely mourn his loss.

    If it is possible to find out anything definite of his fate I will let you know. I would have written sooner but never had an opportunity to do so until I was sent back sick to this place.

    Sincerely sympathizing with you in your sorrow I remain your true friend

Peter G. Tait
1st Lieut. Co. G
89th Ill.

The chronicle of Thomas Berry's letters ends here. His regiment pressed on to other engagements adding further glory to its noble service under the flag of the United States. The 89th Illinois regiment moved through Georgia with Sherman's army seeing action at Kennesaw Mountain, Peach Tree Creek, and in the flanking movements around Atlanta.

Confederate President Jefferson Davis, in another of his customary rash decisions, replaced General Johnston on July 18, 1864 with General John B. Hood as commander of the Army of Tennessee. General Hood attempted in vain to defend Atlanta, evacuating that city on September 1, 1864. Sherman occupied Atlanta the following day. Sherman continued to Savannah on his famous "march to the sea" leaving the army commanded by General Thomas to contend with the Army of Tennessee under General Hood.

Hood marched his army north into Tennessee in an attempt to shatter Union railroad communication lines and retake territory previously lost by the Confederacy.

The following excerpt is from the Illinois Adjutant General's Report:

> "After the unsuccessful attempt of the rebel forces to destroy the railroad communications of the army between Atlanta and Chattanooga, the (89th) Regiment rendered very important service, while on detached duty, in repairing the damages on the railroad inflicted by the enemy."
>
> "On the 30th of October, 1864, the Regiment was ordered to rejoin the command at Pulaski, Tenn. It participated in the brilliant achievements of Spring Hill, Columbia, Franklin and Nashville, in the latter of which fell Lieutenant P.G. Taite (sic), of Company G. pierced by a cannon ball..."

At Nashville on December 15, 1864, Hood encountered the Union army under General Thomas. A two day battle ensued involving the 89th Illinois regiment. It was that battle in which, on December 16, 1864, First Lieutenant Peter G. Tait was killed.

Further from the Report:

> "Subsequently it (the 89th Regiment) pursued Hood's shattered forces in their flying retreat across Tennessee."
>
> "It passed winter quarters at Huntsville, Ala., in January, 1865, and on the 1st of February traveled by railroad for Nashville, and after lying there five days, returned to Camp Green. About the middle of March, the command embarked on the cars for East Tennessee, to reestablish communications through to Virginia, and prepare to repel rebel invasion."

Hood's army suffered heavy loss at Nashville. The Army of Tennessee was down to 5,000 men when it was once again, by order of General Lee on February 23, 1865, placed under the command of General Johnston. Two weeks earlier, Lee had been made general-in-chief of all Confederate armies.

The Civil War was rapidly winding dawn. The Confederates could no longer afford the waste of men when Lee surrendered his Army of Northern Virginia to

General Grant at Appomattox, Virginia, April 9, 1865. With the surrender of the South's largest army, the war for all practical purpose was over, since the remaining rebel armies could not possibly stand up to the huge Union forces remaining active.

A relaxed and joyful air permeated the North, and particularly was experienced by the Federal administration, when on the night of Good Friday President Lincoln attended Ford's theater to enjoy the play, Our American Cousin. There he was shot by an assassin. He died the next day, April 15, 1865. The evil of slavery had extracted yet another payment for its undoing, and would continue its demand long after the truce.

The surrender of Johnston's Army of Tennessee took place near Raleigh, North Carolina, on April 26, 1865 following ten days of cease fire negotiations. The remaining Confederate armies soon followed in surrender. During the four year war, over two and one half million men had enlisted in Union military services, suffering a loss of more than 360,000 dead. Confederate military services enlisted approximately one million losing one fourth in death.

The majority of those losses were suffered at the hands of men trained in the military and naval academies of the United States, men whose fidelities became divided by their sympathies, and took opposite sides in a war. Had all those men remained loyal to the Federal Government, the Confederacy would have been hard pressed to assemble forces able to stand long against the additional talents Generals Jackson, Johnston, Beauregard, Lee, Bragg and the many others who defected.

Despite the pain and prolonged agony despicable action of those turncoats, on some is arrogantly bestowed the title 'hero'.

Excuses for desertion were varied. Many like Beauregard had a personal dislike for the North, others like Bragg owned plantations which were thought in need of protection, and some such as Lee, felt devotion to the state of their birth was more deserving than devotion to the only mother country concerned with their liberty. Lee rationalized defection by his claim of the need to protect against invasion of his State of Virginia, yet he commanded an army marching on the offensive into the new State of West Virginia, the State of Maryland, and on to the Gettysburg, Pennsylvania.

Commanders of the surrendered armies enjoyed liberal terms and were free to return to their homes and families, paying no penalty for defection. Defecting soldiers under command of those same liberated officers paid with their lives for their action, as did defecting Union soldiers under Federal Command. No such payment was extracted from those practicing treason in command of rebel armies nor from anarchists in the Confederate administration.

President Jefferson Davis was captured in his attempt to escape Federal officers. He was indicted for treason, jailed, and after posting a bail bond signed by Horace Greeley and others, was released May 13, 1867. Legal proceedings against him were withdrawn the following year during the administration of President Andrew

Johnson, a southern Democrat.

More from the Illinois Adjutant General's Report on the history of the 89th Illinois Railroad Regiment:

> "On the surrender of Lee's army, further movements in that section (East Tennessee—Virginia) were abandoned, and the Fourth Corps returned by cars to Nashville, to muster out of service its Non-veterans.
>
> "On the 10th of June, 1865, the Regiment was mustered out of the United States service, in the field near Nashville, Tenn. Left there June 10th, by Louisville, New Albany and Chicago Railroad, and arrived in Chicago on the night of June 12th, 1865, and was discharged at Camp Douglas, on the 24th of June, 1865, making its term of service two years, nine months, and twenty-seven days."

Thomas never learned that his brother George Berry, after being taken prisoner at the Battle of Chickamauga on September 19, 1863, was sent to Andersonville Prison. At that infamous prison, George died on August 6, 1864. The cause of his death is listed as "desease". He could have died of a bullet wound delivered by a trigger-happy guard, or from malnutrition, or from wounds received at Chickamauga, wounds which at best would have received slovenly medical attention by officials who took delight in letting the sick and wounded suffer until death. All of the above conditions including untreated disease have led to thousands of deaths in Andersonville Prison, and documented as practice attributed to the administration of that prison, an administration which looked upon the incidental death of a Yankee prisoner as a Confederate gain.

Such deliberate acts of bestiality should have been traced to the source which allowed that cruelty, and to that source, penalty justly applied. Instead, only one man paid with his life for those crimes against humanity, the commander of Andersonville Prison, Captain Wirz, who worked with orders from higher authority.

Forty-one men from the 89th Illinois Regiment alone died at Andersonville Prison. Privates from Company G of the 89th regiment who were taken as prisoners from battlefields and confined at Anderson are listed with their Illinois home town, date of death within Andersonville's prison walls, and the assigned grave number.

Of the 93 men who had enlisted in Company G. of the 89th Illinois Railroad regiment in August of 1862, thirty-five men were mustered out of service from that Company at war's end. None of the 34 recruits were mustered out of Company G, for various reasons including transfers to other regiments (22), killed in action (2), death from wounds (6), discharge due to medical disability (2), and desertion (2). Mustered out of service from Company G of the 89th Illinois Regiment at the close of the war were the following:

Captain	William H. Howell	Walnut Grove
First Lieutenant	John W. Swickard	Walnut Grove
Sergeants	Richard J. Burneson	Walnut Grove
	Harrison G.O. Wales	Walnut Grove
	John B. McLaughlin	Walnut Grove
	Orange G. Hayward	Walnut Grove
	William S. Fiten	Walnut Grove
	Richard H. Lyman	Lynn
Corporal	Edward W. Stephens	Walnut Grove
Privates	Schuyler Atherton (musician)	Walnut Grove
	Charles V. Bainbridge	
	Jacob Borkhart	Walnut Grove
	John Campbell	Walnut Grove
	Henry C. Collinson	Walnut Grove
	James H. Dillworth	Walnut Grove
	Michael Doyle	Walnut Grove
	Albert W. Elsworth	Lynn
	William Ferman (musician)	Clover
	Levi Hager	Lynn
	James Livingston	Walnut Grove
	James W. McLaughlin	Walnut Grove
	William H. Nesbitt	Walnut Grove
	Charles Rowe	Henderson
	Benjamin F. Riner	Walnut Grove
	Isaac Roosa	Walnut Grove
	Matern Spohr	Lynn
	Arad C. Stowell	Walnut Grove
	Thomas Sprouse	Weller
	Isaac Sprouse	Weller

The end result of the Civil War occurred on December 18, 1865, with the 13th amendment to the Constitution of the United States, which forever abolished slavery from the land of the free.

Civil War Glossary
Referenced to Thomas Berry Letters

Abolitionist	advocates abolishment of slavery, and trading or ownership of slaves illegal
Copperhead	resident of northern state in sympathy with slave—holding states
Democrat	predominant sympathizer with southern cause of slavery, divided on issue of Union and Constitution
Dixie	land of the United States below the Mason and Dixon Line. The Mason—Dixon line is the border between Pennsylvania and Maryland surveyed by Charles Mason and Jeremiah Dixon, 1763—1767, considered the demarcation between free and slave colonies. With the formation of states the line was extended in theory to the west to provide the same separation.
Firebrand (south)	activist advocate of slavery in pursuit of unrest and war with abolutionists
Fire eater	belligerent advocate of slavery
Freedman	once bonded person who fulfilled contract of indenture and became free of bondage, also one given certificated freedom from slavery by former owner
Indentured servant	a person under contract for specified service and time period
Northerner	resident of non-confederate state
Rebel	one who revolts from the government to which he owes allegiance; one who defies and seeks to overthrow lawful authority
Republican	predominant advocate of abolition, the Union and Constitution
Secesh, sesesh	colloquialism for secessionist citizen or soldier
Secessionist	advocate of secession, resident of Confederate state, Confederate soldier, or any person actively engaged in rebellion
Separatist	advocate of separate nations by division of states and territories
Slave	human chattel with no legal means to freedom
Southerner	resident of confederate state
Unionist	advocate of Constitutional government
Yank, Yankee	resident or soldier from non-confederate state. Of disputed origin, thought to be Indian corruption of the word 'English', also from an early settler D. Janke, a northern soldier of Colonial times. Post Civil War, any native or citizen of the U.S.